Praise for the Second Edition

"Ricky Jones's *Black Haze* is an important study of black male identity development. By examining black men's relationship with fraternities, he uncovers larger and brilliantly penetrating insights into issues of masculinity and political identity among African American males in the post-civil rights era."
— Peniel E. Joseph, author of *Waiting 'Til the Midnight Hour: A Narrative History of Black Power in America*

"*Black Haze* is a compelling survey of black Greek-letter organizations, their history, purpose, and their most damning traditions. This is an examination of how the virtues of brotherhood and civic service coexist with brutal violence and cruelty within some of the oldest organizations in black America. Professor Jones has produced a vital contribution about a crucial and enduring problem."
—William Jelani Cobb, author of *The Substance of Hope: Barack Obama and the Paradox of Progress*

"*Black Haze* is a riveting *coup de grâce* against ritualized violence in black fraternities. The second edition of *Black Haze* is the most penetrating, illuminating, and articulate sociopolitical and cultural analysis of the chilling legacy of violence in black Greek-letter fraternities. As one of the world's leading authorities on black masculinity and organizations, Ricky Jones intelligently confronts traditional verities, social norms, and myths that seek to justify and continue ritualized violence in black fraternities through the courageous prism of a reformed insider dedicated to the preservation of black dignity and life."
—Jeremy I. Levitt, author of *Black Women and International Law: Deliberate Interactions, Movements and Actions*

BLACK HAZE

Second Edition

BLACK HAZE

Violence, Sacrifice, and Manhood in
Black Greek-Letter Fraternities

Second Edition

Ricky L. Jones

Published by State University of New York Press, Albany

For information, contact State University of New York Press, Albany, NY
www.sunypress.edu

Production, Ryan Morris
Marketing, Kate R. Seburyamo

Library of Congress Cataloging-in-Publication Data

Jones, Ricky L.
  Black haze : violence, sacrifice, and manhood in black greek-letter fraternities /
Ricky L. Jones.—Second edition.
      pages cm. — (Suny series in African American studies)
  Includes bibliographical references and index.
  ISBN 978-1-4384-5673-7 (hardcover : alk. paper) — ISBN 978-1-4384-5672-0
(pbk. : alk. paper) — ISBN 978-1-4384-5674-4 (e-book) 1. Greek letter
societies—United States. 2. African American college students—Conduct of life.
3. Hazing—United States. I. Title.
  LJ51.J66 2015
  371.8'5—dc23
                                                                          2014027655

10 9 8 7 6 5 4 3 2 1

For my daughter, Jordan. May you never belong to a group
that places your humanity or your life at risk.

Contents

Preface to the Second Edition:
Black Haze Revisited

In 2004, the first edition of *Black Haze: Violence, Sacrifice, and Manhood in Black Greek-Letter Fraternities* became the first (and remains the only) scholarly monograph specifically dedicated to analyzing violent hazing in these groups. The book was the last in an important trilogy on black Greek-letter organizations (BGLOs) published at the turn of the century. The first two were Lawrence Ross's *Divine Nine* in 2000 and Walter Kimbrough's *Black Greek 101* in 2003. Both books were essential historical primers for anyone interested in black fraternities and sororities. *Black Haze* completed the set with a targeted exploration of the myriad motives behind the organizations' most troubling and persistent ill—violent hazing.

A number of other books on BGLOs have surfaced, as the subject has grown in popularity over the last decade. They have ranged from works targeting particular organizations to broader interrogations of different aspects of the groups. They have also run the gamut in quality. A few have been thoughtful, whereas others have been little more than shortsighted "brag pieces" written by BGLO-affiliated apologists. The market for these books has grown because black Greeks have often found themselves in the news in recent years—for all the wrong reasons. To be sure, sex, dysfunctionality, and death sell in America. Black Greek culture has its share of all these.

Dramas surrounding black Greeks and subsequent analyses have carved out space for a new and small category of people classifying themselves as "black Greek scholars"—a label I personally reject. Neither *Black Haze* nor any of the other work I have done concerning BGLOs in general or black Greek fraternities (BGFs) in particular has been intended to only be about or for black Greeks. My purpose has always been greater. At the end of the day, I am not a "black Greek scholar," but a political philosopher with rather different intellectual, social, and political interests than many of my peers. So, it makes sense that I would produce an exploration rooted in the ideas of the likes of Antonio Gramsci, Jürgen Habermas, and René Girard, rather than theories deployed by historians, sociologists, or student affairs professionals. Consequently, *Black Haze* is a very different book from those that preceded or followed it. The fact that both the book and I are anomalous animals that do not neatly fit into the normal black Greek genre has caused problems.

Like many works, *Black Haze* is a classic example of the old adage, You can't judge a book by its cover. Understandably, anyone looking at the original jacket, adorned with the Greek symbols of every major black fraternity, would think the book was only about these organizations. Those who actually read it realize this initial assumption is wrong. Admittedly, the misunderstanding (which has resulted in frustration for me as well as others over the years) was just as much my fault as that of the willfully anti-intellectual people who drew flawed conclusions without reading.

Writing is an artistic exercise. Like all art, books never turn out exactly as the artist originally envisions them. The process of research and writing takes one down unforeseen paths, presents new possibilities, and yields epiphanies *and* quandaries by the end that are simply not in the author's sightline at the beginning. If I am to criticize my readers (or nonreading critics) for making assumptions about or downright misunderstanding *Black Haze*, I must also admit that almost two decades ago a part of me really didn't understand exactly what was to come. One must remember that the original edition of this book was the culmination of work started ten years earlier, following the death of Michael Davis at Southeast Missouri State University in 1994. In my mid-twenties at the time, I was quite romantic about the prospect of producing a study that would ultimately help BGFs and their stakeholders figure out ways to quell or eradicate violent hazing. Years later, a more realistic (even more cynical) me must admit that I failed miserably in that respect.

Although neither *Black Haze* nor anything else has stopped or even slowed BGF hazing, it had another purpose that continues to make it relevant. As stated above, the original work began with the Michael Davis story. This edition ends with the brutal 2011 hazing death of Florida A&M drum major Robert Champion in a band incident that mimics the behavior of black fraternal groups. The deaths of these young men and others are no less disturbing than they were ten, twenty, or thirty years ago. *Black Haze* was not meant to be simply an endeavor in historicism or a police blotter of murder.

Ultimately, the recounting of incidents was secondary to *why* individuals and organizations allowed them. What are the micro- and macrofactors that open the door for the brutality we find in BGFs? What creates the type of men who inflict and endure this violence, hurt and even kill one another . . . and never apologize? The questions themselves were troubling; some of the answers even more so. I make no claim to having uncovered every personality permutation of black men or a definitive bottom line for violent hazing. The unending search for answers led to interesting intellectual and individual odysseys. The philosophical inquiry itself ultimately prompted me to question not only my subjects' identity formations and definitions of manhood, but my own as well. The process prompted interrogations that drill deeply into soil far outside of BGF's fields. For both good and ill, it has forced me to seriously explore my own past and the baggage it has left.

Well before I joined a BGF, my socialization in violent and masochistic cultures produced distinct (and largely dysfunctional) ideas about manhood. Outside of the Preface of the original edition of *Black Haze*, I never divulged too much about my own life and how I came to self-select (and in many ways embrace) BGF mores. I suppose I avoided too much self-injection, in part in an effort to maintain (or at least present the facade of maintaining) the position of the dispassionate, neutral researcher. Like most academicians, that is how I was trained. It is also highly probable that I was simply not in touch with the impact of my own past earlier in my intellectual life. Either way, the nondisclosure was a mistake that needs correcting for current readers to understand how I fit into this story.

My mother, Betty Jones, was impregnated the first time she had sex by a man almost twenty years her senior when she was fourteen years old. To this day, my father, Shelley Stewart, is a very prosperous businessman in Birmingham, Alabama. His parental performance has not been as stellar. In the mid-1960s, he was a relatively popular disc jockey in Atlanta, who branded himself with the radio moniker Shelley "the Playboy." He worked diligently to live up to the name—having a penchant not only for women, but, obviously, for very young ones. While my father continues to maintain the image of a man who cares about the fortunes of children, he has not been a very good father to at least one of his own. By self-admission, he does not have the best relationship with his other progeny (though I have never met any of my siblings).

Either before or soon after I was born, Stewart left Atlanta and never returned to meet or check on me. All I knew of him was his name. I was thirty-four when a dear friend finally decided to track him down (which was not difficult), and I submitted to meeting him. Her argument was that I had gone far too long without knowing my father. She saw it as a source of trauma with which I was not in touch but needed to face. By this time, I was an adult and considered myself tough and self-made. I was not enthusiastic about immersing myself in what I saw as childhood problems. I sincerely felt that many years earlier I had laid to rest the subject of a father who unapologetically abandoned me. I was wrong, and I am thankful that I was prompted to admit it.

That story does not have a happy ending. Even though we sporadically interacted for a few years, I have not spoken to Shelley Stewart since 2009. He has met my daughter only once. He never visits or calls to check on her. For his part, Stewart maintains that he never knew he left a son behind in Atlanta, in that he was unaware of my birth. My mother and late grandmother brand this as a falsehood, but little more can be expected from a man who has a well-crafted reputation to maintain and an equally strong reluctance to deal with the darkness he has brought into the world rather than what he has overcome. Despite my father's failures, I grant him a bit of grace only because he had a traumatic childhood of his own, which he meticulously chronicles in his autobiography, *The Road South*.

Even though some people contest the veracity of his story, Stewart writes vividly about how at five years old, he witnessed his father murder his mother. By seven or eight he was on the streets of Birmingham alone. He speaks of his father, Huell Stewart, in almost demonic terms. Huell is portrayed as a man with few, if any, redeeming characteristics and a willingness to subject his sons to unspeakable indignities. Shelley Stewart's triumph in the absence of a benevolent, humane father is an impressive story. It is ironic that he did not reject his father's example of indecency, but in some ways replicated it. Although Shelley "the Playboy" returned to Birmingham to seek his fortune, he left his own son fatherless and impoverished to battle his way through the housing projects of Atlanta. And so my life began.

By the time I was born, my mother was fifteen years and three months old, and in no way prepared for parenthood. Consequently, the responsibility fell to my grandmother—Linnie Mae Jones. My grandmother, who died in 2009, was a titan of a woman. Born in 1933 (a year before my father), in rural Georgia, she never attended school and could read only enough to struggle through passages of the Bible. In her twenties, after a tumultuous childhood of her own, she journeyed to Atlanta with her two young children. She remained there until her death. My grandmother supported us by cleaning homes in Buckhead—Atlanta's wealthiest area—where I would eventually be bused to Northside High School. Though I attended high school on the north side of the city, I grew up in the Carver Homes housing projects in Southwest Atlanta. Carver Homes was not an easy place. Like most public housing it was marked by shoddy maintenance, pest infestation, crime, addiction, disproportionately poor education, dysfunctional socialization, and a general sense of nihilism.

Contrary to popular belief, though, most residents of the projects are not oblivious to their conditions or supportive of the cultural underbelly that seizes their communities in a vise. Many, in fact, work doggedly to construct better lives against unimaginable odds. Of course, others succumb and turn to compensatory behavior. Those who are broken and lose hope often tumble into lives where they have only one tool left available to them—their bodies. Women use sex, men use violence, and a great percentage of both use drugs to escape. This was an everyday reality that adults and children alike normalized. It was simply the way of things.

Those fortunate enough to survive rough-and-tumble projects and ghettos often speak of their exits from these neighborhoods as "escapes." I am among that number. Unfortunately, we are in the minority. Many others remain in these environs from birth to death. Most are not shiftless, unmotivated pariahs—they are simply members of America's growing underclass, continuously crushed by the boot of a nasty brand of American capitalism and individualism that invariably benefits a few and disenfranchises, dismisses, and demonizes the many. This was the world in which my grandmother struggled to raise me. Illiterate, she made sure I learned to read. Not well traveled, she watched as I left home at seventeen years old to explore the world. Not educated or professional, she smiled as I finished college, a PhD, and made my bones in a notoriously elitist and clannish profession.

For all the negatives, fatherless project kids who ultimately become successful develop positive skill sets as well. Among other things, by necessity we are vigilant, tough, smart (streetwise and otherwise), fiercely independent, and unfailingly pragmatic. For example, I graduated from the Naval Academy's Preparatory School in Newport, Rhode Island, and then attended Annapolis for the first half of my undergraduate career, ultimately graduating from Morehouse College. In certain circles, I am complimented for attending reputable schools. The truth is I had no idea about the pecking order of institutions as a teenager. Being the first to graduate high school in my immediate family, I had no idea that some considered the Naval Academy or Morehouse to be elite colleges. Navy was simply the only one of the many institutions that recruited me to offer me a free education *and* a paycheck while I was in school. This gave me an opportunity to go to school, send money home to my grandmother, and have a guaranteed job on graduation. It was just that simple.

I transferred to Morehouse for my junior and senior years after a tumultuous time at Annapolis. My brief military career was marred and eventually ended by burgeoning self-awareness and racial consciousness that led to constant defiance and rule-breaking. At the end of the day, military life held an untenable level of misery for me, and I was not an acceptable midshipman or future officer for my superiors. As I grew into manhood, I developed an even deeper inquisitiveness, a newfound disrespect for authority, and an abiding skepticism about the status quo. The factors that would eventually make me a good scholar made me a terrible military man. My propensity to question everything was completely out of place in an environment that mandated personnel to "Follow the last order given."

Like Navy, Morehouse held no particular intrigue for me. It was simply convenient—a place to finish my undergraduate career. I had no knowledge of Morehouse's history. I did not know that Maynard Jackson, Julian Bond, Calvin Butts, Martin Luther King Jr., and many other iconic black men attended the school—and quite honestly, I did not care. Though I was a native, I grew up in a different Atlanta. I was a project kid. The first time I set foot on Morehouse's campus was when I arrived to apply for admission. It was a pragmatic choice. Again, it was just that simple.

Despite my lack of awareness of it, both Navy and Morehouse

were contributing to my development in peculiar ways. I am certainly one of a small handful of men to attend both schools, and it gives me a unique perspective. On the surface, the two institutions seem incredibly different. Founded twenty-two years apart (Navy in 1845, and Morehouse in 1867), one school is a military academy with a history of racial exclusivity, governmental support, and the production and maintenance of American empire; the other is a predominantly black, all-male proving ground that has produced men who have fought against everything Annapolis stands for. To be sure, Morehouse men such as Maynard Jackson, Martin King, and others have been at the heart of changing the course of cities, the country, and the world.

There are also deep-seated similarities when one looks closer. Both schools are old and very traditional. Dress codes, chapels, monuments, and an unrelenting dedication to the past define both. Both schools have "systems" designed to take students from disparate environments and ultimately graduate "products" that are indistinguishable from one another. When pressed, neither institution tolerates much variation from their institutional norms. Both painstakingly socialize their students and demand such dedication that it is difficult to find current or former students who do not know the words to the school songs—"Dear Old Morehouse" or "Navy Blue and Gold." Most important for our purposes here, both are male dominated and have pronounced ideas about manhood that largely remain unaltered.

By the time I joined Kappa Alpha Psi, I had endured an absent father and broken mother, survived Carver Homes where physical prowess defined men, gone through the hazing of military preparatory school, faced a full year of hazing as a plebe (freshman) at Annapolis, and witnessed the fanaticism and arrogance of black Greek life and school spirit at Morehouse. Not surprisingly, I did not question hazing at this point in my life. It was, again, simply the way of things. All these very important events in my life were combining to produce a new level of reflection by the time *Black Haze* was written. Even I was not completely in touch with how deep it would run. The product was a book that was not solely about fraternities—they were only used as vehicles to examine more substantive philosophical subjects. At the end of the day, *Black Haze* was more about manhood and identity.

I am under no illusion that my life story (only partially relayed here) is unique or particularly exceptional. Many black boys are left without fathers and must endure the drudgery of blighted neighborhoods. Many of us grow up seeing physical prowess and athletics valued over intellect and academics. We endure poverty, racism, mistreatment, and low expectations from teachers. Our childhoods are often ripped from us prematurely as we are saddled with the responsibility of being the "man of the house" before we have any inkling of what being a man entails. We are "trial-and-error" men. We have no example of what being a man looks like. So, like musical artists, we improvise. This is at the heart of why Cornel West has often labeled black folk "blues people."

Even young black men who grow up in better circumstances are immersed in a society that provides few examples of black male power and success. Whether rich or poor, we all are inundated with a societal view of black men that sees us as underachieving, uneducated, unemployed, criminal-minded ne'er-do-wells. Many who theorize on America's greatest problems regard us as being among *the* problems. Those of us who "make it" are not considered the norm, but the unexplainable exceptions.

Over a decade ago, *Black Haze* asked what compensatory behavior black men engage in to form what they see as healthy identities and senses of manhood in the pressure cooker of America. Also, how should we handle the sometimes dangerous organizations these men create as a result? This is the reason ideas and movements such as Du Bois's "double consciousness," Mele's "akrasia," Girard's "liminality," and Bly's "man camps" are so important to our subject. Whether this is your first reading of *Black Haze* or you are revisiting it as 1 am, read it knowing that it is not just about the search for membership or preservation of Greek-letter organizations. It is about the quest for acceptance, comfort, reaffirmation, and manhood. It is about boys and men searching for identity in a world where their footing is often unstable. It is an intriguing story, but like many stories in the real world, it does not have a happy ending.

Ricky L. Jones
Atlanta, GA
May 2014

Preface to the First Edition

In September 2002, police officers in Playa del Rey, California, pulled two college students to shore from the Pacific Ocean. Police attributed the deaths of Kenitha Saafir, twenty-four, of Compton, and Kristin High, twenty-two, of Los Angeles, to their inability to swim back to shore after being caught in a powerful undercurrent. No one could explain exactly why the women had been in the water in the first place. Within a month after the young ladies' deaths, High's family filed a $100 million lawsuit against Alpha Kappa Alpha (AKA), the nation's oldest black Greek-letter sorority. The suit alleged that Saafir and High had died in a hazing ritual gone awry while trying to join the AKA's ranks.

Battle lines were immediately drawn inside and outside of black Greekdom. A national black Greek Internet listserv exploded with opinions ranging from outrage at more deaths possibly attributable to hazing to cries for black Greeks to close ranks. One sorority member warned Greeks who thought it wise to talk to outsiders and media outlets, "I say a mistake is being made to welcome people that have *no* idea of the history and processes in. There is no going back from that. All it's gonna take is one Bill O'Reilly type to take a stance on something he/she doesn't understand and we might as well hang it up." This member's perspective certainly prompted the question, among non-Greeks at least, if Greeks were indeed involved in these deaths, what processes could one understand (outside of murder) that could explain the deaths of these two students? A member of Alpha Phi Alpha, the oldest black Greek fraternity, went so far as to take an approach that simultaneously introduced deceit and God into the equation when addressing the deaths of High and Saafir: "To be honest, if I knew that what I said could cause harm to any BGLO (black Greek-letter organization), *I would lie* in an effort to avoid causing harm to that institution. . . . Again, not to sound cold or ignorant, but the matters of life and death are in the hands of God. If someone can show me where any other spiritual being has the might to take a soul before our God deems its time . . . please correct me."

At the writing of these words, the exact circumstances surrounding the deaths of High and Saafir were still undetermined. Despite the protestations of many black Greeks who are undyingly protective of their fraternities and sororities, if it does come to light that these women did indeed die trying to join a black Greek organization, it would not be the first time. In this case, hazing simply crossed the gender line and involved the ladies, but black fraternity men are all too familiar with landscapes littered with pledging and death. The unfortunate and abusive marriage of black Greek-letter fraternities (BGFs) to hazing prompted this book. Whether or not High and Saafir perished as a result of it, hazing in black Greek organizations is all too real and its arm is long. In spite of the almost certain rancor they will engender among many black Greeks, the following pages examine violent hazing, the single most unfortunate legacy of Alpha and the black Greek-letter fraternities that followed it. Most members of these organizations know this tradition well.

My personal trek into the sometimes-surreal world of black Greekdom began when I was a thirteen-year-old student in Atlanta, Georgia. At Martin Luther King Jr. Middle School, I met social studies teacher James Terry.[1] Now, more than two decades later, I do not remember very much of what Mr. Terry taught me in that classroom at King. I do, however, remember his sheer presence and the impact he had on the youngsters in his charge. Many of the students at King were from single-parent households headed by women and had very few positive male role models. Personally, I did not meet my own father until I was well into adulthood. In spite of the sometimes decent relationship I have been able to establish with him, Terry remains my model of what a perfect father should be. As a boy, Mr. Terry seemed like a giant among men to me—calm, collected, intelligent, handsome, charismatic, and always in control. He was the epitome of black manliness. He was also a member of Kappa Alpha Psi. Over a decade after his initiation, Terry still wore his Kappa Life Membership pin on his jacket lapel daily. He explained what the pin was, but few, if any, of us understood the concept of fraternity at that time. All we knew was that if Mr. Terry was a part of this thing, it must have been good.

As I matriculated through my high school and college years, I gained a personal understanding of fraternity. Eventually, I had my own pledge experience and was initiated into Kappa Alpha Psi. As fate would have it, Mr. Terry wrote one of my letters of recommendation and subsequently became *Brother* Terry. Just as Brother Terry exposed me to the beauty of Kappa, he alerted me to its dark side before I pledged. As a father would, he sternly warned me about hazing and advised me to steer clear of illegal and dangerous situations that ran counter to the purposes, mission, rules, and statutes of the fraternity. I did not wholeheartedly heed his warning, but was fortunate enough to have big brothers who never came close to injuring me before I could be initiated. Not all the young men attempting to join a BGF have been so lucky.

The most disturbing hazing incident of my young fraternity life did not happen to me directly. It happened in 1994, while I was working on my PhD at the University of Kentucky (Lexington). Hundreds of miles away at Southeast Missouri State University (Cape Giradeau), members of our beloved Kappa Alpha Psi beat a pledge to death. The fraternity was thrown into a tailspin. We were subjected to harsh public scrutiny, a moratorium was placed on the initiation of new members, and we finally lost more than $2 million in a lawsuit surrounding the death of Michael Davis.

The Davis case was one of the most publicized instances of black fraternity hazing in the 1990s. It provides a rich case study of the factors that drive the ritualized process of initiation in BGFs. At first look, the choices of Davis and his potential fraternity brothers seem almost nonsensical and, individually as well as collectively, sociopathic. This initial observation, however, deserves a revisit. The activities of the young men in the Davis case are good illustrations of what often takes place during the pledgeship of new members into BGFs. Unfortunately, Davis's plight is not an anomaly. It is a rarity only in the fact that he was actually killed and the events leading to his death were made public.

In January 1994, Davis, a Southeast Missouri State University junior, attempted to join Kappa Alpha Psi for the second time in his college career. A few years earlier, he had tried to join the fraternity and engaged in an illegal process known as "underground pledging." "Underground" is a highly secretive period (not officially condoned by the fraternity) that "combines goofy pranks with rough-house physical and mental abuse designed to break you down as it builds you up."[2] Although this statement is generally correct, it does not even begin to capture the truly brutal nature of many underground pledge lines. The levels of physical abuse during such periods in some chapters of BGFs are almost incomprehensible.

In the spring of 1991, Davis participated in his first underground pledge line. Before he could be initiated into the fraternity, however, the chapter's alumni adviser traveled from St. Louis to Cape Girardeau and placed the chapter on "cease and desist" (a halt in chapter activities) on grounds that hazing—outlawed by Kappa Alpha Psi, as well as other BGFs—was taking place. After an unsuccessful graduate investigation, underground started up again, but Davis did not rejoin. Instead, he went home to St. Louis to raise his tuition for the upcoming year. He carried the stigma of being an "Eternal Scroller" (a Kappa pledge who was never initiated). In January 1994, Davis again joined a Kappa underground pledge line. In mid-February, a concerned neighbor entered his apartment to find a faint-pulsed Davis clad only in his underpants face-up on the floor. His body was covered with cuts and bruises.

Meanwhile, a Kappa and a pledge were frantically tossing a number of Davis's possessions into a trash bag. As events unfolded, paramedics would be called in, but Davis would eventually die. It was determined that he sustained broken ribs, a lacerated kidney, a torn liver, and finally died from a blow to the head that caused a fatal brain hemorrhage. To make it plain, Davis was beaten to death. The Kappas claimed he was injured during a pick-up football game. In reality, he was killed during an underground pledge session beating. Active member Carlos Turner and pledge Tabari Wayne had returned to the apartment to recover any evidence of the dying student's fraternity ties. If the Kappas had succeeded in fooling the police and Southeast Missouri State authorities, the facts behind the death of Michael Davis may never have been known. Unfortunately for them, they failed.

The question of blameworthiness is not quite as simple as it initially seems. Certainly, the casual observer would immediately say the Kappas should be held responsible for Davis's death. Deeper examination proves this to be incomplete. A good deal of blame, according to Kappa Alpha Psi's Past Grand Polemarch (National President) Robert Harris, must be laid at the feet of these individual "renegade members," and the courts seemed to agree.[3] Six of the seven fraternity members charged with involuntary manslaughter were found guilty. Nine other members were charged with various counts of hazing, and penalties ranged from probation to thirty days in jail.

I make no effort here to re-adjudicate the case of Michael Davis, but will attempt to provide some explanation for the existence of the environment in which his death occurred. To begin to understand this environment, we must examine a world rarely exposed to non-Greek-letter fraternity members. The almost impregnable tenets of BGF tradition that include secrecy and violent hazing run deep. Michael Davis became embroiled in the mystique of pledging and the organizational "respect" it supposedly brings. Alarmingly, even in the face of this incident and others like it, underground pledging continues. Active members persist in requiring it as a rite of passage. More disturbingly, pledges continue to subject themselves to a process they know is dangerous and illegal. The pull of pledging is so strong that some potential members risk being "blackballed" from the organizations they wish to join for submitting to illegal, underground activities.

Four years before the death of Michael Davis, four major BGFs along with black Greek-letter sororities came together, ironically in St. Louis (Davis's hometown), and outlawed pledging as a prerequisite for joining their organizations. This controversial move was largely prompted by another death—that of Morehouse College (Atlanta) student Joel Harris in 1989, while pledging Alpha Phi Alpha.[4] Kappa Alpha Psi Grand Polemarch Robert Harris took the condemnation of pledging and hazing a step further. He issued a series of executive orders mandating the suspension or expulsion from the fraternity of any active member who hazed, and the blackballing for life of any prospective member who allowed himself to be pledged or hazed. The fraternity's public stance on pledging and hazing was absolutely clear. In spite of this, Davis still allowed himself to be hazed and was subsequently killed.

Disturbingly, this was a case of a promising young black man being beaten to death by other promising young black men. These were not gangsters, drug dealers, or underachieving juvenile delinquents. These young men were Kappa men, supposedly our best and brightest hope for the future! We all knew that hazing occurred in our fraternity—it had traditionally been regarded as simply being the way of things. This loss of life, however, was disturbing. Davis's death marked one of the few opportunities that gave the media and the public the initiative to deeply examine what we considered a part of our private affairs—the rite of hazing. They placed a mirror of condemnation to our faces and made us take a long, hard look.

Reasonable brothers eventually had to admit that many of the practices we accepted and normalized over the years to test the mettle of our new initiates were nothing short of barbaric. It was clear to them that something had to be done. Many other brothers were not nearly as open to change. Maybe to put my own demons to rest, I embarked on a two-year study of BGF hazing for my doctoral dissertation. The work was so psychologically draining that I considered relinquishing active membership in the fraternity more than once. Ultimately, I stayed and even became Polemarch of my chapter for a time.

In 1996, I finished graduate school and accepted a professorship at the University of Louisville. I put the stress and strain of the dissertation behind me and moved on to teaching. In the spring of 1997, the hazing monster resurfaced—this time in Louisville. In early April, the campus and city were shocked to learn that yet another black student had fallen victim to an alleged hazing involving a BGF. Shawn Blackston, who would later become one of my students, sustained serious injuries that left his kidneys badly damaged. He was hospitalized, and at one point, doctors were unsure whether he would survive. Blackston did not initially admit to school or law enforcement officials how he was injured, but it was eventually revealed that he was the victim of hazing at the hands of members of the Omega Psi Phi Fraternity.

My life had changed greatly by 1997. I was no longer Mr. Terry's student waiting for a turn to become a Kappa, nor was I a graduate student trying to earn a doctorate and in turmoil over whether Kappa was helping or hurting young black men. I was now a professor who was not only a fraternity member, but also one of the few scholars who had conducted serious research on BGF hazing. My office and home phones were inundated with reporters' inquiries and requests for interviews. I submitted to the ones I thought were worthwhile and turned others away. Meanwhile, another promising young black man had nearly been beaten to death. The fraternity colors had changed from crimson and cream to purple and gold, but the end result was the same. In one radio interview, I commented to the host that he should be applauded for talking about the issue more than a week after it initially made its way into the news. I knew this incident and Shawn Blackston would soon be all but forgotten until the next time something like this happened.

A few months later, *Black Issues in Higher Education* dedicated almost an entire issue to BGF hazing and my fraternity brother, Jason DeSousa, appeared on the cover. He was quoted, "I specifically want to go on the record and say that unless we get control, or end undergraduate pledging, it's only a matter of time until someone else gets killed."[5] I had interviewed Jason a few years earlier for my dissertation. He had given me positive encouragement on the research, because it was more than a study to both of us—it was something that could possibly help "good old Kappa Alpha Psi." If Jason said he felt someone else would be killed, it was not said for effect—he meant it. Unfortunately, the coming years would prove his prediction accurate. Granted, Jason is no Nostradamus. The reality of the situation was that anyone with a modicum of rationality coupled with knowledge of the abuse involved in BGF pledging could have made the same prognostication with little risk of being wrong.

Three years later, hazing struck my beloved Kappas once again. This time it was much closer to home. The University of Louisville's chapter, with which I had been involved since my arrival at the university, was suspended. Many of these young men, brother and pledge alike, had been and were my students. I had even written letters of recommendation for some of them to join the fraternity. Beyond this, they had been named Provincial Chapter of the Year for the previous two years. How could something so good have gone so bad? I knew then that it was time I returned to this project and try to disseminate it to the masses in hopes of getting at the root of the problem where BGF hazing is concerned. What follows are my scholarly and personal observations and conclusions. Hopefully, they will help in the continuing struggle to save lives in our Greek-letter organizations.

Ricky L. Jones
Louisville, Kentucky
October 2002

1

Hazing Then and Now

To say that no one has known that hazing has been a problem in BGFs for a very long time would be patently false. Concern grew as the twentieth century ended, largely because of shocking Greek-related incidents and the media exposure that followed.[1] Unfortunately, the Michael Davis tragedy was not the result of atypical violent behavior in BGFs. The fact that violence in these groups is not isolated is further supported by injuries and deaths across organizational and regional lines every year. As a result, certain cases involving black Greeks and historically black college and university (HBCU) bands have gained great public attention over the last few decades. In addition to the deaths of Davis and Joel Harris, Omega Psi Phi pledges Van Watts and Joseph Green were killed at Tennessee State University (Nashville) in 1983 and 2001, respectively. Phi Beta Sigma pledge Donnie Wade died at Prairie View A&M University (Prairie View, TX) in 2009. By far, the most high-profile case was the brutal beating death of Robert Champion in 2011 at Florida A&M University (Tallahassee). Many more young men and women have been physically injured, hospitalized, or both during this time. The psychological damage visited on potential initiates is not easily quantified.

Despite the seemingly endless parade of organizational and institutional initiatives, hazing perseveres. It apparently baffles college and university administrators, Greek-letter officials, and an increasingly concerned community at large. Whether they are truly perplexed or simply have neglected the issue is debatable. To be sure, hazing organizations and their supporters have been taken to task in multiple mediums, but hazing incidents continue and remedies remain elusive. This book not only recounts hazing incidents, but explores possible individual, organizational, historical, and societal factors that lead to them. Normatively, it would seem that the "end" of building the complete fraternity man (or band member, etc.) through ritualized physical and mental rigor should dissipate when the ceremonial "means" reach such a level as to not only present life-threatening motifs, but actually cause death. In such instances, potential initiates can no longer be viewed as pledges; they must be considered victims. This victimage, however, does not begin or end with individual initiates or their pledge leaders. It is a social, cultural, and political process that involves people in a multilevel network of relationships leading to reification of belief in the BGF pledge/haze process as necessary and generative.

CONCERN, CHANGE, AND QUESTIONS

In response to elevated concern with hazing, BGFs have conducted a number of internal organizational studies since the late 1980s, seeking to explain its continuance in many of their chapters. I contend, however, that the motivations behind some of these studies and the data they have yielded are questionable. The changes BGFs have made within their organizational structures regarding the recruitment and initiation of new members are also debatable. The aforementioned studies and changes are suspect, because one may certainly submit that a good percentage of the membership of these organizations on the national, regional, and local levels has been reluctant to change the way in which they actually conduct the business of initiation. Most statements issued by BGF national offices take the stance that hazing continues because of a minority of "renegade members" who have no true allegiance to the ideals of the organizations. But while initiation procedural policy has been altered from time to time, behavior has remained constant.

The very fact that hazing continues in many BGF chapters lends credence to the idea that the practice is condoned—actively or passively—by a significant percentage of black Greek members. Internal studies, supposed changes to the pledge processes, and executive orders mandating cessation of this behavior are perceived by some as little more than smoke screens for the public's eye and legal defenses. Kappa Alpha Psi, for example, went so far as to change its initiation ritual (in the face of strong opposition from its membership) in 1993. The rationale behind this change was that the previous version of the fraternity's ritual had many "gray areas" and statements that could be construed as promoting hazing. Unfortunately, this and other internal changes obviously went for naught, because Michael Davis was killed the very next year.

The fact that the groups' attempts at self-study and regulation have not been successful in promoting real change brings two possibilities to the fore; one concerns utility and the other control. Either the national offices of the organizations are intentionally misleading in their reports on where their members stand regarding hazing in an effort to relegitimate the fraternities or they are out of touch with the members' beliefs and practices and have lost control of a good percentage of the brethren.

No matter which of the above scenarios is true, three questions are brought to bear when considering the indisputable fact that hazing still exists in black fraternities. First, were the activities and purposes of BGF pledge processes autonomously constructed by these organizations? Second, why is physical hazing regarded as such an integral part of black fraternity initiation? Finally, why do individuals continuously submit to this unsanctioned and sometimes dangerous process? My work here revolves around the belief that hazing of the more physically violent sort encountered in BGFs must be addressed sternly, because this type of abuse poses an immediate threat to black life. Consequently, in a practical and moral effort to save lives, the mortal risk inherent in such a process must be regarded as unacceptable. Unfortunately, although most people in the main have reached this threshold of intolerance, we are far from the historical moment when BGF members themselves submit to the cessation of hazing.

To elaborate on why I support the hypothesis that hazing in BGFs is more physically violent than that found in similar organizations, let us refer to Hank Nuwer's classic book *Broken Pledges*.[2] A quantitative analysis of BGF, white fraternity, and military hazing cases cited by Nuwer reveals interesting trends. The military institutions covered in Nuwer's work include the United States Military Academy, United States Naval Academy, United States Air Force Academy, and the Citadel.

It is important to understand that hazing is a very secretive activity and the numbers presented above only represent "reported" cases at the time of *Broken Pledges*' publication (1990). Unfortunately, the majority of cases are more than likely dealt with within fraternal orders or educational institutions without public scrutiny, so the actual instances

Black Greek, White Greek, and Military Academy Hazing Since 1838

Total Cases of Hazing	441
Cases involving military academies	31
Cases involving white Greeks (WGFs)	241
Cases involving black Greeks (BGFs)	31
Hazing deaths at military academies	4
Hazing deaths involving WGFs	47
Hazing deaths involving BGFs	4
Cases of physical hazing at military academies	7
Cases of physical hazing in WGFs	13
Cases of physical hazing in BGFs	29

of hazing are probably significantly higher than statistics indicate. The reported numbers suggest, however, that hazing has historically been and continues to be a problem in white fraternities and military academies as well as black fraternities. What the quantitative analysis does not reveal is the fact that hazing usually has very different manifestations in these groups. WGFs have the highest number of reported hazing cases as well as deaths, but their most extreme abuses have most often been alcohol and food related. There were no reported cases of white pledges dying from physical abuse. All forty-seven reported WGF deaths were caused by choking on raw food (i.e., liver), alcohol poisoning, accidental falls (from roofs, cliffs, etc.), or car accidents (i.e., pledges attempting to return to campus after active members abandoned them in some remote area). Of the 241 cases since 1838 involving white Greeks, slightly more than 19 percent of them resulted in death and only 5 percent of the cases involved any physical abuse at all.

The fact that only thirty-one reported cases involved military academies probably speaks to the fact that information concerning hazing at these institutions has always been even more difficult to access than details on fraternal transgressions at civilian colleges and universities. Hazing has also been regarded by some as a necessary tool to mentally and physically prepare men for war. This preparation has served as one of pro-military hazers' justifications for hazing practices at military academies and ROTC units throughout the country. There also exists an interesting link between military and fraternity hazing. Nuwer cogently points out the potential impact of the military on fraternity hazing as we know it today when he cites the case of young Douglas MacArthur, who was commanded to testify at a congressional court of inquiry ordered by President William McKinley in 1900. "The hearing had two purposes: to deduce whether the unwritten code of hazing had caused the recent death of a young cadet named Oscar Booz of Bristol, Pennsylvania, and to determine if hazing was a significant problem at West Point."[3]

In the end, MacArthur "steadfastly refused to name the upper-classmen who had hazed him, yet he tried to appease the select committee by giving them the names of several men who had already quit West Point for one reason or another. He downplayed the convulsions he had experienced after being seriously hazed, and he most certainly lied on the stand when he said that he could name with certainty only those hazers who had already left the service academy, a Mr. Dockery and a Mr. Barry."[4] Nuwer concludes: "The importance of this study, in retrospect, is the striking similarities revealed between many latter-day hazing practices and West Point abuses. These similarities raise the possibility that military academy drop-outs introduced hazing practices into the colleges they later attended and, thus, played a leading role in the history of hazing on American college campuses."[5]

Just as it stands to reason that military academy dropouts may have influenced hazing at civilian colleges and universities, it is also quite logical to conclude that military academy graduates helped reinforce the hazing of soldiers, sailors, airmen, and Marines as they went through boot camp. A Kappa Alpha Psi member commented on this historical progression:

A lot of people wonder how hazing started in our groups and why it looks like it does today. I'm old enough to have been initiated before all of our founders died. I also know people who were pledged by some of the founders. From what they tell me, most early members were not overwhelmingly concerned with physical hazing or an extensive pledge period. Remember, even though our fraternity was founded in 1911, there was no official pledge club until 1919. Even then, physical hazers were of a particular type. This was even true when I was made in 1963. There were three basic types of guys. The smart ones made you remember a lot of information. The athletes exercised you a lot, but they did that stuff along with you. Then there were the guys who weren't very smart and weren't athletic either. These guys were usually the hazers. It was their claim to fame. Also, activities in the process changed a lot after World War I and again after World War II. This is because a lot of guys went to the military and then returned to school after the wars. They brought things like dressing alike and walking in line, along with a few other "unmentionables" back with them.[6]

Although the military may have contributed to hazing in all fraternities, BGF hazing seems to have become the most physically intense variation of the practice. The first of the 241 white fraternity cases reported by Nuwer occurred in 1873 at Cornell University. The first military case was the 1900 case cited involving MacArthur. The first BGF cases do not appear until 1977. Glaringly, between 1977 and 1990, BGFs are cited for the same number of hazing cases as military academies are in a span of 90 years. Furthermore, only 23 percent of the reported military cases involved physical abuse. In contrast, almost 94 percent of the black cases involved physical abuse—with all four deaths being caused by physical hazing. Almost a quarter of a century after *Broken Pledges*' publication, the number of incidents has obviously increased, but the trends in these groups remain steady.

It must be clear that I do not contend that physical hazing only occurs in BGFs. Nuwer's study illustrates that this is not the case. It is also probably true that men who seek to join organizations such as fraternities and the military through violent means belong to a particular personality group. Admittedly, membership in this personality group crosses racial and organizational lines. It should be emphasized that men who seek affiliation with hazing fraternities, bands, or high-risk units of the military are not totally coerced, but are largely self-selected. The striking point of departure is that, at least where fraternal orders are concerned, there seems to be a higher frequency of this type of personality found among black males than any other group under consideration. If true, this helps explain why the prevalence of physical hazing in BGFs is much higher than in WGFs or even the military. Certainly, an important epistemological question must follow such an assertion. If, in fact, there are more black men in this personality group, how did they come to be this way? This is an issue of paramount importance that chapter 6 engages in depth.

THE INFLUENCE OF THE ANCIENT
AND MODERN WORLDS ON BLACK GREEK VIOLENCE

Regardless of the answer to the aforementioned question concerning the personality types of black men who engage in hazing, the theory of BGF violence offered here posits that the pledge process is not a phenomenon unique to (or invented by) black Greek-letter fraternities, but finds its true roots in the ancient world. Black fraternities were created by black collegians in an effort to provide interpersonal, social, educational, and professional support denied to them in many American social and political structures, but they did not autonomously create the process of violent initiation. The manifestation of violence found in BGFs is really another form of sacrifice that has been passed down to black fraternities through multiple ritualistic traditions. As chapter 4 illustrates, ancient sacrificial ritual was usually mortal and public because people believed it impacted the entire community. These rituals were established to intervene in what was seen as inevitable violent social interaction so that violence could be redirected and even legitimized. In societies where the notion of human sacrifice was considered "uncivilized," the tenets of sacrificial ritual were transferred to social and secret organizations that ultimately served many of the same purposes.

Although the underlying purpose of sacrificial ritual never changed, it was presented in different guises. These altered avenues for sacrifice usually appeared as secret and semisecret orders such as the Egyptian Mysteries, Eleusinian Mysteries, Orphic Mysteries, Mithraism, Freemasonry, and the military. According to some thinkers, these structures (whether secret or not) always serve a societal purpose. By legitimating violence through ritual, one "can precipitate the forging of new social forms that address violence as an autonomous, culturally generative, and meaning-endowing practice."[7] Though all sacrificial rituals demand some form of sacrifice, they all do not demand death in the literal sense. This does not mean that the notion of death is absent from any sacrificial ritual. Contrarily, it is forever present. All sacrificial ritual hinges on the expectation of some type of death and subsequent rebirth. In modern times, this death-rebirth process is usually symbolic. This is the case in fraternities, but it does not change the purpose of the ritual.

Violence in these rituals has become integral in BGFs, because it is now regarded as an important tool in the construction of black male identity and manhood. BGFs problems are not only rooted in the fact that they are Greek-letter organizations with unique practices or that their written rituals somehow mandate violent behavior (as is evidenced by the death of Michael Davis in spite of ritualistic alterations). BGFs have historically been concerned with the construction of a particular black American male identity that affirms and continuously reaffirms black manhood. Unfortunately, violent physical struggle is regarded as a key ingredient in the building of this manhood. The dependence on the physical often occurs because many black men feel (rightfully or wrongfully) that they are not privy to the same opportunities to define themselves as their white counterparts in American society. This perception (and reality) will be explored in depth in later chapters. Before reaching these passages, however, I hope the reader will temporarily accept my hypothesis that social and political marginalization help to promote the black male's search for alternate arenas in which he can be regarded as a man. One way to define manhood that has emerged, particularly in black intraracial interaction, is to be physically dominant or able to withstand physical abuse. In this manner, physical toughness is eventually equated with manliness and this phenomenon carries over into BGFs.

This reality helps explain why many individuals continue to submit to hazing—they feel it affirms their toughness and manhood. It must be noted that BGFs do not force black men to join their organizations. Contrarily, a large number of men go to great lengths to convince current members that they are worthy of membership. Many of these men submit to, and even seek, pledging and hazing, because modern BGFs have developed an interaction of domination that largely centers on the narrative of the pledge process. This phenomenon is rigorously engaged in chapter 5. The hegemonic struggle between pro- and antihazers within BGFs has effectively established parameters that define individual fraternity brothers as legitimate or illegitimate. The criteria for legitimacy are primarily based on whether or not a member has participated in the traditional BGF pledge process. Many black men see membership in a fraternity as one way to respond to negative societal factors and carve out space that truly belongs to them. Along with this space comes some degree of (or perception of) power and camaraderie not easily accessed by the majority of black males in American society. Some of these men see the traditional pledge process that includes hazing as the only way to gain uncontested admittance into this zone of power and brotherhood.

Although the pledge process may have its roots in sacrificial ritual, the current extreme nature of violent hazing in BGFs is augmented by the unique identity of many modern black American males, be they Greek affiliated or not. Some believe this identity may be a historical construct of conscious and unconscious oppression of this group by Anglo American–centered structures of governance and determinants of social and political power. Louis Knowles and Kenneth Prewitt described this system as *institutional racism*.[8] They saw it as one in which the institutions and rules of American society were based on the values of the dominant white racial group and society's goods and services were distributed according to these values. They subsequently concluded that continuing discrimination against African Americans has been one of the most powerful expressions of institutional racism in the society and the most devastating legacy of the white supremacist ethos.

Following this admittedly contested logic, the black male Self created by these realities is only further fragmented by the assault of modernization and the economic and psychological problems it brings to bear. This phenomenon changed the realities and life chances of most Americans during the twentieth century, in that old familiar social forms disintegrated before the new and highly aggressive forces of urbanization and industrialization. In relatively quick succession, family links in America weakened, religious authority waned, face-to-face communal life was replaced by competitive, atomized city life, and custom and tradition were displaced by the cold, brutal rationality of the modern marketplace.

Black Greek-letter fraternity hazing and the particular black male identity that leads to it are bound up in the upheavals of these various trends in general, rather than the dynamics of fraternal interaction in particular. The historic psychic trauma of black males resulting from chattel slavery and continued post–Civil War marginalization increases the toll of modern American society that often occasions painful dislocations economically, socially, and psychologically. This book seeks to examine and ground the hypothesis that it is in the societal realm, rather than the fraternal, that we can locate many of the realities that allow us to more completely understand violence among black men in BGFs.

FALSEHOODS AND FAILURE:
THE EPISTEMIC DOMINO EFFECT AND ETHICS IN GREEKDOM

Though it is often ignored or misunderstood, inquiries such as this are ultimately concerned with the intersections of epistemological engagement and axiological shifts in cultures. Observers often attempt to separate these matters of the mind into distinct, disconnected entities. The reality, however, is that if one interrogates a culture's epistemic modes of inquiry while disregarding its conclusions concerning values and ethics, a critical link that can help explain behavior is lost. It must be clear that epistemology is not simply the authority by which one purports to base his or her knowledge. Certainly, the questions of What do I know? and How do I know it? are asked in epistemological inquiry, but the real power of the engagement does not end there. Once people draw conclusions about what they know and how they know it (whether the answers are right or wrong), they use this knowledge to construct, affirm, and reaffirm individual and group modes of behavior and traditions. Ultimately, these behaviors and traditions are based on, and subsequently help to create, ethical constructs.

Troubling questions rise out of this progression. What if the answers to the initial epistemic questions are wrong? What if an individual draws conclusions and inferences from skewed, flawed, or even outright false information? Beyond this, there exists the possibility that the formation of identities and the axiological foundations upon which they necessarily rest could be exposed to an identity domino effect. Such an effect occurs if inquiries and answers concerning the authoritative legitimacy of knowledge are not grounded in fact, but in fiction. Carried far enough and reified for long enough, not only do the answers to questions become wrong, but the questions themselves become flawed.

If epistemological inquiry is necessarily related to the construction of ethical systems, then it may very well be mandatory that our study of the subject at hand be rooted in epistemological means with the purpose of influencing axiological and ideological ends. To be sure, our charge here is not only to encounter, know, and understand, but also to practically impact the behavior, politics, and power structures within the groups in question. Ultimately, difficult challenges must be presented and answers demanded. What is the purpose of BGFs in the modern age, when the black community continues to face overwhelming forces of negativity? It must be acknowledged that black Greeks have built a great historical legacy of placing powerful black men and women at the forefront of the black freedom struggle. The list of names is endless: from W. E. B. Du Bois to Martin Luther King Jr., from Jessie Jackson to Johnnie Cochran. If twenty-first-century black Greeks, however, lose sight of the fact that the community looks to them to behave with decency and integrity—the groups have lost their way.

We must understand that the mission and meaning of black Greekdom can only be respected and needed insofar as they speak to the mission and meaning of black life in general. Black Greeks' worth must ultimately be affirmed by the people they produce and the communities they serve. If some members of the community now hold them in disdain, there is a reason why. The perspective that many people (on campuses and in communities at large) have distanced themselves from Greekdom completely out of ignorance and jealousy simply does not hold under critical analysis. At some point, BGFs must not only address what they are doing right, but also what they are doing wrong. Such intellectual exchange, unfortunately, is largely emptied of its quality by a lack of direction and courage to speak to issues of import to BGFs and the larger community with strength, clarity, and purpose.

When engaging activities within BGFs, we must recognize the strong possibility that what members actually do today is largely a result of the manipulation of identity construction from within as well as from without. The end result of this manipulation is often the production of people who do what many consider to be wrong. This is simultaneously a simple and difficult admission. We would be hard pressed to find someone who would not admit that the violence, damage, and death visited upon young men such as Joel Harris, Michael Davis, Shawn Blackston, and Robert Champion are wrong. Regardless of this fact, there is an almost immediate attempt by many Greeks to convolute the issue by shifting blame and refusing to take responsibility for their personal involvement in similar violent activities.

When crimes are committed in these organizations, a project almost totally dedicated to the maintenance of the fraternal structures is mobilized. These structures are often maintained through the use of blatant lies and the deception of other members, educational officials, and legal authorities. Often, this deceit is undertaken because of the ethical orientation of members largely borne of epistemic questions and answers provided during their own pledge periods. The ploys are often successful, not because they are well thought out or believable, but because many of the investigators either tacitly condone the actions of the Greeks (sympathetic fraternity officials) or seem to not really care whether groups of black men beat one another to death. The deceptions and those who allow them must be stopped. There is no room for neutrality on this point. Our bias, however, must be guided by care and concern for the preservation of life rather than degenerative judgment grounded in misunderstanding and contempt. Certainly, prejudice fueled by blind rage and folly is negative, but so is the ineffectual stance of the neutral observer in instances such as this. Stands must be taken, and this work is intended to be one.

Consequently, in the following pages I hope to move beyond simply condoning or condemning the BGF pledge process and the hazing that usually comes with it (though this volume certainly condemns it). I will endeavor to transcend the traditional questions as to whether hazing or pledging are morally right or wrong; whether they need to be eradicated or maintained; whether fraternities have outlived their usefulness or not. The thrust of this work is to question why the particular type of violence in BGFs exists, how it relates to the political situation of black males in America, and what can be done to counter it. As a consequence of this engagement, I hope fraternities, university officials, and individual members will revisit their approaches to hazing and their organizations in general.

This is, no doubt, a political project and process. When speaking to the "political" here, I am addressing the process by which any group or community decides who gets what, when and how.[9] The political, therefore, moves quickly from its colloquial position of referring to electoral politics and distribution of material resources. It is, critically, the process by which not only the allocation of economic and material resources is determined, but it also dictates how different groups in a society see themselves and others and subsequently determines what is acceptable (and in some cases necessary), unacceptable, and even human. This inquiry into humanity is not limited to that which is considered human physically, but also culturally and psychologically.

The way in which this work adds to the body of philosophical, theoretical, and practical knowledge is that it seeks to help us understand a process among a group of men that may at times seem sociopathic and barbaric. My personal feelings about the endurance or demise of the pledge process notwithstanding, before policy can be influenced, a clear epistemological understanding of the true forces at work must be reached. Some may be disappointed that I do not have answers to all the questions posed in this work. Admittedly, no surefire solutions to solving the problem of BGF violence *and* preserving the organizations are offered in these pages. The sad reality is the ritual of hazing is probably too deep-seated in the groups to be halted—short of eradicating them. What this work does offer is a study that draws a distinct line between fact and the fantastic and gets at the root of the phenomenon by being very clear as to why this violence takes place.

There is no doubt that something is amiss here, but it is probably not some intrinsic evil found in black males. The need for perceived power, respect, and acceptance is more than likely the culprit. The quest for these social goods—borne of psychosocial anxieties—plays itself out in fraternities, but would (and does) manifest itself elsewhere if (and when) the fraternal vehicle were not present or accessible. BGF policies change, but behavior among many members and initiates remains constant, because of one simple fact—the fraternities do not produce potential initiates, society does. BGFs simply augment their madness. BGF national organizations continue in the struggle to identify and solve their problems from the wrong perspectives—practical (organizational hierarchies, dues structures, individual chapter and national chapter power relations, etc.) and individual-psychological (levels of active participation, personal approaches to the organizations bred by particular pledge processes, etc.)— rather than examining the more telling relationship between sociopolitical systems and black male organizational and personal interactions and identities. As a corrective, this study takes a new approach to an old problem that has plagued BGFs for most of their existence.

My research here suggests that oppression is societal in that it is a reality that has been historically integrated into everyday American life through political, economic, and social means. This everydayness has, over time, desensitized us to the very real dehumanization that American structures have fostered where their African-descended citizens are concerned. Black Greek-letter fraternities have not been immune to the effects of this progression. We must, therefore, trace out the true links between the production and cultivation of the inhumane and its effect on black male identity and action—inside as well as outside of fraternities. The reasons for the failure of fraternal policy are multivariate, with the various causes reinforcing one another. Most of these causes are usually (if not always) societal—not individual—and it is there that we must search to change present fraternal realities into generative forces in modern black life.

2

Men, Media, and Movements

For three years of my graduate school career, I served as the adviser to the University of Kentucky's black Greek-letter fraternities and sororities. One of my duties was chaperoning the groups' parties, which were the primary social outlets for the campus's African American student population. During one event, I met and casually chatted with a fraternity brother who had recently come to the university to work on an MBA. This particular brother had graduated from the University of Georgia the previous spring and seemed decent enough. His home chapter, however, had encountered a problem the previous school year. As the media reported it, the brothers at Georgia beat one of their pledges so extensively that his buttocks split. Unfortunately, the young man did not keep the wounds cleaned well and they eventually became seriously infected. Ultimately, surgery was required to halt the inflammation in his rear end. The idea of a pledge having an operation on his hind-parts was simultaneously comical to some of us at my chapter (for obvious reasons) and sad. Either way, it became a topic of conversation with my new acquaintance.

"You're from ZI [Zeta Iota], huh?" I asked.

"Yeah," he replied, "You know any bruhs there?"

"No. I know an Alpha from UGA [University of Georgia] who pledged in the eighties, but I don't know any bruhs there. I'm from Georgia though, and spent a little time in Athens when I was an undergrad. So, you were there when the kid got his behind busted last year."

"Yeah, I was there," he replied.

"So, what happened with that?"

"Man, that little bastard dropped dime on us. It was fucked up. He got the whole damned chapter in trouble 'cause he couldn't take a little heat."

Even though blame-the-victim rationales and rhetoric were

common when hazing was exposed, I thought it was almost insane in this instance. After all, these brothers had literally busted this kid's buttocks! I told the brother so. "Bruh, don't you think you're being a little unfair? I mean from the way this thing came to us, he pretty much had to eventually tell what happened. I mean you all busted his butt!"

"Yo bruh, he knew what he was getting into."

"Bruh, do you think he really knew? I mean, do you think he would have pledged if he knew bruhs were going to bust his ass and he would have to go under the knife?"

With that my fraternity brother looked a bit perturbed, and then nonchalantly but firmly restated, "Yo, he knew what he was getting into."

"All right, frat. Good meeting you," I said as I took my leave. I walked away and took another spin around the party to make sure everything was in order. I thought to myself that this brother's approach to the situation at Georgia was disturbing at best and psychotic at worst. But was this brother really crazy, or had we established a culture in Kappa that reinforced this type of sentiment when we harmed pledges? I have since concluded that he was probably not a psychopath. In fact, to look at the violent acts in BGFs as the separate actions of individual lunatics would be flawed. It would be closer to the mark to suggest that, in studying the behavior of individuals or even organizations, societal factors are a more appropriate focus than individual factors.

An example of such a strategy where violence is concerned is the medically oriented work of Deborah Prothrow-Stith. Prothrow-Stith's study of teenage violence, *Deadly Consequences*, proposes more partnerships between enforcement agencies and communities that emphasize community responsibility to handle wayward teens.[1] From her perspective, we must change our entire ethos in an attempt to move away from a system designed for intensive, acute care toward much greater concern with prevention and maintenance. Change will occur only if society sees violence as a distinctly societal problem, and individual fields of technically oriented professionals see themselves as part of the answer rather than the entire solution.

Emile Durkheim also did important philosophical and sociological work that linked society and individual behavior. He claimed that there are "ways of acting, thinking, and feeling that present the noteworthy property of existing outside the individual consciousness."[2] Durkheim's belief that socialization had a disproportionate impact on the individual extended to the point that he even examined the act of suicide in societal rather than individualistic terms. He saw society at large and the thoughts and conduct it yielded as not only external to the individual, but coercive as well. It is so because society imposes itself on a social agent regardless of his or her individual will. In Durkheim's view, contrary to what many people believe, most of our ideas and tendencies are not developed autonomously but come from without.

I contend that this is the case for many BGF members. They certainly suffer from societal psychoses that are not wholly products of the individuals themselves. Undeniably, these external attacks burden some individuals to a greater degree than others, but these "social facts" and "currents" serve to form "collective habits" and are always present. Durkheim argued that "collective habits are inherent not only in the successive acts which they determine, but by a privilege of which we find no example in the biological realm. They are given permanent expression in a formula which is repeated from mouth to mouth, transmitted by education, and fixed even in writing."[3] This perspective has great explanatory power and requires us to examine the plight of BGFs on the macrosocietal level rather than the microindividual one.

HABERMAS, THE PUBLIC SPHERE, AND A CRITICAL APPROACH TO THE MEDIA

One important issue that must be considered is where in society we locate most of the current discussions concerning BGFs. Looking back on the situation at Georgia, even though we were in the same fraternity, my chapter did not hear about the incident from brothers. We initially heard of the hazing through newspaper and television news reports, via what is often called the "public sphere." The fact that the acts of these brothers were negative cannot be denied. Unfortunately, this particular debacle aside, most of the media attention brought to BGFs has been negative, and at least where hazing is concerned, deserved. The fact that so much attention has been paid to the underbelly of black fraternities by local and national media forces us to look there as one starting point in our examination. Simultaneously, it is wise to note that the media are probably not the best place to get at the heart of the problem of violence in BGFs, because they rarely place hazing in a larger context that includes the histories and doctrines of the organizations.

Of course, media myopia is not limited to BGF coverage. Earl Ofari Hutchinson, for example, has done notable work on the narrow portrayal of blacks in general—and black men in particular—across various outlets. In *The Assassination of the Black Male Image*, Hutchinson includes negative reports on black males from the nations' most powerful news outlets: television, the *Boston Globe*, the *Boston Herald*, *Newsweek*, the *Los Angeles Times*, *Time*, the *Washington Post*, the *New York Times*, and the *Wall Street Journal*, among others.[4] Although he admits that black men are sometimes at fault and deserve negative reporting (as do people from all groups), Hutchinson is shocked by the dearth of positive images presented. Media narratives are usually devoid of historical or societal references that help explain the *why* instead of merely reporting the *what.* This failure to examine deeper reasons behind violent acts, by blacks or others, happens for several reasons. One is pure capitalist economics. American media may not be worthy of absolute public trust, because they have a tendency to simplify and sensationalize news in an attempt to increase the sale of papers, magazines, television shows, and movies. This practice inevitably contributes to the disappearance of meaningful rational discourse among a country's citizenry.[5] Such anaesthetization and dialogical eradication immediately brings to mind the social criticism of the media by Jürgen Habermas in *The Structural Transformation of the Public Sphere.*[6]

Habermas saw the media as playing a key role in influencing the technological and social organization of a society's communications, but felt they should be distrusted because they often pander to political agendas fraught with propaganda and economic manipulation.[7] *The Structural Transformation of the Public Sphere* is an effort to understand the history, foundations, and internal processes of public discourse; it makes inquiries about the constituents of the bourgeois public sphere over time and what has caused its erosion. Habermas ultimately concludes that the rise of new media forms—telegraph, telephone, film, and especially television—undermine a society's discursive relations.[8]

In today's cynical society, people do not come together to discuss and rationally evaluate books, movies, television programs, or media personalities. Though families may convene to engage in social and cultural consumption by watching television, very rarely do they subsequently immerse themselves in discourse about the substantive issues presented by (or absent from) television shows, films, or speeches—political, religious, or otherwise. Passive consumption blurs lines between the public and the private by allowing both to be colonized by the social. Publicity is lowered amid professionalism as critics and so-called "experts" (not the citizenry) become arbiters of taste in that they decide what and who is worthy to be deemed art or trash, shallow or substantive, trustworthy or suspect.

Theoretically, the very concept of the public sphere assumes that participants have equal access to information and opportunities to participate in decision making within a particular sociopolitical space. In this framework, governing bodies are open to the people as true mediums for voicing public opinion. The reality, however, is that these bodies are usually not open. Contrarily, information is often intentionally held back, sometimes temporarily, sometimes permanently, and the populace cannot engage in informed dialogue. Thus, the governmental vehicle is not really public; rather, it enunciates preset opinions and compromises made behind the scenes by political conspirators (whether or not they know they conspire). Media machines are integral to this process in that they often report the symbolic agreements, not the underlying critical issues. Ownership of such media tools in the modern capitalist society is concentrated, and they are run as profit-making businesses rather than ideological instruments for public enlightenment and change.

Problems with Habermas

Even though Habermas presents powerful points relevant to the purposes of this paper, his work has glaring shortcomings. Some concerns are products, not of issues Habermas includes in his writings, but rather of the ones he ignores. First of all, *The Structural Transformation of the Public Sphere* is true to its name—structural. It is so structural, in fact, that it disregards important cultural issues that have historically influenced the public sphere. Craig Calhoun comments, "He [Habermas] does not consider the continuing transformations of subjectivity wrought not only in literature but in a host of identity-forming public spheres."[9] Without this cultural analysis, Habermas's explanatory power is limited.

He also ignores the plight of women and is content to collapse the plebeian public sphere into the bourgeois.[10]

My points of contention with Habermas's work have more to do with his failure to incorporate consideration of race into his model rather than relying on a somewhat mechanical paradigm centered on class. These criticisms considered, Habermas's work still helps flush out the issues under consideration here where the media are concerned.

Succinctly, the public sphere ideally serves as a forum for communication aimed at mutual knowledge and understanding among a democratic society's populace—whether exploring BGFs or any other issue of import. Unfortunately, the media do not always positively contribute to this project. The "dumbing" effect of the media is compounded by the fact that BGFs are populated by black men, who have always been somewhat alien in the imagination of America's core culture.[11] Black men have been historically considered the "Other"—either superhuman or subhuman—depending on the situation. This peculiarity sits at the heart of the construction of the black fraternity man's psyche.

BGFS, SOCIAL MOVEMENTS, AND IDENTITY

If we follow Prothrow-Stith, Durkheim, and others and historically contextualize our argument by moving from the individual to the societal level, it becomes readily apparent that BGFs originated within a larger social movement. Just as early white fraternities had strong political interests, the activities of BGFs were political on various levels. An Anglo American fraternity man commented on the political nature of fraternities: "They all came out of a political environment. They were in some cases political by claiming to be anti-political. My fraternity itself, Phi Kappa Tau, was founded as the Anti-Fraternity Association. They were responding to the power that fraternities wielded at Miami (OH) in SGA, intramurals, and other campus activities. What they ended up doing was going into that same movement when they saw that any students effectively banding together could come up with that type of power base and still foster the brotherhood."

Black fraternities have always been populated by college-educated men and, for the most part, have been relatively conservative in their approaches to social and political change. This is not to say that early members were not conscious of prejudice or discrimination, for this would be untrue. Their goal, however, was not to somehow break away from or destroy American mainstream culture, but to integrate blacks into it. Consequently, BGF strategies for bringing about change largely fell within the plural-integrationist school of thought. Beyond this, when we address BGFs as social movements, we must also address the identity issues involvement in such activities inherently brings to the fore.

Examining the formation of BGFs within the U.S. collegiate and social realities that produced them illustrates that they were firmly entrenched in the wave of black social movements and struggles of the early twentieth century. One reason the five organizations under consideration were formed was that white Greek organizations would not allow black participation. This was a direct result of the political repercussions of chattel slavery and Jim Crow social structures. In actuality, many men who joined BGFs may not have had any powerful racial identification, loyalty, or strong desire to change the political environment for the black collective. It is possible that some of these individuals simply yearned to be part of a Greek-letter organization that offered collegiate activities similar to those of their white counterparts. We cannot know what motivated every member to join during the early 1900s, though one thing is for sure—if they wanted to be part of a fraternity, America mandated that they form and join their own.

If members were not political before joining these movements, the relationship between movements and identity probably politicized them. This assertion becomes clear when we note that the effort to form and join fraternities is not as important as the reality that social movements extend beyond obvious struggles into the realm of identity politics. As Craig Calhoun posits, "One could read the history of social movements as the story of efforts to bring social concerns into political contestation."[12] It is through this process of politicizing the social that change can be determined "from the bottom up" and not only by rulers. This change is inescapably tied to identity, though this fact may not be realized:

Identity politics have more generally been basic to a whole range of movements that sought to use the public sphere to challenge existing arrangements or bring forward new possibilities in religion, sexual relations, the human relation to nature, community life, work and economics, and a host of other dimensions of social life.... Different understandings and valuations of pressing social concerns were not just matters of fixed interests. They were—and necessarily are—matters of the constitution of identities. Neither identities nor interests neatly come before the other; the struggle to achieve what we believe to be in our interest shapes our identities as much as the identities determine what we see as in our interests. The point is that neither is altogether fixed. Both are produced and altered in the course of everyday social projects and collective mobilizations of varying scale. There is always some politics to this process.[13]

THE POLITICS OF PERSONAL INVOLVEMENT: GAZING THROUGH FRATERNITY MEN'S EYES

To be sure, this project considers many issues, but it is ultimately concerned with the question of identity. Although one particular method was not used, the overall work is ethnographic. This approach was employed in an attempt to reexamine BGFs at least partially from the perspectives of men involved in the organizations. The naturalist-ethnographic paradigm used here includes four major factors: anthropological descriptions, naturalistic research, field research, and participant observations.[14] Through the use of these methods, the ethnographer attempts to capture and understand specific aspects of the life of a particular group via prolonged immersion in the setting of interest. Over the years, some modern researchers have tended to drastically shorten their time of immersion, which has produced a bit of debate over whether these studies bred of brief exposure of researcher to researched are truly ethnographic. The ideal, of course, is for the researcher to stay with the researched long enough to have an informed, but not biased, opinion. He must endeavor to balance involvement with detachment, familiarity with strangeness, and closeness with distance.[15]

Admittedly, my immersion in this subject is deep. For a number of years I have been a BGF member. I personally experienced my own initiation process and have held a number of posts in my organization as well as in Greekdom on the university and national levels. This immersion has, since my initiation, made me a complete participant in BGFs, so I am aware that the possibility of personal bias certainly exists. I hope the reader will feel (as I do) that this personal involvement adds spirit and love to my handling of this sensitive issue. I sincerely hope that my Greek brothers will not be overly offended by the passages that seem to be too hard on them, and that critics of BGFs will forgive me for sections of the text that appear to not be critical enough.

Whether my readers forgive me or not, I believe I would have done this work a great disservice by not drawing on personal experiences to add meaning and lucidity. The use of narratives is important, because they relay the lived experiences of BGF members and take the theories I put forward out of their philosophical vacuums. As Donald Polkinghorne states, "The products of narrative schemes are ubiquitous in our lives: they fill our cultural and social environment."[16] Thus, all people create narratives about their past actions for themselves as well as for others. These narrative descriptions not only relay experiences, but also aid in giving the experiences meaning—"we develop storied accounts that give sense to the behavior of others [and ourselves]."[17] Once the parameters of sense making are established, the narratives we encounter then "carry the values of an entire culture by providing positive models to emulate and negative models to avoid."[18]

Practically, the core of this study revolves around narratives received from extensive interviews and focus groups with actual BGF members that give us a "firsthand" glimpse into the life-worlds of these men—how they see their fraternal and extrafraternal realities. Michael Carpini and Bruce Williams give a fine summary of the utility of interviews and focus groups in the social sciences in their article, "The Method Is the Message."[19] They cite Richard Krueger as noting, "the focus group is a carefully planned discussion designed to obtain perceptions on a defined area of interest in a permissive, nonthreatening environment."[20] It is a technique that has rarely been used in the social sciences, but for the purposes of this study it is much more suitable than methods that rely on cold, lifeless numbers.

During these interviews, I was particularly interested in finding out what members think the pledge process actually does and how it influences the fidelity and viability of members. Beyond this, I was concerned with how members view the political progression of BGFs since their inception. Do they think the groups have a continuing political mission for the advancement of the human condition to any particular point, or are BGFs now simply social outlets? One could certainly argue that the impetus for joining the organizations has changed to such a degree that present day BGFs only vaguely resemble the organizations founded in the early 1900s. Certainly, social change (modernization and its many consequences) has altered the "type" of member encountered in contemporary America, but why do the groups endure?

The interviews and focus groups included more than 170 graduate and undergraduate members of BGFs. They ranged from national officers to undergraduate members who held no elected position. These members are students or graduates both of predominantly black and predominantly white institutions, both public and private. Group member initiation dates range as far back as 1953. The study also includes nonblack respondents, who could more effectively address issues concerning white Greek organizations. Consequently, there is a good mix of opinions from national leaders as well as mass followers initiated in various parts of the country.

Members of four of the five major BGFs give comments in the text. I was in no way interested in which of the five organizations these men belonged. Although perceived group differences are certainly extolled by a good percentage of each groups' members due to competitive and egoistic concerns, outside of colors, signs, and grips (secret handshakes), I do not believe there are any substantive dissimilarities among members of Alpha Phi Alpha, Kappa Alpha Psi, Omega Psi Phi, Phi Beta Sigma, or Iota Phi Theta. In this engagement, they are all regarded as black men who suffer from the same societal and organizational ills.

Even though I have sought to make this inquiry as open and honest as possible, like any work it has a number of natural and self-imposed constraints. I addressed my primary self-imposed limitation in the previous chapter: choosing to center on hazing in black fraternities and not fraternities in general, high schools, bands, or the military. The research is African-centered in that it seeks to examine phenomena impacting African-descended realities. My approach to these problems, however, differs from that of a few ideological extremists who feel that a person must be of African descent to provide models that help explain the African-descended experience. Consequently, I do not hesitate to draw on intellectual engagements rarely used in examinations such as this (i.e., Antonio Gramsci, Jürgen Habermas, Lawrence Grossberg, and Harry Frankfurt, to name a few).

Another self-imposed limitation is the use of actual fraternity rituals.

Although I do have access to specific knowledge concerning the written ritual of my own fraternity and others, I do not feel it is appropriate to utilize such knowledge for this study. I do, however, cite rituals made public over the years (for example, the initiation ritual of the Society of Redmen of the nineteenth century), and attempt to draw links between relevant motifs.

A non-self-imposed limitation is that even though I am a member of a BGF, I am perceived as an outsider by many members of the remaining four organizations (and even by some members of my own fraternity who belong to different chapters). This divisiveness caused problems when I attempted to secure historical information on these groups. For example, even though the history books of each organization are public documents, many chapters' members steal them from campus libraries so nonmembers cannot access them. This strong "gatekeeper" tendency was obviously problematic, so it was essential that I capitalized on relationships with sympathetic members of these organizations.

These groups all have rich traditions of achievement, but current abusive trends in the organizations are disturbing to many observers. An Alpha commented, "Somewhere in this historical experience, there has been a failure to communicate properly and to impress upon those who have since gained membership what are the real ideals and objectives of black Greek life." The traditions of BGFs that have been communicated, be they productive or destructive, are difficult to halt. Studying the destructive ones is an imposing task. Because of the secretive nature of fraternal societies, the media and scholars alike have been (and are) faced with restricted access to information. BGFs are no different in that members see anyone who is not a part of the organizations as an out-group member, and organizational knowledge is therefore closely guarded. This reality is one of the greatest obstacles faced by a researcher. Such circumspection, combined with a historic lack of concern on the part of America's core culture (including institutions of higher learning that house chapters of these organizations) with the progress, histories, and activities of BGFs, yields a dangerous witches' brew.

Before 2000, there were few scholarly engagements centering on the five major BGFs. The publication of Lawrence Ross's *The Divine Nine* filled a yawning gap.[21] While acknowledging that Walter Kimbrough did the lion's share of speaking and writing on black Greeks in the

1990s, Ross produced the first study that included the histories of the nine black major fraternities and sororities in one volume.[22] For all its positives, Ross's historical piece (by design) was simply that—an endeavor in historicism. *The Divine Nine* made no real effort to examine the underpinnings of hazing within BGFs. The definitive study on hazing was Nuwer's *Broken Pledges*. Although Nuwer mentions BGFs in one section of his work, he only gives serious attention to the death of Joel Harris at Morehouse. He too fails to adequately deal with what produced and sustains hazing in these organizations.

Directly, we shall endeavor to eclectically combine the best intentions of Ross and Nuwer to place black Greek-letter fraternities in their proper historical framework and render a solid examination of the particular type of hazing encountered in these groups. Our course shall be guided by an approach that frames hazing as only one variable within a complex system that has historically driven the activities of these fraternities and the men who populate them. In our search for the true foundations of these violent pledge practices, a logical starting point would seem to be the history of black Greek-letter fraternities and the American fraternal movement itself.

3

The History of Black Greek-Letter Fraternities

Much historical and contemporary discussion has revolved around the American idea of "manliness." Although the notion itself transcends lines of race, its attainment presents unique challenges for African American males. Ellis Cose remarks that, unlike the majority of white males, the black male does not receive comfort from the thought that America has a "prepared place" for him.[1] Of course, many believe that over the last few decades, individual societal space has also decreased at an alarming rate for white males. Whereas the colonization of all life-worlds cannot (and should not) be denied, the supposition that discrepancies between the life chances of black and white males exists is difficult to refute. For both groups, fraternal orders have provided solace and one form of manly reaffirmation.

Although black Greek-letter fraternalism, to a great degree, evolved as a response and contestation to white privilege, racism, and elitism, many would argue that these organizations have been guilty of promoting intraracial social stratification themselves. Whereas the early twenty-first century saw a noticeable shift in the socioeconomic status of America's black college population, no more than 19 percent of any generation of black people has earned as much as a bachelor's degree.[2] Because college attendance has been a prerequisite for membership in most BGFs, this group of men has always had a proclivity toward exclusivity.[3] Indeed, in Lawrence Otis Graham's controversial examination of the black upper-class and its occasional real or perceived snobbery, *Our Kind of People*, he dedicates an entire chapter to "The Right Fraternities and Sororities" to which the upper crust belongs. Graham comments:

Most blacks who attended historically black colleges had hopes of joining one of the black fraternities because that was one of the surest ways to become accepted among the campus elite. In the early 1900s, the groups were small, intellectually elite, and rather secretive in their activities. By the 1930s and 1940s, the fraternities and sororities had become more dominant on campus, offering large social gatherings and serving as a magnet for not just the intellectual elite but also the social elite, who looked to the groups as a way to distinguish themselves from non-members who could not afford the membership fees or pay for the kinds of clothes, parties, and automobiles that were de rigueur for members.[4]

Disturbingly to some, there even exists a pecking order among black Greeks themselves, though it is considered in poor taste to speak of it in "mixed" black Greek company. Be this as it may, black Greeks and non-Greeks alike generally acknowledge these tiers in black Greekdom. Although the National Pan-Hellenic Council (NPHC) today houses five male fraternal organizations, Graham asserts that only three are considered "acceptable" by black blue bloods:[5] "A great deal of what has determined the prestige of specific fraternities and sororities depends on the age of the organization, its size, and the wealth and prominence of its members. In fact, many among the old-guard black elite would argue that only three of the fraternities—the Alphas, the Kappas, and the Omegas—and two of the sororities—AKAs and the Deltas—actually fit the 'society' profile."[6]

As we shall see, some form of elitism has always been present in black Greekdom, and this fact has historically and contemporarily caused a certain level of angst in the black community. In their early years, a number of prominent black schools were reluctant to allow the organizations on their campuses, for several reasons.[7] Some blacks were even opposed to these groups because they actually viewed them as antithetical to black struggle and sociopolitical consciousness. E. Franklin Frazier's critique in *Black Bourgeoisie* of the organizations' outrageous frivolity and extravagance at conventions is one of the most famous of these commentaries.

To the chagrin of critics such as Frazier, black Greek-letter fraternities and sororities endure. Even though the social and political status and orientation of their memberships have broadened, the organizations still claim to attract the best and brightest that black America has to offer. Whether this assertion is accurate depends on whom you ask, but few would deny the groups were indeed born of struggle. One need look no further than the origins of American college life and fraternalism itself to prove this point.

AMERICAN GREEK-LETTER FRATERNALISM

The fraternity system in the United States has been present since America became a nation. When colleges and universities began in United States, student life was very restrictive. As a result, various organizations were formed to create avenues for discussion, thought, and social activity. The first of three different organizations that catered to the students was the *academic class structure*. In many instances, academic class societies eventually formed highly organized structures, elected officers, and had their own secret colors, symbols, and mottoes. In fact, we find one of the precursors to hazing in fraternities here. An Alpha Phi Alpha member comments on this class structure:

> In discussing hazing, we still refuse to acknowledge the historical aspects of it outside of fraternities. Hazing has been a part of American higher education since its inception. Up until the 1920s, a lot of freshmen were hazed. They had events known as freshmen rush where the sophomores beat them down as part of this ritual. Colleges eventually decided that this was not good and began phasing it out in the '20s. The practice continued well into the '50s, though. For example, freshmen at Hampton wore beanies in the '50s as a part of this hazing ritual.

The *secret literary society* eventually took the academic class structure to a different level. According to a university dean of students and Phi Kappa Tau member, these societies were "a response to the strict curriculum management of administrators of the time. It gave students the opportunity to debate outside of the classroom, to raise philosophical questions and to consider issues in politics in a manner which was more acceptable to the students." These societies trained members in drill and composition. The respondent observed that radical views among students were expressed because colleges and universities, in most instances, prohibited students from openly discussing anything other than prescribed work. The component of critical thinking, ideally cherished in today's U.S. higher education system, was largely nonexistent. Students could not question what was academically proper. The meetings of these organizations were usually secret and each organization had its own color, motto, and badge.

The last of these college societies was the *secret college fraternity*. The purposes of the early fraternities were very similar to those of the literary societies. They came into being because many literary societies ultimately fell under faculty influence. The first such secret college society was the Flat Hat Club, founded in 1750. Thomas Jefferson was a member of this organization. It is believed to have thrived for at least twenty years; after 1772, there is no record of the Flat Hat Club's existence. The PDA Society, founded in 1751, was the first society to use the letters of its motto ("Please Don't Ask") as its name. The members of this organization are reported to have had little regard for scholarship and preferred the more social aspects of college fraternities. The PDA Society took its disdain for the nonsocial so far that it refused to admit anyone who considered himself a "Greek" scholar. An offended "Hellenist" then organized his own secret society—thus beginning the trend of using Greek letters in the names of organizations.

U.S. Greek-letter fraternities are generally divided into three groups: Era I, Era II, and Era III. Era I fraternities continued from 1825, when members of Phi Beta Kappa founded the first Kappa Alpha Society (not the same as today's Kappa Alpha Order) until 1859. Five characteristics must be considered to understand the commonalities in these groups. First, college was almost exclusively for upper-class WASP (white Anglo-Saxon Protestant) males studying for the ministry, medicine, and the legal profession. Second, all were founded by undergraduates, without assistance from adults. Third, most of these fraternities were founded in response to domination of student activities by administrators. As one group formed, others were organized to compete. Students wanted control over their lives and desired to create organizations that would complement and enhance what they learned in the classroom, because college life at the time included highly structured days, meager physical environs, and inflexible rules and regulations. Fourth, all these groups were highly secretive. Faculty felt threatened by them and would enforce retribution on members whenever possible through a variety of means—including expulsion. Fifth, all of these groups were sectarian.[8]

Greek-letter fraternities in the United States were thus clearly born of a spirit of rebellion and agency in an attempt to create intellectual and social space for students. They were a response to restrictive societal conditions that were reinforced at colleges and universities. Indeed, both black and white Greeks came out of a tradition of opposition, and were founded on similar principles of developing young men. Just as black fraternity men would later respond to racism and the restrictions made salient by its cleavages in U.S. higher education, white fraternity men also waged war with administrators and student groups that sought to maintain the status quo. Ironically, just as administrators sought to deny white Greeks the opportunity to affect change, white Greeks eventually sought to deny black students equal access to fraternal organizations.

Phi Beta Kappa is recognized as the first society in America to bear a Greek-letter name. It was founded in 1776 by some accounts, 1778 by others, at the College of William and Mary. It had all the characteristics of the modern fraternity. Francis Shepardson notes that these characteristics are, "the charm and mystery of secrecy, a ritual, oaths of fidelity, a grip, a motto, a badge for external display, a background of high idealism, a strong tie of friendship and comradeship, and an urge for sharing its values through nationwide expansion."[9] Explanations for the founding and perpetuation of fraternities vary. Shepardson argues they were originally social outlets, but always held a commitment to intellectual matters. Others, such as Helen Horowitz in her book *Campus Life*, hold that Greeks have always been either on the fringes of intellectualism in campus life or even blatantly anti-intellectual.

In separate studies, James Brunson and Bobby McMinn put forward the view that Freemasonry strongly influenced American fraternities, beginning with Phi Beta Kappa. Brunson notes, "one of Phi Beta Kappa's founders, Thomas Smith, originally belonged to the Williamsburg Lodge and in 1778 nine other members of this fraternal society joined the Masons. It was through this affiliation with the Masonic order that Phi Beta Kappa found models they could adapt for the society's grip, sign, and other rites."[10] The first black Greek-letter fraternity, which strongly resembled these groups in structure and practice, was not founded until 1906. These organizations, founded on noble principles, are the forefathers of the groups that today seem, at least to some, to be almost irrelevant and even destructive in many respects.

Creation of land-grant colleges by the Morrill Act of 1862 strongly influenced Era II fraternities, which were founded between 1860 and 1899. This led to much more diversified curricula with the addition of agriculture, engineering, and the sciences to the traditional classics—theology and liberal arts. The faculties of many schools became more tolerant of student self-governance. Enrollment grew rapidly during this era and institutions could not house and feed everyone, so the presence of fraternity houses actually aided colleges and universities logistically. The Civil War marked the end of many southern chapters, and some groups were reluctant to return to the South. Hence, a few fraternities (e.g., the Kappa Alpha Order and Pi Kappa Alpha) were originally formed specifically to expand in the South and capitalize on the absence of chapters that were once powerful. More importantly, the student population of the United States began to diversify at an incredible rate, which led to Era III fraternities. Many of the post-1900 Era III fraternities were founded for persons who were racially, culturally, or religiously different, or whose sexual preferences or ethnicities kept them from being offered membership in existing groups. BGFs fall into this category.

BLACK ENTRANCE INTO AMERICAN COLLEGE LIFE

After their founding, BGFs eventually expanded into an area that their white counterparts did not. As BGF members left college, they formed graduate chapters of their fraternities that grew in strength and influence over the years, to such an extent that the true centers of the organizations are currently in doubt. Some members, while recognizing that the fraternities were founded as undergraduate chapters and organizations, feel their focus has long since shifted from these chapters to alumni chapters. These members contend that for over half a century, the fraternities in question have operated primarily as graduate fraternities, with their undergraduate components contributing little. Be this as it may, we must locate the genesis of black fraternity life in the same place we find the roots of white fraternity life—in U.S. college life itself. At this point, we must note how American college life received its African American population.

Bowles and DeCosta note in their historical study of African Americans in higher education, *Between Two Worlds*, that only 28 African-descended Americans had received baccalaureate degrees by 1860. These graduates attended northern universities because the political and social climate of the proslavery South made matriculation in that part of the country unrealistic and, in many cases, legally impossible. The first black college graduate seems to have been Edward Jones in 1826. Jones graduated from Amherst College two weeks before another black student, John Brown Russworm, finished graduation requirements at Bowdoin College. Even though these two schools can rightfully claim the first two AfricanAmerican college graduates, neither would produce additional graduates before 1860. This gulf in graduation illustrates that there was no real place set aside for African Americans in higher education, which reflected their position in American life as a whole. The growing demand for African American collegiate training immediately prior to, and especially after, the Civil War was addressed by the establishment of Negro colleges and universities.[11]

The first of these schools was Cheyney University in Pennsylvania, established in 1837. For a number of years, however, schools such as Cheyney were not effective in constructing and delivering true college curriculums. In reality, they provided little more than elementary and secondary education for students. By 1865, America's population of African Americans totaled 5 million (4.5 million having been recently freed from slavery), with more than 90 percent of them remaining in the South. The number of college graduates began to escalate for the next thirty years, with northern schools again taking the lead. These institutions had graduated some 194 African Americans by 1895. Oberlin led the way with 75 black graduates.

The Exclusion of Blacks from White Greek Life

Student life inside and outside the classroom for this new influx of African American collegians provides the backdrop for the establishment of BGFs. Bowles and DeCosta report that African Americans apparently made considerable initial efforts to participate in the larger campus communities of predominantly white institutions through athletics, literary societies, musical groups, and fraternities and sororities. But, like many things in America at this time, participation in these groups on most campuses was continuously restricted according to race. The politics of exclusion in white Greek-letter organizations have long been incorporated into the inner workings of the groups. In *Fraternities Without Brotherhood*, Alfred Lee writes that by 1928, more than half the national white fraternities and sororities had specific rules requiring membership to exclude along racial and religious lines. Most white Greeks "had the [exclusionary] policy, but did not find it necessary or in good taste to say so formally."[12] Phi Delta Theta's constitution, however, included the following statement regarding membership: "Only such persons as are contemplated in the bond of Phi Delta Theta may be admitted, and only male, white persons of full Aryan blood not less than sixteen years of age, shall be eligible."[13]

This policy of exclusion, whether de jure, de facto, or by virtue of "gentlemen's agreements," effectively excluded Jews, Catholics, Italians, Asians, blacks—and, ironically, even Greeks. This practice continued well into the twentieth century. As late as 1954, the Williams and Amherst College chapters of Phi Delta Theta were suspended for pledging "non-Aryans."[14] Louis Foley, an editor of Sigma Pi fraternity's *Emerald* magazine, addressed this practice by writing, "our traditional attitude of superiority toward non-Aryan races is something which most Europeans have found difficult to understand."[15]

Barbara Collier Delany's problems at Cornell University in 1956 illustrated that racism in Greekdom also knows no class lines:

Delany made national headlines in 1956, when, as a student at the Ivy League campus, she was offered membership in the white sorority of Sigma Kappa. She remembers being one of only a handful of blacks at the college at the time. "I was the first black ever to be offered membership in a white sorority," says Delany, who had grown up in a family of privilege. She belonged to Jack and Jill, debuted with the Girl Friends, and graduated from the elite all-girl Hunter High School in Manhattan. "The girls in the sorority were very nice to me, but the officials at the national headquarters were furious, and they told the students that they had better reject me or headquarters would shut down the sorority's chapter at Cornell," says Delany, who still corresponds with some of those classmates. "When the white students refused to kick me out, headquarters shut down the sorority."[16]

Even today, although there is a rhetoric of humanism and inclusion that comes from the white Greek-letter community, discriminatory practices remain somewhat constant. M. G. Lord refers to white rushing policies (recruitment) as a "codified white exclusionary ritual. . . . Nothing, in fact, has changed [as far as white views on racial purity in their organizations is concerned]."[17] Take, for example, the case of the University of Michigan's chapter of Kappa Alpha Theta, the oldest white women's sorority. When the group pledged its first black woman in the 1980s, many of the chapter's "traditional white, Anglo-Saxon Protestant" women were unhappy that this student received a "bid" (invitation) to join their organization. This prejudice was further evidenced by actual discrimination when a number of white fraternities informed the Thetas that they would no longer party with them.[18]

In 2013, fifty years after segregationist Alabama governor George Wallace stood at the "schoolhouse door" to prevent the integration of the University of Alabama, student members of Alabama's Alpha Gamma Delta chapter reported that a sorority recruiter and alumnae members overruled their desire to induct a new member simply because she was black. M. G. Lord quotes anthropology professor Susan Harding: "It is tacky to be verbally racist, but perfectly acceptable to discriminate through your behavior; through your choices. Elite racism is implicit, acted out, behaved—not expressed in language. And fraternities are training ground for that kind of elite practice."[19]

In 2001, in a rather bizarre development, white members of three different fraternities at Auburn University, the University of Mississippi, the University of Wisconsin (Whitewater), and the University of Louisville took this behavior to a different level by dressing in blackface and racially offensive costumes at various Halloween festivities. The cases at Auburn and Mississippi received the most press, because members actually posted pictures of their antics on the Internet. At Auburn, Delta Sigma Phi and Beta Theta Pi were the culprits. Members of Delta Sigma Phi were shown wearing Ku Klux Klan robes, wielding rifles and a noose, with a confederate flag in the background. A few members were photographed pretending to hang another member in blackface garbed in a mock FUBU shirt (For Us By Us—a popular clothing line in black youth culture at the time). The members of Beta Theta Pi blackened their faces, wore Afro wigs, shirts with the Greek letters of the Omega Psi Phi fraternity, and bulky jewelry. Some members flashed simulated gang signs as a number of white female students joined in for pictures.

In the less-publicized Louisville case, members of Tau Kappa Epsilon (TKE) engaged in similar activities, blackening their faces and arms and dressing in costumes they said portrayed: Snoop Doggy Dogg, a rapper, with an Afro wig and convict's orange clothing; a nurse who used heavy black slang; Shaft, portrayed as a 1970s pimp; a 1980s pimp who used slang such as "Don't you be getting fresh with my women"; and a Ku Klux Klan member.[20] Strangely, the Klan outfit was actually worn by one of the five African American members of the fraternity. Some members of the fraternity later contended the party was actually a display of antiracism, because the Klan robe was burned later in the night to the uproarious applause of the TKEs.

All of these cases are interesting, not necessarily because of the blackface incidents, which angered most people in the black campus communities at these schools, but because of the white response. Almost immediately after the incidents were publicized at Louisville, for instance, and demands for punishment levied, many in the campus' white student, faculty, and staff communities contended that blacks were overreacting. Their stance was rooted in a number of claims: blacks were too sensitive to a simple case of Halloween fun; even if the costumes were in poor taste, the fraternity should not be punished because they had a right to freedom of expression; and maybe most disturbing of all, blacks who were responding to the incident, not the fraternity members, were the real problem in that they were behaving in a racially divisive way.

Jack Levin, an expert on race relations and director of the Brudnick Center on Violence and Conflict at Northeastern University, said the behavior came as no surprise to him:

"Some fraternities have been home to some of the most grotesque and stereotypical acts going back for many decades." Levin said that during the 1980s, when more students of color arrived at universities around the country, "we saw these kinds of incidents increase. . . . It's a defensive position from the point of view of these students, who are what used to be the prototypical college student: White, male and Protestant. . . . But now they have to share with people who are different—Black, Latino, and Asian students—and they don't like losing their advantage and privilege."[21]

These types of events and biases directly led to black men forming their own fraternal organizations over a century ago. Charles Wesley comments in *The History of Alpha Phi Alpha*:

"In the colleges which were attended by both races, they [blacks] were regularly overlooked in the selection of fraternity membership. It was not without reason, therefore, that the Negro college fraternity had a part of its origin in these conditions."[22]

THE FOUNDING OF BLACK GREEK-LETTER FRATERNITIES

A few obscure precursors to major BGFs come to mind when black fraternities are mentioned. Sufficient documentation exists to show that the first Greek-letter fraternity organized by African Americans was Alpha Kappa Nu at Indiana University. Walter Kimbrough notes that different accounts referencing Alpha Kappa Nu's creation exist.[23] Kappa Alpha Psi historian William Crump reports the year of the group's founding as 1903, but Thomas Clark cites 1904.[24] Kimbrough goes on to say that accounts of the fraternity's development and demise differ also. Although Crump chronicles the fraternity as lasting roughly a year after its inception, Clark and the school newspaper of the time, the *Daily Student*, agree that it continued to grow through at least 1911. The local newspaper, the *Bloomington Telephone*, indicates the fraternity even bought a house in 1911. The campus paper concurs in reporting that Alpha Kappa Nu was the first black fraternity chapter to own its own house. These discrepancies may be a result of some confusion of Alpha Kappa Nu with Kappa Alpha Nu (the original name of the Kappa Alpha Psi fraternity), but this is not certain.

Another early black Greek-letter fraternity, Sigma Pi Phi (better known as "the Boule," which is a Greek word designating a council of community leaders who advised kings), is obscure for different reasons. Although this organization still exists and is probably the most elite BGF, it was not founded as, nor did it ever become, a college fraternity. Beyond this, Sigma Pi Phi has always been a highly secretive organization. One of the first widespread public reports on it came as late as 1990, in a brief newspaper article by Los Angeles journalist Karen Bates. She reports, "The Boule is an organization that celebrates the professional and material success of black men."[25] Sigma Pi Phi was established in 1904 in Philadelphia by black men who had graduated not only from college, but from graduate and professional schools. These graduates were already the elite of the black community in that they were, to a man, doctors and dentists.

The fraternity was organized so that the tiny number of black men with graduate degrees could network with one another and help younger men. Boule member and past president Benjamin Major commented, "It [the Boule and networking] was important back then, because the only avenues of professional discourse in society as a whole were closed by segregation."[26] Major recalls that as a young man he would see older men in the community as they quietly left to attend monthly meetings. "I saw these black professional men, doctors, judges, lawyers, put on their tuxedos every fourth Saturday and disappear. I wanted to know what was going on."[27] He found out when he became one of the few invited to join the group. Bates notes that "like Yale's Skull and Bones secret society, to which George Bush belongs, the Boule has been criticized by some as a social anachronism."[28] Be this as it may, the membership of this organization (whose average age is around sixty) is quite impressive as far as notoriety is concerned. It has included such luminaries as former Virginia governor Douglas Wilder, chief judge A. Leon Higginbotham, publishers Earl Graves and John Johnson, former U.S. secretary of Health and Human Services Louis Sullivan, former Los Angeles mayor Tom Bradley, past NAACP director Benjamin Hooks, U.S. secretary of commerce Ron Brown, and scholar extraordinaire W. E. B. Du Bois.

The Boule has not been threatened by accusations of violent behavior, because their selection process has apparently never included a traditional pledge period. In contrast, the five NPHC fraternities are very much imperiled by destructive violent behavior. The origins of these organizations are not deeply rooted in Bloomington, Indiana, or Philadelphia, Pennsylvania, but in Ithaca, New York, on the campus of Cornell University. It was there that seven black Ivy League undergraduates—Charles H. Chapman, George B. Kelly, Henry A. Callis, Eugene K. Jones, Nathaniel A. Murray, Robert H. Ogle, and Vertner W. Tandy—would found Alpha Phi Alpha.

Alpha Phi Alpha

Founded: December 4, 1906
Alpha Chapter: Cornell University (Ithaca, New York)
Colors: Old gold and black
Motto: "First of all, servants of all, we shall transcend all"

Alpha Phi Alpha, the first collegiate black Greek-letter fraternity, today has over 290,000 members and more than 800 chapters throughout the United States, Africa, Asia, Europe, and the Caribbean. Over the years, rather pervasive stereotypes have developed regarding the images members of several BGFs present—especially the Alphas, Kappas, and Omegas. Although many individuals in these fraternities do not "fit" their organization's personality profile, it is not unusual to hear, "You look (or act) like a Kappa (Q, or Alpha)." Graham comments on Alphas: "Some say that the stereotypical Alpha is professionally ambitious, bookish, not overly gregarious, and 'safe.' My father-in-law, who pledged Alpha in 1947, says, 'He's the *mensch*—the nice guy—that everyone wants his sister to date.'"[29]

Alpha Phi Alpha was originally a social studies club that shared many of the same goals as earlier collegiate literary societies. Walter Kimbrough comments, "The initial goals of the group were to create a forum for closer relationships through a social and literary society."[30] Several of the students, however, worked in campus fraternity houses, which fueled thoughts of creating a similar organization for black men.

This aspiration had its dissenters, according to fraternal lore. Though it is not written about often, history tells that at least one member felt the club would lose its direction if it were to become a fraternity, and he did not participate in the founding of Alpha Phi Alpha. The group did, however, move forward and explored other attempts to form a fraternity. Founder Robert Ogle followed up on a newspaper report from Chicago that a black fraternity called Pi Gamma Omicron existed at Ohio State University. When questioned about this group,

Ohio State officials responded that no such fraternity had ever existed. The group of Cornell students persevered and established Alpha Phi Alpha on December 4, 1906. Subsequently, the members of the new fraternity considered expansion and took a somewhat elitist position from the start. Wesley comments, "Strong opposition developed to the establishment of chapters in schools that were not of Grade A recognition. This opposition was directed at this time particularly to Negro institutions other than Howard."[31]

Even though the chapter at Cornell was Alpha's first, it may not be the one that carries the most historical significance for BGFs. That distinction belongs to the second chapter established in Alpha Phi Alpha in December of 1907—the Beta Chapter at Howard University—for it is at Howard that three of the other four BGFs, directly or indirectly, have their origins.

Kappa Alpha Psi

Founded: January 5, 1911
Alpha Chapter: Indiana University (Bloomington)
Colors: Crimson and cream
Motto: "Achievement in every field of human endeavor"

Two years after Alpha Phi Alpha established a chapter at Howard University, two students, Elder Watson Diggs, a native Kentuckian, and Byron K. Armstrong of Indiana, matriculated at Howard. At the request of Armstrong's cousin Irvin, Diggs and Armstrong transferred to Indiana University for the 1910–11 school year. Ironically, this was the same campus where Alpha Kappa Nu had been founded in 1903–04, but Diggs and Armstrong knew of fraternity life from their experience at Howard. Crump states that "both were approached by a fraternity, and both declined pledgeship because they disapproved of the attitudes and actions of certain members."[32] Although Crump never mentions the name of this fraternity or the specific attitudes and actions that Diggs and Armstrong disliked, logic dictates that it must have been Alpha Phi Alpha.

In December of 1910, Diggs and Armstrong began to work with the nine other black male students at Indiana to form a fraternity of their own. One of these men, Frederick Mitchell, did not return to

Indiana for the spring semester and the fraternity, initially known as Kappa Alpha Nu, was founded on January 5, 1911, around the stated fundamental purpose of "achievement."[33] The names appearing on the charter of Kappa Alpha Nu's Alpha Chapter were: Elder Watson Diggs, Byron Kenneth Armstrong, John Milton Lee, Guy Levis Grant, Ezra Dee Alexander, Henry T. Asher, Marcus Peter Blakemore, Edward Giles Irvin, Paul Waymond Caine, and George W. Edmonds. Kappa filled an important void, because it was the only BGF founded in the Midwest and therefore has a number of older chapters at schools where other black fraternities would not arise until much later. Today the fraternity has more than 150,000 members in over 700 chapters.

Whereas Alphas are regarded as "bookish" and "safe," Kappas are widely stereotyped as somewhat arrogant, smooth-talking ladies' men. Admittedly, Kappas themselves do a bit to enhance this image. For example, when questioned as to why Alphas are often historically linked with AKAs, Omegas with Deltas, and Sigmas with Zetas, but Kappas are associated with no particular sorority—many Kappas devilishly respond, "We don't discriminate, we love them all."[34] No matter how pervasive it is today, the "pretty boy/playboy" image is really not very old in Kappa Alpha Psi. Older Kappas cite the early 1970s as the period in which that persona became popular. Before this time, Kappas were widely regarded as athletes and heavy social drinkers. Long before either stereotype was cultivated, the founders of Kappa Alpha Psi toiled alone in Bloomington. Meanwhile, in November 1911, the black fraternity spotlight moved back east to Howard.

Omega Psi Phi

Founded: November 17, 1911
Alpha Chapter: Howard University (Washington, DC)
Colors: Purple and gold
Motto: "Friendship is essential to the soul"

On November 17, 1911, three Howard University undergraduates—Edgar A. Love, Oscar J. Cooper, and Frank Coleman, with the assistance of young biology professor Ernest E. Just—founded the Omega Psi Phi fraternity. Just was a Dartmouth graduate with a doctorate from the University of Chicago, and many "Omegas will quickly tell you that Just is the only fraternity founder to appear on a U.S. postage stamp."[35] The name of the fraternity, derived from the initials of the Greek phrase meaning "Friendship is essential to the soul," was selected as the motto of the fraternity. Just as the Kappas rallied around the purpose of achievement, the Omegas adopted "manhood," "scholarship," "perseverance," and "uplift" as their cardinal principles.

Omega Men, or "Que-Dogs" as they are sometimes called, are often stereotyped as the most boisterous, rambunctious members of black Greekdom. One can safely say that the Omegas promote the exact opposite of the Alphas' "safe" image. Many members—especially younger ones—can regularly be seen adorned with dog collars, spray-painted gold boots with purple laces, and military camouflage pants to reinforce the "hardcore, wild" persona. Contrary to widely held belief, however, the dog is not Omega Psi Phi's official mascot, nor does the national fraternity officially endorse or condone barking or any other canine references. In fact, among many older members, the Que-Dog moniker is actually considered retrograde. Instances have occurred in which the Que-Dog/Omega Man dichotomy has fomented rather bitter intrafraternal confrontations between members of Omega Psi Phi. For example, I personally witnessed an incident in 1986 when a basketball coach at a southern black college was so offended by Que-Dog bravado that he threatened his younger fraternity brothers with expulsion from the venue if they continued to bark during the game.

Whether one chooses to refer to the members of Omega Psi Phi as Que-Dogs or Omega Men, the fraternity has a strong history of which it can be rightfully proud. Currently, Omega has more than 750 chapters and over 175,000 members.

Phi Beta Sigma

Founded: January 9, 1914
Alpha Chapter: Howard University (Washington, DC)
Colors: Blue and white
Motto: "Culture for service and service for humanity"

The four early BGFs are rounded out with the founding of Phi Beta Sigma. The founders of this organization were Howard students A. Langston Taylor, Leonard F. Morse, and Charles I. Brown. Like Kappa principle founder Elder Watson Diggs and the Omega's "Three Musketeers"—Love, Cooper, and Coleman—A. Langston Taylor had no interest in joining an already established organization. Sigma has always seen itself as the black fraternity that shunned the bourgeois inclinations of the Alphas, Kappas, and Omegas. It has publicly proclaimed that not only is its membership not based on race, creed, or national origin, but also that it has never discriminated on the basis of family affiliation and physical characteristics: "The founders deeply wished to create an organization that viewed itself as 'a part of' the general community rather than 'apart from' the general community. They believed that each potential member should be judged by his own merits rather than his family background or affluence . . . without regard of race, nationality, skin tone or texture of hair. They wished and wanted their fraternity to exist as part of even a greater brotherhood which would be devoted to the 'inclusive we' rather than the 'exclusive we.'"[36]

To some degree, the contention that this fraternity has an aversion to elitist exclusivity is not simple rhetoric. Sigma, more than its three predecessors, has a history of broadening its membership base and visibility through the initiation of honorary members who do not hold typical fraternity credentials, but have distinguished themselves in other walks of life. Honorary initiates include President Bill Clinton and activist Al Sharpton. The fraternity has also established an honorary chapter, the Distinguished Service Chapter, to which members are elected on the basis of their achievements either scholastically or through community and national service. Today, Phi Beta Sigma has over 650 chapters and more than 200,000 members.

Iota Phi Theta

Founded: September 19, 1963
Alpha Chapter: Morgan State University (Baltimore, Maryland)
Colors: Charcoal brown and gilded gold
Motto: "Building a tradition, not resting on one"

Almost half a century passed between the founding of Phi Beta Sigma and the next major BGF, Iota Phi Theta. Iota is the only black fraternity that has the distinction of being founded in the middle of the civil rights movement. On September 19, 1963, at Morgan State, twelve students—Albert Hicks, Lonnie Spruill Jr., Charles Briscoe, Frank Coakley, John Slade, Barron Willis, Webster Lewis, Charles Brown, Louis Hudnell, Charles Gregory, Elias Dorsey Jr., and Michael Williams—founded the last of the currently recognized National Pan-Hellenic Council fraternities.[37] This group of fraternity founders was a bit different from the founders of Alpha, Kappa, Omega, and Sigma because most of them did not meet in college, but had been friends since childhood. Spruill, Coakley, Dorsey, and Gregory had known one another since grade school. Spruill and Coakley's friendship extended back to their preschool years.

Many of Iota's founders were what are now referred to as "nontraditional students" and were three to five years older than the average college student. Gregory, Willis, and Brown were all service veterans. Brown, Hicks, and Briscoe were married with small children. Several worked full-time jobs and all were full-time students. The fraternity's public history asserts, "Based upon their ages, heightened responsibilities, and increased level of maturity, this group had a slightly different perspective than the norm for college students. It was this perspective from which they established the Fraternity's purpose, 'The development and perpetuation of Scholarship, Leadership, Citizenship, Fidelity, and Brotherhood among Men.' Additionally, they conceived the Fraternity's motto, 'Building a tradition, not resting on one!'"[38] In just over 50 years, Iota Phi Theta has expanded to more than 300 chapters and has initiated over 70,000 members.

BGF's POLITICAL INVOLVEMENT

Of the beginnings of black Greekdom, an Alpha Phi Alpha initiated in the 1960s comments:

> The little I know about the history of black fraternities, at least in the case of my own, is that they were kind of a means to help black students cope with climates of isolation, alienation and in some cases hostility on these predominantly white campuses. I know that's the history of Alpha Phi Alpha at Cornell. This was the coming together of a very small number of black men to try to cope, to bond, to give them . . . ; the fraternity history describes it as an effort to create some sort of social life, but I tend to think that the agenda was probably a

little broader than that. From what we know about these men, they were very involved in a lot of the cultural and political activity of the time, so I would tend to think that they were thinking about more than social life—they were really organizing around common political interests.

Historical evidence supports the view that a great number of early members and chapters were active politically. Although they had minuscule resources compared to present-day BGFs, their level of political participation both local and nationally was noteworthy. The members of Kappa Alpha Psi, for example, led by Elder Watson Diggs, were well aware of national and world events. They constantly publicly expressed their opinions on many issues and lent their support to America in word and action. When the United States declared war on Germany in 1917, Diggs immediately drafted the following letter to Woodrow Wilson:

May 25, 1917

The President
The White House
Washington, DC

Sir:
   The national Negro college men's fraternity known as Kappa Alpha Psi, having chapters at Indiana University, the University of Illinois, the University of Iowa, the University of Nebraska, Wilberforce University, Lincoln University, Ohio State University and Northwestern University, begs to assure you that the organization is in full sympathy and accord with the purposes of the government in waging the present war against the Imperial German Government in defense of the principle of International Law and the protection of our citizens upon the high seas, and hereby pledges its unswerving loyalty to the President and the flag in the great struggle which now confronts us.

> Respectfully yours,
> Elder Watson Diggs, Grand Polemarch
> Kappa Alpha Psi Fraternity[39]

The reply read: "The President thanks you cordially for the good will that prompted your kind message. It has helped to reassure him and keep him in heart."[40] Soon after this, Diggs, along with many of his fraternity brothers, entered the armed forces and fought for America. Unfortunately, this dedication to American ideals did not change the approach of many Americans to the black man. Crump notes, "America reacted violently to the confusion that followed the end of overseas hostilities. There was sporadic rioting. Blacks were murdered for the 'grave offense' of wearing the uniforms of soldiers. But in spite of this, Kappa Alpha Psi, a fledgling Fraternity of seven years, gathered up the fragments and rallied once again around the Purpose of Achievement."[41]

It is probably not coincidental that BGFs were formed during the early twentieth century. In addition to the fact that the late 1800s saw a great increase in African Americans attending U.S. colleges and universities, this violent period in U.S. history witnessed the founding of other black collective action groups with sociopolitical goals emphasizing black uplift. Maulana Karenga notes:

> In the wake of the failure of Reconstruction, African-Americans were confronted more and more with discrimination and mob violence. By the end of the century, Jim Crowism, the racist system based on the separate-but-equal doctrine and the political, economic and social subordination of Blacks, was firmly in place. Most of the Southern states had passed such discriminatory laws and in 1896 in the *Plessy v. Ferguson* case, the Supreme Court had upheld and enshrined such practices, a ruling that would last until the 1954 *Brown* decision. In the areas of politics, economics, and justice, African-Americans were excluded from voting, jobs and unions, and jury duty. And white terrorist societies rose to ensure such exclusion and subordination.[42]

To aid in the fight against discrimination, a number of black-oriented movements and organizations were founded in the early 1900s. Notable among these were the Niagara Movement, the NAACP, the Black Women's Movement, and the Urban League. The original members of BGFs seem to have had goals very similar to those of the members of these organizations, as is illustrated by a high frequency of cross-organizational membership. Hence, at their inception, BGFs were solidly political and belonged to the larger Negro social movement of the time. These groups were the children of a long-standing tradition of black social and political ideologies and actions ranging from Frederick Douglass and Harriet Tubman to W. E. B. Du Bois and William Monroe Trotter. An Alpha Phi Alpha member comments,

"These men had to be political. These were the black Intelligentsia, they came out of a background that really impressed upon them the responsibility of the black intellectual class so they had to be political. I think it would have been the exceptional black man that went to college at that time and tried to pursue an agenda that was purely personal or frivolous. They were products of the times and the times were serious times."

Graham comments in *Our Kind of People*:

For my aunt, my uncle, and many other blacks, their sororities and fraternities are a lasting identity, a circle of lifetime friends, a base for future political and civic activism. Continuing throughout their adulthood, membership means lifetime subscriptions to publications like the *Sphinx*, the *Ivy Leaf*, or the *Oracle* [the official publications of Alpha Phi Alpha, Alpha Kappa Alpha, and Omega Psi Phi, respectively]. It means regulated funeral programs with unique fraternity services that are specifically outlined for surviving members in attendance. Having attended a college that permitted neither black nor white fraternities [Princeton], I have long felt alien to—and envious of—the experience that my friends received at other colleges. For many of them, these black Greek-letter organizations provided a forum, post-college, through which some of the best-educated blacks in America can discuss an agenda to fight racism and improve conditions for less-advantaged blacks.[43]

Succinctly, black fraternities are products of ongoing social movements (including the black freedom struggle and American fraternalism) that have existed in one form or another since the founding of the country. Thus, BGFs did not construct a new social movement; they simply created another entity in movements, black as well as white, that ultimately addressed the same issues. Unfortunately, the linkage between BGFs and black sociopolitical struggle has changed over the years, for a number of reasons—some within BGFs and others external to them.

THE DEPOLITICALIZATION OF BGFS

Just as surely as BGFs were sociopolitical movements historically, to a great degree they have ceased to address these concerns in contemporary America. When questioned about whether Greeks are more or less political today than they were in the past, interviewees answered unanimously that they were less political. One interviewee commented that he felt a major factor in the depoliticalization of black fraternities has been the overall loss of a national black political agenda and leadership:

It is the rare Greek organization today that has a political agenda. I mean, what's happening in black Greek life are aspects of what's happening in black life period in this country. There is no clear black political agenda in the main. The unfortunate thing is when it comes to looking at those parts of our community where people have the greatest expectations in terms of change for us it generally comes from those of us who've had the opportunity to be more educated or had the opportunity for access. So, I think it is legitimate still that people who find themselves in places where they can think of something as luxurious as being involved in a fraternity or pursuing a college education will have a special responsibility. There has been an erosion of clarity around questions of leadership. We can romanticize about masses doing things, but leadership has always come from those few of us who have gotten the opportunity to be educated. So, part of our dilemma is over this question of black leadership and the fact that there is no coherent, serious agenda coming from our educated ones.

This statement seems to be largely based on the supposition that from the beginning of the last century until the post–civil rights movement and black power era, black Americans have had a distinct leadership with which to identify. Although this leadership's philosophies and tactics were often sharply contradictory, their simple existence and overlapping goals gave almost all blacks something they felt comfortable affiliating themselves with psychologically or through membership.

Locating black leadership has become more and more difficult as the years have progressed, and BGFs are yet another place where leadership is weak. A 1994 *Time* article on Louis Farrakhan reported that a Time/CNN poll of African Americans found that 73 percent were familiar with Farrakhan. This was more than any other black political figure except Jesse Jackson and Clarence Thomas. Of those polled, 9 percent named Farrakhan when asked to identify "the most important black leader today." This very small percentage was higher than that for everyone except Jackson and was three times as high as Nelson Mandela. These results obviously "reflect a lack of broad-based, high-profile black leaders," and this vacuum may be one of the root causes of black American nihilism.[44] The emergence of Barack Obama a decade later has not changed this reality appreciably. Many people just may not know where to turn for political direction.

A Kappa Alpha Psi member who also served as executive director of the National Pan-Hellenic Council commented on BGF leadership in particular, "I cannot remember the last time that we have had any strong, dynamic, charismatic leadership that was capable of giving our young people any kind of vision—political or otherwise." Although this depoliticalization seems to be a trend in BGFs, it has also influenced white fraternities. A Phi Kappa Tau member addresses this issue: "White Greeks and black Greeks are pretty similar in most ways, but saying that is inflammatory—especially to the black Greeks. This does not stop with their current political involvement—they both are less political. The way in which they exist today, they have a skewed emphasis that concentrates more and more on social aspects and the surface things we see as far as what *is* fraternity."

Some contend that the effects of this failure by white fraternities are not as drastic as the failure by black ones because the realities of blacks and white are, again, not wholly compatible. In the black case, as James Brunson notes, "There may well be close to a million people initiated into black fraternities and sororities," and a struggling people simply cannot afford to lose this cadre of educated individuals to frivolity.[45]

We have seen that the historical genesis of black fraternities was inevitably influenced by the WGF movement in the United States, and also by the larger black American sociopolitical movement. We have observed that some of the founding members of Alpha Phi Alpha worked in white fraternity houses and were certainly influenced by white fraternities. The blurring of early black and white lines becomes so extreme at points that even fraternity social rituals and customs are intermingled. Kappa Alpha Psi's "Loving Cup Song," for example, is borrowed from the Beta Theta Pi fraternity (except in the verses where Kappas sing "Kappa Alpha Psi," Betas sing "Beta Theta Pi").

In fact, very few glaring differences exist in the reasons for the founding of black Greek-letter fraternities and white Greek-letter fraternities, although black societal marginalization, outside and inside college walls, was more extreme. Even so, both black and white fraternities were movements among college students that sought to carve out space for intellectual discourse and social and political opportunity on college campuses. Although obvious differences exist—mostly products of the racial segregation of the time and the discriminatory attitudes and practices that came along before and with it—there are no differences related to the founding and evolution of the organizations that can account for the divergence in the pledging and hazing techniques of black and white Greeks.

4

The Pledge Process as Sacrifice

If solutions to the destructive behavior that sometimes manifests itself in BGFs are to be found, we must begin to take different approaches to understanding the impetus at the heart of the pledge process. Critically speaking, when engaging the pledge process one must work diligently to frame it such that it is not necessarily viewed as a directionless anthropological aberration of black men who wish to impose violent behavior on one another. On the contrary, one must approach it as an activity that has been historically viewed as functional.

The fact that injured pledges are victims of violent physical aggression is indisputable.

However, we will focus our attention for a moment not on these injured individuals, but on the fact that the modern pledge process is an operation of historical social import as well as a powerful aspect of black fraternity legend and lore. We must then understand that, contrary to the beliefs of many BGF members, this process is at its heart a sacrificial rite that was not created by BGFs. Therefore, the BGF pledge process is not unique in and of itself. These factors combine to support the thesis that the modern BGF pledge process is a form of sacrificial ritual and such rites (be they mortal or not) are largely inaccessible to intellectual explanation, unless one can locate some basis for them in historical and contemporary social reality.[1]

VIOLENCE VEHICLES: RITUALS AS SOCIAL STABILIZERS

As long as we insist on interpreting the violence of initiation rituals in purely individual psychological terms, we can only assume (in this case) that BGF members are dysfunctional sociopaths. This view must consequently suggest that members seek some sort of moral justification for their acts after the pledge process is completed by showering the newly

51

initiated neophyte with "love" in the form of verbal and social acceptance or gifts. On initial observation, it would appear that the pledge is simultaneously disdained and coveted, because such quick movement from a position of loathing to one of love seems implausible. Pledges are often told by their deans of pledges (members who are primarily responsible for the progress and well-being of potential initiates), "None of the brothers like you. You have nobody but each other and me." Although an illusion of aloneness and adversity is created, the reality must be that the pledge is somehow loved all along (whether this type of love is pure or healthy is arguable)—even when he is the object of violence from his fraternity-brothers-to-be. This love/loathe ambivalence would seem, on its face, to be nonsensical. When examined more closely, however, it can indeed be explained.

Fraternities are filled with rituals. These rituals (written or not) are nothing more than forms of behavior or interaction repeated again and again for the fraternal vehicle to function in a particular manner. Ritualistic processes are often employed to open and close fraternity meeting years; others are used at weddings, and still others at funerals. Many are performed with no threat of dissolution of the fold if they are neglected for one reason or another.

The fraternal pledge process, however, is unique in two ways. First, it stands alone as the ritual many fraternity men perceive as mandatory. The belief exists that if the pledge process is tampered with too extensively or eradicated, the very fabric of the organization will certainly unravel.[2] If proper protocol is not followed at meetings or weddings, the fraternity is not necessarily in danger; the pledge process alone is viewed as having the power to inevitably determine the course of the group, because it is seen as having an inordinate impact on what the neophyte *is*.

The second reason pledge ritual is unique directly relates to the first. It is the only rite in fraternities that does not ask for, but *demands*, sacrifice. This is not necessarily sacrifice of the altruistic type, but of the sort that places the pledge in positions that threaten him emotionally and physically, in many cases at levels unequaled in intensity and largely unacceptable in the larger society. The fact that the pledge process falls into this category moves it to a very different place from which it must be engaged.

Most supporters of the ritualized pledge process defend it as central to fraternities' purposes. Whether this is a truism or not does not invalidate the fact that, in one sense, fraternity rituals have the same purposes as the rituals found in everyday life. These include religious ceremonies ranging from marriage, baptism, and weekly worship to modern rites of passage such as graduations. Rituals, although they often contain some emotive messages, exist to define the traditions of an organization. When paired with ceremonies unique to particular groups of people, they forge a standard formula for the organization's activities and teachings. When taken together, ritual and tradition form almost impenetrable barriers that determine whether a person is accepted into the bond or denied access. Bonding rests on the supposition that every member participates in the same ceremony, hears the same words, and lives the same experience.

If successful, this common experience gives the organization continuity and structure. Because of this uniformity, a fraternity brother from one part of the world should be able to meet a member from anywhere else and instantly have a connection. This is central to fraternities' notion of brotherhood. Consequently, rituals seeking to achieve such an attachment are strongly functional. Fraternity initiation rituals (of which the pledge process is only a part) are meant to bring about solid, concrete results. If the functional nature of this operation is not understood, the moorings of this historic phenomenon will continue to be misunderstood, and the particular type of violence that has become a part of it will never be resolved.

Anthropologically, initiation rituals and rites of passage occur in contexts other than those involving racial and social disfranchisement. Even though they are often veiled, all rituals of this type have a sociopolitical component in one way or another. In fact, common threads run through this variety of sacrifice that bind participants regardless of religious, political, or fraternal affiliation. According to René Girard, sacrificial ritual is always social, whether or not this fact is realized. In *Violence and the Sacred*, Girard advances a hypothesis regarding the development of ritual and culture positing that ritual arose from what he calls "mimetic desire and ritualized scapegoating" to prevent universal violence. He sees violence, in one form or another, as inevitable. There are, however, good or legitimate violence and bad or unacceptable violence. The task of societies is to choose through which vehicle they will allow violence to manifest itself:

Fieldwork and subsequent theoretical speculation lead us back to the hypothesis of substitution as the basis for the practice of sacrifice. This notion pervades ancient literature on the subject—which may be one reason, in fact, why many modern theorists reject the concept out of hand or give it only scant attention. Hubert and Mauss, for instance, view the idea with suspicion, undoubtedly because they feel that it introduces into the discussion religious and moral values that are incompatible with true scientific inquiry.[3] And to be sure, Joseph de Maistre takes the view that the ritual victim is an "innocent" creature who pays a debt for the "guilty" party. I propose an hypothesis that does away with this moral distinction. As I see it, the relationship between the potential victim and the actual victim cannot be defined in terms of innocence or guilt. There is no question of "expiation." Rather, society is seeking to deflect upon a relatively indifferent victim, a "sacrificeable" victim, the violence that would otherwise be vented on its own members, the people it most desires to protect.

The qualities that lend violence its particular terror—its blind brutality, the fundamental absurdity of its manifestations—have a reverse side. With these qualities goes the strange propensity to seize upon surrogate victims, to actually conspire with the enemy and at the right moment toss him a morsel that will serve to satisfy his raging hunger. . . . *Violence is not to be denied, but it can be diverted to another object, something it can sink its teeth into.*[4] [emphasis mine]

This supposed link between violence and ritual will certainly seem implausible to some. The notion that all sacrificial rites are more similar than different at their cores will breed even more debate. This will cause dissent particularly among BGF members who hold fast to the belief that their organizations and fraternal experiences are so radically different from those of their white counterparts that the differences mandate the particular pledge process under consideration. One BGF member interviewed for this study stated:

There's no real respect for their [white fraternal] groups, you know? Just look at how they view their organizations when they graduate. You hear them all the time saying, "I **was** a this" and "I **was** a that." You never hear us say that. I'm a Sigma and I'm going to be a Sigma until the day I die. So we always say "I **am**" instead of "I **was**." They just don't have to work for it, man. I guess that's why you see them running around with their Greek letters on their butts. How are you going to put your letters on your ass? How disrespectful can you get? We respect our organizations more because we work for it! They just walk in. They can't love and respect it.

My stance calls into question what I see as a fallacy of association. The tendency to couple the intensely physical brand of hazing in BGFs with greater regard for the fraternities and a stronger sense of brotherhood is illusory. But to accomplish this task, a cursory glance at rituals located in different mediums is necessary. This examination illustrates that the pledge process belongs to a historical ritualistic genre that is not unique to BGFs.

Some scholars, directly or indirectly, posit that what we today regard as fraternity ritual has its roots in Freemasonry, which can be traced back to ancient Africa. Various Afrocentrists assert that ancient Egyptians developed a complex religious system called "the Mysteries," which was the first religious system whose structure was geared toward the achievement of salvation.[5] George G. M. James notes that this system regarded the human body as a "prison house of the soul," which could only be liberated from its "bodily impediments" through the disciplines of arts and sciences and advanced from the level of a mortal to that of a god.[6]

The belief that structured initiation rituals have their roots in Africa is certainly disputed. The rage, however, is not necessarily over ritual, but over a more central and pressing Afrocentric claim. That claim is that modern Western society is based on the faulty assumption that Greek tradition is at the heart of what we presently know as religion, the arts, and sciences, and maybe most disturbing of all, philosophy. Wellesley professor Mary Leftkowitz led the strongest anti-Afrocentric attack over the last few decades in her book *Not Out of Africa*.[7] Whether or not one accepts the Afrocentric stance, the works of James, Molefi Asante, James Brunson, Maulana Karenga, and others include additional ritualistic processes of the type we are concerned with. We find rituals of historical and social significance in other locations as well. Notable ritualized initiation appeared outside of Africa in several instances. Mysteries systems in the Greco-Roman tradition, for example, included Eleusinian and Orphic orders.[8] The Eleusinian mysteries included four elements: purification, communication with the mystics, exposition of holy objects and symbols, and investiture by crowning with a garland. People are said to have traveled from around the Roman Empire to take part in these rituals. The most important part of the festival included a play based on the Greek myth dealing with the abduction of Persephone, daughter of the goddess Demeter, by Hades, god of the underworld. The events that unfold in the myth explain why seasons change. Subsequently, the theme of death and rebirth was central to the Eleusinian initiation.

The Orphic mysteries were performed by ancient Dionysian cults.[9] In these rituals, Dionysus represented productivity and destruction, the sacrificed and the sacrificer. These cults continuously sought to affirm that true individuation could not be achieved without interaction between the individual and the collective. Only the initiate who could move beyond the individual Self to an affirmation of Dionysus was able to achieve a transformation that illuminated the transitive interaction between the individual and society. The Dionysian Mysteries aimed to restructure the individual so that he was no longer tied to the minimal "I," but to a larger community. This commitment to a larger cause falls neatly in line with Girard's hypothesis, because this commitment called for individual sacrifice to maintain the well-being of the whole.

Mithraism provides another example of ancient ritual that ties into our study. This cult, which worshiped the Persian god Mithras, had a wide following across Europe and parts of Africa, as is evident from the numerous temples of Mithras excavated in Germany, the United Kingdom, Algeria, and Italy.[10] In this ritualized system, the initiate went through seven degrees representing the seven spheres through which the soul passes on its way to perfection. Much like in modern Freemasonry, the neophyte was considered a "servant" until the third degree was completed.[11]

Despite their different geographic locations, all of these rituals display commonalities passed to today's fraternal world in one way or another. These include (1) *purification* of the neophyte; (2) some type of *symbolic journey* that includes symbols, objects, or other means of identifying initiates (these may include a crown, tattoo or scar, jewelry, etc.); (3) *inspiration* by lecture on the expectations of future behavior based on the values presented in the initiation; and (4) *degrees or multiple levels of initiation*, which usually demand a waiting period.

These ancient and modern rituals illustrate that the themes of death, rebirth, and perfection are quite common. These themes hit closer to home in the West when we consider rituals in Christianity that survive today. The symbolism of death and rebirth is quite clear in the Christian baptism-in-water ritual. Ceremonies still exist that mark the attainment of different levels of achievement in the church—the ordination of priests, deacons, confirmations, and similar rituals. In the sacred as well as the secular realms, ritual participants are, in one way or another, past-oriented and continue to long for a sense of enlightenment and community through the completion of prescribed rites.

THE COMMONALITIES OF MODERN FRATERNITY RITUAL

Modern fraternity initiation rituals are no different than ancient ones in that they also seek to maintain some form of stability within organizations. They are not unique, but rather they are syntheses of materials from a number of sources, including historical rituals from other civilizations (especially Africa, Asia, and Greece); Freemasonry; other adult lodge groups such as the Knights of Pythias, Knights of Columbus, Order of Odd Fellows, and Knights Templar; and religious books and liturgies. Some Greek organizations also developed commonalities because men in one fraternity assisted those who were starting new ones. Kappa Alpha Psi historian William Crump recounts that the founders of Kappa Alpha Psi found white Greeks at Indiana University quite agreeable about aiding them in certain fraternal endeavors when they determined the new black organization was no threat to them.[12]

Bobby McMinn summarizes modern fraternity rituals as having five basic ritualistic precepts and seven common steps or components. The precepts include (1) *character* (honor, leadership, morality, truth, and loyalty); (2) *scholarship* (academics, intellectual development, and the pursuit of knowledge); (3) *fellowship* (brotherhood, group unity, and shared values); (4) *service* (to the less fortunate, and/or to a particular profession); and (5) *religion* (respect for a higher authority, sometimes a particular denomination's views). Without divulging the particulars of any surviving fraternity's initiation ritual, the work of McMinn illustrates that most fraternities use some or all of these precepts as part of the themes of their initiation ceremonies.[13]

McMinn posits that initiation rituals usually progress in a very deliberate manner. The following steps may occur at different points in different rituals, but they are almost always present. The first step is *preparing the candidates and creating a procedure for admitting them into the initiation room.* This usually consists of dressing the neophytes in robes and often blindfolding them. They are then led to a door by an already initiated guide where there are knocks on the door, an exchange of dialogue, and sometimes an exchange of signs, grips, or passwords to gain the neophyte and guide entrance. Next, *the initiation oath is administered.* In most groups, the chapter president administers the oath. The neophytes are often standing, but may be kneeling, and may have their right hand raised. Some of the items included in the oath may be to keep the secrets of the fraternity, to promote the fraternity's interests, to obey orders from superiors, to strive to improve oneself in areas of the precepts of the fraternity, to not join any other college social or service fraternity, and to promote the interests of the host institution (when applicable).

Third, the neophyte is *taught the secrets and symbols of the fraternity.* These usually include passwords, a motto, recognition signs, the symbolism of the coat of arms, the significance of the titles of officers, and the interpretation of the fraternity flag, flower, whistle, call, song, and so forth. Fourth is the *investiture of the badge or pin*, which is usually done by the big brother sponsor or president. If a more prominent fraternity officer (national or regional) is present, he may assume this duty. Fifth comes the *charge of responsibility*, which is often read to the new initiate(s). This, again, is usually done by the president. These charges may include encouraging the initiate to fulfill the ideals of the fraternity, complete his college education to the best of his ability, pursue lifelong learning, strive for unity, and serve the fraternity in the future. Most fraternities say a *prayer* at some point in their ritual.

Finally, and most important to our study, is the practice of requiring the neophyte to undertake a *symbolic journey*, which has two important purposes. On one hand, it teaches the neophyte the ideals and virtues of the fraternity through the use of personification and sound and sight effects. Second, it affords him the opportunity to prove his allegiance to the organization by presenting him with situations in which he must sacrifice himself for the good of others and the fraternity. This ordeal ideally determines whether the neophyte is prepared for membership and impresses upon him the necessity of guarding the fraternity's secrets. It is here, within the symbolic journey, that we locate hazing's lair.

HAZING AND THE SYMBOLIC JOURNEY

It is important to understand that the pledge process of fraternities *is* what McMinn calls the "symbolic journey" and is nothing more than another dramatization of the death and rebirth theme passed down to us from the ancients. Completing this ordeal symbolically represents the replacing of a life of hopelessness, selfishness, and solitude with one full of hope, light, and fraternal love. All of these aspects, along with the desire to attain and affirm manhood, serve as the carrots dangled by secret orders to attract men. One examiner of initiation ritual, Mark Carnes, sees the initiation rites of fraternal orders as a distinct product of Victorian American culture and society.[14]

Although this assertion is debatable, Carnes provides valuable information on specific events that take place in fraternity initiation rituals that attract men. He opines that whereas thousands of rituals were written for different orders, "probably no more than twenty were successful." These particular rituals, which struck a responsive chord in members, "were shamelessly pirated or slightly modified by rival orders, and certain themes reappeared in scores of ceremonies."[15] The purpose of all these rituals was to establish not only a fraternal identity, but to forge a vision of a complete Self to help men take their places in society.

To support his hypothesis, Carnes examines the attempt by the Improved Order of Red Men to attract members in the mid-nineteenth century. Former Freemasons initially established the Order of Red Men in 1834. Its original initiation ritual included little more than the initiation oath and charge of responsibility components. Absent from this ritual was anything resembling the symbolic journey. After quick initial growth, the Order began to falter, and by 1850 had little more than 3,000 members. During the following two decades, the fraternity concentrated primarily on developing a ritual that would effectively attract and retain members. The Red Men finally settled on the Adoption Degree of 1868 as the initiation ritual, and fraternity officials credited it with the order's renewed success.

Carnes feels "the question as to why earlier rituals failed to elicit 'general approbation' while the Adoption Degree of 1868 gave 'excellent satisfaction' is ultimately unanswerable."[16] Contrarily, I feel this question is very answerable. First, however, it would be useful for us to recount the Adoption Degree that was published verbatim by the National Christian Association, an organization that sought to destroy the appeal of secret ritual by making it public. The major difference in this ceremony from that of Greek-letter orders is that the characters are "red men" and "palefaces" instead of "Greeks" and their symbolic opponents. Carnes summarizes the initiation ceremony as follows:

> It began with an invocation by a sachem, who prayed to the "Great Spirit of the Universe" to bring harmony to the tribe, to preserve the Indians' homes, and to "shed Thy boundaries upon all Red Men of the forest." Despite these hopes, however, the ritual's main theme was death. The sachem called upon the Great Spirit to give each Red Man the "holy courage" to paddle his canoe safely to "that undiscovered country from whose bourne no traveler returns." During the invocation he returned to the subject of death:

> > Teach us the trail we must follow while we live in this forest, and when it is Thy will that we shall cross the river of death, take us to Thyself, where Thy council fire of love and glory burneth forever in righteousness.

> Then the council fire was kindled; in the preparation room the candidate—a "paleface"—removed his shirt and shoes and put on moccasins. A scout rapped at the "inner wicket" and motioned for the candidate to follow. They padded silently around the lodge room, avoiding a group of Indians who were "sleeping" at the far end. Then the scout tripped over one of the sleeping Indians. The awakened Indian shouted, "Spies! Traitors in our Camp!" and the group captured the candidate; the scout escaped. The Indian "hunters" then conferred around a fire:

> > FIRST BRAVE: This paleface is of a hated nation: let us put him to torture!
> > SECOND BRAVE: He is a squaw, and cannot bear the torture!
> > THIRD BRAVE: He fears a Warrior's death!
> > FOURTH BRAVE: Let us burn him at the stake!

The discussion continued in a similar fashion. At last the initiate was informed that he would indeed be consumed by fire.

They proceeded to the opposite end of the lodge, where they were led to a tepee. Just after they had been admitted, another Indian rushed at the candidate with an uplifted knife, only to be intercepted by a hunter, who assured him that [the] paleface would soon be tortured. "Then let us proceed, pale face, and unless some Chief interposes, you perish at the stake. . . . Why do you tempt your fate? Or is it your wish to become a Red Man? The candidate was prompted to answer yes. The hunter warned: "Know, then, that Red Men are men without fear, and none but such can be adopted by our tribe." After more questions the hunter demanded proof of the candidate's courage: "The honest and brave man meets death with a smile—the *guilty* trembles at the very thought."

The initiate was bound to the stake, and the hunters were encouraged to prepare their scalping knives and war clubs. The Indians commenced a scalp dance and fagots were lit. Another Indian ran to summon the prophet. The prophet, however, emerged from the tent, halted the execution, berated the hunters for their impulsiveness, and pronounced the candidate a "man without fear." The prophet then lectured the candidate on the family of Red Men, explaining that they held property in common and were dedicated to their "brothers," the "children of the forest." However, he warned the candidate that the final decision about his adoption rested with the sachem. The prophet gave the candidate an eagle's feather as proof of his courage.

After more speeches and a pledge of secrecy, the candidate was led to another tepee in the far corner of the lodge. As he approached, the sachem threw open the flap and upbraided his guards for sleeping on duty, thereby allowing a paleface to come in[to] his presence. The warriors did not immediately respond and the sachem started to throw a tomahawk at the initiate. One of the hunters then grasped the sachem's arm. "No, Sachem, no! Thy children when on duty never sleep!" The hunter added that the initiate had passed the ordeal and been endorsed by the prophet. He produced the eagle's feather as proof. The sachem, realizing his error, tossed his tomahawk aside and shook hands with the candidate: "Then you are welcome to our bosom." The sachem deliver[ed] a welcoming speech stressing the protection that the order afforded members of the tribe, much as "the eagle shieldeth her young and tender brood."[17]

The common threads of fraternity ritual covered by McMinn are clearly evident in the Adoption Degree of 1868, which differed from the group's other proposed ceremonies in two important ways. First, it included a symbolic journey. Second, the symbolic journey incorporated the motifs of sacrificial death and rebirth, just as the ancients had. This ritual death moves the initiation to a special zone. The ritualistic rebirth of the initiate not only marks his entrance into the fraternal order, but also the birth of a new Self. The symbolic threats of death are not easily overlooked in the Order of Red Men initiation ritual, and they should not be overlooked in any sacrificial rite, for it is the threat of death that gives the rites their appeal. This fact answers Carnes's earlier query about what made the Adoption Degree of 1868 particularly successful.

In the Red Men case, although the neophyte is twice spared from execution at the hands of his brothers-to-be, he does experience a metaphorical death. His former Self does not really survive the ritualistic symbolic journey. His previous life course has been proven flawed. With the help of the ritual and the guidance of the Red Men, he has chosen an alternate route. Simply put, the life of the paleface has come to an end and the life of a new Red Man has begun. The attraction of the death motif can be clearly linked to René Girard's hypothesis that regards sacrifice as utilitarian in that it is necessary for the good of the community. In the Girardian sense, the fraternity is not the community, but a symbol of the community. Social and fraternal rituals, however, ideally serve the same purpose—they maintain order, continuity, and goodness. Through the trials of the ritual, the new initiate becomes able to contribute to the maintenance of order and the continuous survival of the fraternal community. This is so because he supposedly moves from his place of individualistic egoism to one of altruistic sacrifice and bonding with his brothers. Only in this way can brotherhood and the vitality of the whole be kept alive.

The purpose of initiation ritual is not to reform the initiate, but to *remake him entirely*. Not surprisingly, then, BGF members often refer to their date of initiation as the day they were "made," and members who initiated other members will say, "I made him" or "I made you." In the case of the Red Men, Carnes remarks, "Though apprehended for the crime of trespass, he [the Initiate] was to be put to death for a failing of character: He was a 'paleface' and a 'squaw' who 'could not bear torture.' He was excluded from the tribe which consisted of 'men without fear,' because he was unfit. Through the transformative power of the ritual, the initiate's courage was confirmed."[18] This confirmation not only confirms the initiate's fitness for membership in the fraternity, but more deeply confirms his manhood and fitness to undertake greater endeavors in life. Ultimately, the reborn neophyte is expected and expects to be quite different from the candidate who began the process. In most cases, just as the journey in this ordeal is symbolic, the tests and threats embedded in it are also symbolic. In modern hazing, however, members take tests out of the realm of symbolism and catapult them into reality. Instead of the initiate being *threatened* with torture to prove his fraternal worth and manliness, he is actually tortured.

Specific hazing tactics are nothing more than creative variations deployed by individual fraternity members to push initiates to their limits in a supposed effort to establish their worthiness. Although the components of initiation rituals are usually consistent, we find a clear difference between BGFs and WGFs in the tactics of testing and hazing. Although pledging and hazing do not necessarily go hand in hand, many modern Greeks see them as synonymous. On this issue, a Kentucky university administrator comments, "Those two words [pledging and hazing] have become so intertwined, even over the last ten years, that in many instances they are the same thing. Especially in our black organizations and for some of our white ones. If you look at the NPHC men's groups, they've done away with the terminology of pledging in an effort to get rid of hazing, but hazing continues."

The rise of hazing to prominence in BGFs has made it the rule instead of the exception in the journey of the pledge. Again, some black Greeks attribute this progression to the fact that their organizations are much more important to them than white groups are to their members. A member of Alpha Phi Alpha comments, "I think Greek life is a totally different experience for white people. I mean, they don't really care about who is allowed to join their organizations. Look at their rush process. How can you get to know someone in a week? These people are freshmen who have been on campus for a week and you use that to decide who's in and who's out? That's crazy. It's no wonder they use their groups to just drink and party. That's all its about for them. We offer a lifelong commitment. Brotherhood forever. That's something worth struggling for."

Such stances are probably born of minimal interaction with WGF members and do not hold true when white fraternity allegiance is examined critically. In actuality, white fraternity members also display tenacious adherence to fraternity tradition and have pushed for autonomy from administrators and outsiders. Michael Gordon, the long time executive director of NPHC, commented that he "sees very little difference in the fanaticism of some Greeks toward their groups, be they black or white."[19] But, even when similarities are rightfully acknowledged, differences can sometimes be profound. A member of Phi Kappa Tau summarizes differences in black and white hazing accurately when he states that physical hazing occurs much less frequently in white groups:

> In reviewing cases and reading things, I think there are differences in what the [hazing] vehicles are. There is very little difference, though, in commitment to the groups. I see the black groups as being a lot more physical. I see the white Greeks using alcohol more frequently and playing more mental games, especially some of the groups you would not consider as being very large physically. But all these things happen across the board, just with variations in regards to the means. A lot of this goes to definitions of manhood, masculinity, what it is . . . what it means to be a man—in the black sense it means to be strong, defend yourself, stand up for yourself physically. Many times we have the skewed sense in whites that the more alcohol you can drink, the more manly you are. . . . "You drink like a girl," "You're a skirt if you're not drinking on Saturday night," "Can't hold your liquor?"

Study of WGFs does not bear out the notion that they care less about their organizations. Nor does it prove in any way that they do not haze. On the contrary, white Greeks haze extensively in an effort to demand that new members prove their worth and appreciate the fraternity. The levels of physical abuse found in black groups, however, are rarely reached. For example, a common practice among the members of the Klan Alpine fraternity at Alfred University during the 1970s was for a brother to wield a paddle before pledges and aggressively ask, "Who wants to be the first to get paddled? Who thinks he can take it?" When pledges volunteered for the paddling, the big brother would throw his hands up in disgust, pour lighter fluid on the paddle, and fling it into the fireplace exclaiming, "We don't do that at Klan Alpine."[20] White Greeks' adherence to ritualized pledge processes as the essential element that ensures the well-being of their groups, however, is no less powerful than blacks'. For example, too brief of a look at hazing in Klan Alpine can be misleading, for although members took pride in their disdain of paddling, they constructed a number of alternate methods to test their pledges' mettle.

One such activity was the tradition of forcing pledges to smoke large, foul-smelling cigars in the small confines of a broom closet. Small pledge classes endured this ritual in a phone booth. Often, when breathable air vanished as cigar smoke filled the rooms, pledges panicked. On one occasion, a couple of pledges hyperventilated, another vomited, and another began to turn green. The pledges furiously banged on the wall of the closet to be released before someone died or became ill from smoke inhalation. One alumnus of the fraternity remarked that the embedded purpose of the ritual was to teach blind obedience, "The ideal pledge was a boot-camp recruit who followed orders without question." Other hazing rituals included having pledges repeatedly take mouthfuls of water "filled with soggy cornflakes and other objectionable materials" and crawl down a flight of stairs to put out a fire in the fireplace by spitting on the flames. Another favorite of this group was a game called "Bombs Away" in which members dropped beer kegs from windows as pledges attempted to dodge them.[21]

Such hazing activities are not unique to Klan Alpine. One member of the Sigma Alpha Epsilon fraternity commented, "Many of my fraternity brothers feel that pledging and hazing are bases for what we are. They are parts of what we are and you can't take them away from us." This mentality has endured for so long in the fraternal world that abuse during the pledge period has, in many circles, been normalized. For example, University of Lowell spokesman Oliver Ford commented that Stephen Call had been subjected to "ordinary harassment" when Call died from hypothermia while pledging Delta Kappa Phi in 1980. Ford stated, "The only thing we found that is even reminiscent of the old days of hazing is a bit of paddling that was done with a piece of carpet. The paddling is routinely applied. There is a certain amount of indignity involved but that's what being a pledge is all about. It's nothing compared to the horrible days of the past when fraternity pledges went through Hell Week."[22] This fascination with the past is present in both black and white groups and is one of the most powerful tools used to keep hazing alive.

THE LURE OF LIMINALITY: THE RITUALISTIC REMAKING OF THE SELF

Whether the past-oriented ritualistic initiation process truly holds transformative power is debatable. A good percentage of members strongly endorse the hazing that often comes with the BGF pledge process. In the black instance, hazing practices certainly take on a different face within the symbolic journey in that they are often intensified through the use of physical violence. The physical violence involved in the BGF pledge process is the element that, to many BGF members, positions the ordeal as particularly sacrificial and even legitimate. Outside of the vehicles of hazing, however, there is a unity of purpose in most fraternal initiatory rituals—black, white, or other.

Whether the acts during the symbolic journey are threatened or real, sacrificial rites of passage for all Greeks have to do with the initiate's acquiring new status and the organization gaining stability. These rites are designed as processes that confer upon new initiates the privilege of full admission to the fraternal community. That this process is, in and of itself, political, should not be doubted. Just as accepted avenues to achievement in the larger society exist—attending the "right" schools, obtaining the "right" degrees, and living in the "right" neighborhood— avenues of entrance into BGFs that are considered more legitimate and respectable than others also exist.

What has been missed is the possibility that sacrificial processes are political not only on the individual or organizational levels, but also the societal. In our society, which is less and less based on the notion of community, individual passage from one status to another always presents problems of adaptation, but these problems are thought to be limited to the individuals directly involved in the process. This belief is one that potentially serves to limit the modern scope of inquiry into problems of violence. Whereas we in the postmodern Western world tend to largely detach individual existence from that of the society, many earlier societies usually made no such separation. Girard remarks, "In primitive societies . . . the slightest change in the status of an isolated individual was treated as if it carried the potential to create a major [societal] crisis."[23]

To be sure, thinkers such as Girard, Allen Feldman, and Roberto Calasso embrace ritual violence and sacrifice as practices that maintain the stability of a community.[24] In Calasso's view, sacrificial ritual in more civilized societies eventually gives way to less violent, more worldly devices such as romantic stories of adventurous exploits, fantastic journeys, and amazing encounters of love. These fantasies are all very seductive and make for impressive cinema, but they teach nothing about human loss. Ultimately, Calasso sees the societal loss of sacrifice as the root of people succumbing to a material life empty of true ceremonial content.

Modern people are therefore left with a great, aching absence. Hence, nothing seems legitimate, and nothing can be made legitimate once they lose touch with sacrifice—be it physical or emotional. This nebulous feeling is what is commonly referred to as *anomie.* When a society changes rapidly, a cohesive set of values that the majority of people accept no longer exists. This is so, Calasso believes, because it is the primordial act of sacrifice that defines human limits and balances social relations. Only ceremonies of loss and death can teach people how to *live* together. It is the deficiency of legitimacy, brotherhood, and community that Greeks and other groups that employ sacrificial rites seek to eradicate or avoid altogether.

Most criticisms of these groups do not center on the intended ends of the pledge process, but its means. That is, the methods involved in the pledge journey are considered abhorrent. But, the methods endure because just as they are horribly sick to some, they are sacred to others. Again, central to the pledge process is the fact that it is concerned with a change in individual status, or as Arnold Van Gennep coined it, *liminality*, which is involved in all rites of passage. Liminality has two distinct stages.[25] In the first, the initiate loses his previous status, and in the second stage he acquires his new one. The gap between the stages is the void the pledge process must fill.

To members, the process is what moves the initiate from the place of a disconnected individual to that of a connected, metamorphosized fraternity man. At the outset, the initiate is seen as different from his brothers-to-be. The pledge process, like all sacrificial rites, is intended to eradicate this difference. This eradication, however, becomes troubling if Girard is right—"for if all violence involves a loss of difference, all losses of difference also involve violence."[26] Although Girard's conversion may appear a bit flippant, it certainly seems to apply in this particular case. The violence used to eradicate difference can often be extreme, for difference in these spaces is considered contagious. This stance is not disturbing to Girardians because they agree that "perfectly innocent phenomena can provoke fear, but that fear cannot dismiss it as mere fantasy; there is nothing fantastical about its impact or its results."[27]

The love/loathe ambivalence of the pledge introduced at the outset of this chapter can now be explained. The pledge "in passage" is not hated; the difference he represents is disdained. He, therefore, must be regarded in the same light as a criminal or infected individual who could potentially infect the entire fraternal body. His presence alone mandates violence in an attempt to destroy the contagion of difference that, if not treated, can destroy the body. Only through the completion of the process can he be "cured" and subsequently embraced. If we conceive of contagion in terms of microbiology, we miss the point. In this case, the fraternity is the body and the individual is the virus. This, to be sure, is a shift in—or more appropriately, a minimization of—Girard and Calasso's community. Fraternity members are, in the main, not conscious of community in the Girardian or Calasson sense, because the fraternity (all too often) *is* their community and the differentiated individual must be altered or decontaminated before he is allowed entrance. Logically then, the first step is to isolate the infected victim—forbidding all contact between him and the "healthy" members. He is placed on the periphery of the society—in a different, almost surreal, isolated realm where the violence of undifferentiation reigns.

As in other rituals of this type, the initiate is quite often "stripped of his name, his history, and his family connections; he is reduced to a state of anonymity."[28] Violence is the tool that determines the result of this endeavor. The pledge must submit to the violence, but never with full knowledge of the process's outcome. Because much of fraternity life is esoteric, the pledge knows what he is losing, but can only conceptualize a vague silhouette of what he will gain. The mysticism of the process is precisely what affords the pledge journey its appeal. This mystery and the promise of rebirth it supposedly brings aligns the pledge process with ancient sacrificial rites of passage:

Although the prospect of the passage may appear terrifying to the primitive mind, it also offers hope. After all, it was by way of a general outbreak of violence and universal loss of difference—that is, by way of sacrificial crisis—that the community achieved a differentiated order in former times. And it can be hoped that this crisis will achieve the same results. Differences will be restored or established; specifically, the neophyte will gain his new coveted status. A happy outcome must depend on the good will of supreme violence, but the community believes it can influence this outcome by channeling the "bad" energy into prearranged outlets. In order for the final results to match those of the original action, however, every possible precaution must be taken to follow the original model. The neophytes must adhere to the rules laid down by tradition; they must try to shape the new event in the mold of the old one. For only if the ritual reiterates the original crisis is there hope that the outcome will be the same.

Such is the reasoning behind these rites of passage. . . . Instead of avoiding the crisis, the neophyte must advance to meet it, as his ancestors did before him. Instead of fleeing the most painful and terrifying aspects of reciprocal violence, he must submit to each and every one of them in proper sequence. The postulate must endure hardship, hunger, even torture, because these ordeals were part of the original experience. . . . the celebrants in certain festivals are required to perform a number of actions that are normally forbidden: real or symbolic acts of sexual aggression, stealing, the eating of proscribed foods.[29]

Although never referencing BGFs or Greek-letter fraternities of any kind, Girard perfectly describes the psychology, recognized or not, behind the pledge process —it is one that ultimately seeks stability through the liminality of the initiate. Even in the Afrocentric case, the process reappears. Echoing George G. M. James, James Brunson sees initiation ritual as intended to "teach the candidate the secret of making one's self a perfection of God."[30] To accomplish this task, the initiate must endure seven major trials: seclusion, beatings, exposure to cold, thirst, eating of unsavory foods, punishment, and threat of death. Although Brunson makes it clear that he does not necessarily condone the current BGF pledge process, he does use Asa Hilliard's study of African initiation systems to draw comparisons between them and the

BGF pledge process.[31] Compared to our earlier citations of ritual and their components, Brunson's list clearly illustrates that geographic boundaries do not neatly separate such rites:

1. The initiates were physically segregated from the regular activity of daily life.
The "pledge line" is formed. These individuals are required to interact, learn as much about each other as possible, work together, and depend upon each other, with as little assistance as possible from any outside sources; except of course their deans.

2. They retreated from their familiar environment to an environment that enabled them to get more directly in touch with nature. This symbolized a move from the infantile situation into a situation which would allow for more maturity.
The pledge(s) are put into pressured situations that require them to often get in touch with the psychological "inner self" and intellect, utilize their individual and group creativity and resourcefulness towards goals of self-actualization.

3. The initiate joined with other initiates of the same age and shared their lives in common, since common living experience was also a common learning experience.
The pledge(s) at times are required to eat, sleep, and live together, study together, visit their "big brothers," review required learning materials. They get to know each other as one would know a blood brother or sister.

4. The initiates were separated from their parents in addition to being separated from the large community.
The pledge(s) may be put into situations known as "social probation" where they are denied social interaction with anyone outside the classroom or pledge line. They are not allowed to talk, socially interact with, or engage in any form of dynamic that calls into question the dynamic of ostracization.

5. The initiates had to renounce all that recalls the past existence.
The pledge(s) states an allegiance to the tenets of the organization

that they are being initiated into. They are given specific expectations that also demand a fuller respect for humanity.

6. The initiates were then taught by the old men and women of the village or town.
The pledge(s) are taught the philosophic and pragmatic aspects of the organization, as well as its ideologies inherent to Greek-lettered organizations. They learn fraternity and chapter history, poems, information regarding other chapters, myths of the organization, the Greek alphabet, etc.

7. The initiates frequently went nude or wore clothes made of grass to symbolize the clothes of the first men or women.
Pledge(s) is expected to wear uniforms or outfits signifying their status as an initiate as outlined by that organization. The attire may mandate dresses every day or a specific day, shirts and ties, army jackets and boots, beanie caps or hats, shaving one's head or facial hair, etc.

8. The initiates underwent purification baths.
In "crossing the burning sands," initiates often undergo a series of trials designed to bring them from "darkness into the light."

9. During the course of initiation a number of tests of audacity, courage, fasting, flogging, hazing, mutilations, sacrifications were conducted. The purpose was to give the opportunity for the initiate to demonstrate a refusal to take life as it is given as a way of opening the mind to beauty, joy, and ecstasy.
Initiates are sent through a variety of trials during a week-long ordeal referred to as "Hell Week" that are supposed to test their desire to be a member of the organization.

10. Initiate learned a new and secret language.
Neophytes are given the passwords, grips, and signs designed for that specific organization.

11. Initiates were given new names.
During "Hell Week," the candidates are given preliminary names such

as "dog," "probate," numbers, and line names, that are subsequently transformed after the initiation.

12. The initiation process symbolizes a rebirth.
After the "crossing of the burning sands," initiated members become "neophytes" ("new in the light") of their organization.

13. The initiation process included a number of exercises and things to be learned, such as physical and military training, songs, dances, how to handle sacred things such as math and tools.
Pledges learn rituals, songs, poems, history, and Greek literature perceived as relevant to the sustaining and perpetuation of the organization's existence. These ideas are passed on from one pledge class or line to another.[32]

By this point, my hypothesis that there is nothing distinct about the origins or aims of the BGF pledge processes that explain why violence has become such an integral part of them should be undeniable. This is not to say that BGF pledge processes have no distinct characteristics. Clearly, the personas many members of Kappa Alpha Psi have taken on, with cane twirling and the "pretty boy" image, distinguish them in an exteriorized way from Omegas and their infatuation with the "Que-Dog" moniker and all its trappings: dog collars, boots, and barking.[33] The emphasis placed on these differences by the members of each organization is the sole factor that gives each fraternity its particular initiatory quality. Beyond these cleavages, however, there is little difference between Alphas, Kappas, Omegas, Sigmas, and Iotas. Ironically, many members covet and feverishly hold on to these cosmetic differences, even if the most fundamental ritualistic practices and ideals of the organization fall into neglect or disappear from their lives completely.

The reason why Kappas cling to their canes and Omegas bark, even if they are no longer active in their groups, is not really the primary philosophical question here. Our concern lies in locating the unity of sacrificial rites and the link between violence and ritual, and understanding that, although it may not be realized, this ritualized violence originally served a societal purpose. In modern times, ritual violence has lowered societal status, and it is therefore generally minimized, criticized, and rightfully disdained. At the outset, ritual sacrifice was not about the victim or guilt at all, but was concerned with preserving a particular social order. Clearly, the stance that violence is inevitable and that the wise society constructs ways to channel and confine it brings to bear the age-old debate over human nature. Unfortunately for rosy humanists, history (to this point at least) has proven Thomas Hobbes more right than wrong when he argued that men were little more than brutes.[34] Girard must have had this in mind when he opined, "violence is not to be denied."

The pledge processes of BGFs are certainly attempts to recreate ancient sacrificial crises and subsequently maintain community (organizational) stability through the use of ritualized violence. Clearly, the fact that BGF physical violence has risen to inordinately destructive levels relative to other Greek-letter fraternities causes much distress. Although this violence certainly deserves concern, at its core it is nothing more than the use of different tactics during an initiate's symbolic journey to achieve liminality. The very real threat to black life that comes along with these tactics, however, mandates that we not only understand BGF violence, but seek to curb it. Eradicating hazing in BGFs will be no easy task. In fact, it may be impossible.

As we seek solutions to hazing, we must be clear that many BGF members perceive the pledge ritual as an overwhelmingly important force in the preservation of black fraternal orders. To many black Greeks, physical hardship speaks much more thunderously than intellectual challenge, for this suffering is thought to instill fraternal love and also serves as a mechanism that supposedly affords the pledge opportunities to prove his worth. These ordeals make the establishment of the fraternities' hierarchies of respect (those who pledged compared to those who did not) appear to be an extraordinary blessing to members who were "made right." Ritual violence can only be killed slowly—if it can be killed at all. The possibility that violent initiation practices are immortal is quite real, and this realization moves us to the issue of memory engaged by the Dionysian cults so long ago. Ritual and the steady march of time present the potentiality that many members may no longer know why they do what they do anymore. As Walter Kimbrough has noted, some members defend pledging as a construct of black culture that cannot be understood by outsiders:

When faced with challenges from university administrators, they could describe how the unbroken single-file line was seen as slaves marched to ships for the voyage to America, and how current tribes such as the Venda of Southern Africa employ a single-file line during various rites of passage, which include a first menstruation or circumcision. They were able to recount how slave ships were tightly packed, and how it was important for the line to be tight and unbroken. They articulated the importance of carrying bricks, lamps, or paddles in mimicking the behavior of the Kankurand and the Mandinka.[35]

Although such members may exist, Kimbrough also noted that others are not interested enough in this type of historical and cultural knowledge to effectively make such arguments. Pledge ritual today, in many instances, is random, aimless, and degenerative. The purpose of the ritual itself has been lost over the passage of time. With regular repetition and perceptions of success, these rites have gradually been transformed into simple tests or trials that have become increasingly symbolic and formalistic. With this progression, the sacrificial nature of the process has become obscured over time until currently it is hard to say what the symbols are intended to symbolize. Cleansing liminality does not await many initiates—only physical and psychological damage or even death.

5

The Hegemonic Struggle and Domination in Black Greek-Letter Fraternities

A falsehood has been perpetuated about black Greekdom—graduate chapters do not haze. Like many stereotypes, the belief is grounded in a modicum of truth. Usually, graduate chapters do not carry the intensity of their pledge periods to the same levels as their undergraduate counterparts. Admittedly, many have even abandoned the practice altogether. At the same time, however, undergraduates have been wrongfully characterized as the only ones who haze. In some instances, in fact, hazing in graduate chapters can be worse than in undergraduates, because graduate chapters do not have university administrators or fraternity advisors overseeing their activities. If a graduate chapter's membership generally agrees that pledging or hazing should be an accepted practice in their chapter, very few procedures, checks, or balances are in place to stop them.

In the mid-1990s, my own chapter wrestled with the choice of continuing or relinquishing our commitment to pledging. This chapter is a very old one, established in a state with much historical significance in Kappa Alpha Psi. It was founded in 1927 in Kentucky, the birth state of Elder Watson Diggs, the fraternity's principle founder. The city of Lexington itself is notable because it was the city in which Diggs was married a short time after the fraternity's founding. To this day, Lexington Alumni holds a copy of his marriage certificate in the chapter's archives. Many brothers from the area will proudly tell you, "Kappa runs deep in Kentucky." Before the death of Michael Davis, our chapter had always pledged—sometimes harder than others. After Davis's death, however, our chapter and fraternity faced a moratorium on Intake for over a year. Eventually, we were allowed to bring in new members, and the inevitable debate about how these new brothers should be initiated ensued. To put it mildly, the issue was—a bit contentious.

Our direction at this juncture was important for me, because I was now—at twenty-seven years old—the Polemarch of the chapter. A Polemarch so young in a graduate chapter was rarely encountered. Even then, I was by far the youngest graduate Polemarch in our Province. The matter at hand was pressing for a number of reasons. First, it was my first major decision as the chapter's leader and the eyes of older brothers were on me. Whatever I did, I had to make sure that brothers understood that the decision was mine and no one else's. If they got the impression that I was a "puppet king" and not the "sovereign," I was doomed to be challenged and disrespected at every turn for the remainder of my tenure. I also knew very well that any mistakes or violations of fraternity rules would ultimately be my responsibility. At the same time, if we did not pledge "our new boys" and they turned out to be poor brothers or were not accepted by the fold, I could be blamed for that, too. Needless to say, I examined every angle very carefully.

I still remember my former dean sitting in his basement with a number of brothers as opinions bounced back and forth. He listened intently as he inhaled from one of a long line of cigarettes and finally said, "I don't know, brothers. I've never believed in letting people walk into the fraternity. If we do it the way headquarters wants us to, Kappa might as well be a club—not a frat."

He was not alone. The former Polemarch, who had become one of my closest friends, had developed a reputation during his younger years as a brutal hazer. After undergraduate school, however, he set on a path of reform. Although physical hazing had fallen into disfavor with him, he had not abandoned his commitment to what we called "hard" pledging. "I agree," he said, "If we let all of our traditions go, the frat is going to hell in a hand basket. We need to have some kind of process."

Another "old head" brother who had pledged at Old Dominion in 1974 and was now a high-level executive at Toyota Motor Company chimed in, "Brothers, nobody is saying we need to beat the hell out of these guys or anything like that. I'm just saying they need to do some things together. They need the opportunity to bond, you know. We'd be doing them an injustice if they don't have any stories to tell when this thing is over." "Stories to tell," he said . . . "stories to tell." I did not understand the significance of that statement and maybe he did not either—"stories to tell." Over the years, however, as I have thought about that exchange and the decision we eventually made for "our new boys," I have come to understand that this idea of "stories" runs deeper than I had ever imagined up until that point. What this brother was really speaking to was another issue, one that maintains the traditions, the continuity—and also the problems—in our brotherhood.

Substantive intellectual engagement of hazing is hampered partly because studies' scopes of inquiry are often so limited that the real acts that keep the practice alive are never located. Whereas a reconstructed view of the historical and contemporary importance of ritual is necessary, it is not the pull of ritual alone that mobilizes black men to endure and covet the punishment of hazing. Narrative is another powerful and almost always overlooked companion to ritual that also serves as a source of hazing's lifeblood. Narrative is a coercive tool used not only in BGFs, but in many other arenas. Commenting on narrative in his study of conflict in Northern Ireland, Allen Feldman asserts:

> No discursive object exists outside of, or prior to, a discursive formation. The self is always the artifact of prior received and newly constructed narratives. It is engendered through narration and fulfills a syntactical function in the life history. The rules of narration may perform a stabilizing role in the cultural construction of truth, but then self and truth are subordinate to the trans-individual closures of narrative (spoken or written). . . . In a political culture the self that narrates speaks from a position of having been narrated and edited by others—by political institutions, by concepts of historical causality, and possibly violence.[1]

BGF members function within such a political culture. Like all narrative, BGF narrative is coercive in that it is highly influential in shaping the psychologies of the groups' members and potential members alike. The political dimension of the narrative used within the BGF community should not be underestimated, though its impact has never been thoroughly examined. A particularly political, popular discourse is used within the organizations because it inevitably determines modes of interaction between members. BGFs do not, in my opinion, autonomously create violent individuals. They do, however, provide a medium for imposing violence on others. This imposition is sometimes so intense that some argue it borders on the sadistic and sociopathic. Certainly, a significant percentage of BGF members deny that they or the pledge process, as they have conceptualized it, are aimlessly violent or even negative. For example, one 1991 initiate states:

> People act as if no one can get positivity out of pledging. I can say that there were some serious positive aspects to my four-week pledge period. I feel that pledging engrossed in me such skills as conflict resolution, time management, and creativity. I continue to use those skills in my life today—at work, in grad school, in community organizations, etc. Personally, I do not agree with Intake.[2] From talking with some fellow Greeks, their organizations are making changes to the membership Intake process, because it just doesn't work. A lot of people want to make the process seem very primitive, barbaric, and dangerous. . . . and senseless. Well, I disagree and even if pledging presented problems, Intake certainly isn't the right answer to those problems. Intake as an answer in 1990 was not the right answer and it's not the right answer now. Isn't that evident?

VIOLENCE, POWER, HEGEMONY, AND DOMINATION

This study will probably not engender agreement on whether or not the BGF pledge process is generative. It would be difficult, however, for anyone to argue that the presence of some form of violence has been eliminated or even greatly curtailed in these groups during their initiation processes. In fairness to those who do not classify pledge activities as violent, what can be classified as violence and what cannot may not be as clear as it initially seems. As Hussein Abdilahi Bulhan points out in *Frantz Fanon and the Psychology of Oppression*, violence is a difficult concept to define, although a plethora of definitions have been offered. Some are rather conservative and narrowly constructed, whereas others are much broader.

In *Understand Violence*, Graeme Newman asserts that only that which can be observed should be considered violent. He defines it as "that which leads to physical injury or damage, since historically and statistically it is the only aspect of violence that we are able to observe or record."[3] Marvin Wolfgang, on the other hand, sees violence as, "the intentional use of physical force on another person or noxious stimuli invoked by one person to another."[4] Richard Gelles and Murray

Straus argue that violence is "an act carried out with the intention of, or perceived as having the intention of, physically hurting another person."[5]

These definitions are all limited by their preoccupation with the physical dimensions of violence and neglect of the psychological. They all also have a less evident but just as important aim of dichotomizing violence into "legitimate" and "illegitimate." Legitimate violence is the socially sanctioned use of threat of harm, such as police action and war. Illegitimate violence is that which goes against existing laws and the accepted norms of society. Hussein Bulhan provides criteria for what behavioral scientists have typically classified as violence by citing five basic stipulations that combine to label an act as violent. According to Bulhan, there is no such thing as legitimate violence. What some thinkers have labeled "legitimate" violence, would be considered something different altogether and could be defined as *force* or *authority*.[6] Bulhan's criteria for violence are as follows:

1. One must demonstrate the use of physical force against another person.
2. There must be an intensity of feelings, like rage or hate, which prompts the violent actions.
3. One must have some sound ground to infer an intent to inflict harm.
4. The action or intent must lack social or legal sanction.
5. One must demonstrate the effects in terms of physical damage.[7]

On examination, we realize that these criteria leave room to classify some institutions or practices typically thought of as violent as non-violent. Let us take American chattel slavery, for instance. By Bulhan's fourth criteria, to be violent an act must lack social or legal sanction. Slavery had both, but contending that it was not violent would be difficult. Obviously, Bulhan's criteria are strict, and attempts to define violence in such a manner can deteriorate into debates ruled by confusing and sometimes meaningless semantics.

Although universal agreement on what violence means is difficult to achieve, it is essential that we utilize clear definitions of politics and power. Following Harold Lasswell, we will again approach politics as *the process that determines who gets what, when, and how, in a group or societal structure*.[8] Using a variant of this definition, Maulana Karenga notes that the political process is ultimately concerned with "gaining, maintaining, and using power."[9] Power, simply put, is the ability of some agent X to force some agent Y to do something agent Y would otherwise not do. These agents are not necessarily individuals. That is, agents X and Y may be social or political groups as well as individuals. In either instance, the central concern of politics is power and, conversely, any quest for power is (in one way or another) political. Whether the researcher examines this process in system-oriented terms or studies revolutionary structures and processes, the works are examinations of power.

Harold Cruse has asserted that even though America is philosophically based on the notion of individual rights and privileges, real power can only be located in group structures.[10] This stance mandates a de-emphasis of the individual and a resituation of group and societal influence when studying politics and power in their many manifestations. The tendency exists to classify any group dynamics that lay outside the realm of electoral politics as, if not exclusively social, then certainly as nonpolitical. In *Invisible Politics*, Hanes Walton Jr. criticizes this practice as myopic because power and the struggle for it are the essence of the political and extend well beyond electoral activity.[11] Interaction in many areas of everyday life is deeply political and is driven by overriding group dynamics that have been embedded in American society. Everyday life is, in fact, a reification produced by (as well as a producer of) power. There is no innocent moment or inaccessible sanctuary in which everyday life can shield itself from the continuous struggle for power. Try as they may, it is difficult (if not impossible) for individuals or groups to escape this reality.

Although there are very real differences in power potential between collectives and derivative groups, a political choice also exists for both. The choice is whether to act and become agents or succumb to victimhood and continue to be acted on. Here we locate struggles Antonio Gramsci and others refer to as *hegemonic*. Cultural and political studies have often invoked Gramsci's concept of hegemony to describe moments of national sociopolitical struggle, but the term remains ambiguous to many.[12] Probably the most common perception of hegemony sees it as a process through which domination is achieved by constructing an ideological consensus.[13] This formulation of

Gramsci is not altogether correct. Gramsci himself realized hegemony and domination are not necessarily the same, because even though hegemonic struggle always involves coercion and consent, it does not necessarily involve the negativity of domination.

The key variable in this political equation is power and how it is used. Although power is necessary for domination to occur, domination and power are different in that power is not always negative. Unlike power, domination is marginalization marked by an exercise of supremacy over *and* oppression of another. This state is always retrograde. Gramsci speaks of hegemony, however, as having two faces, "*Permanent* hegemony is always bad; *temporary* hegemony of one group or region may be beneficial to all. Hegemony of north over south in Italy has been bad but need not have been so."[14] From this perspective, temporary hegemony may be judged as positive leadership aimed at reaching some noble end for the collective, but permanent hegemony cannot be regarded as such. If permanent hegemony in a sociopolitical space is established and maintained effectively, the ideas of the controlling class insinuate themselves into the lives of the oppressed to the point that subjugated people eventually do not regard themselves as worthwhile beings. Consequently, they base their assessment of their worth on how well they mimic the behavior and life circumstances of the society's dominant group.[15] As Robert Owen and others have realized, "perverse social systems [such as this] create deformed human beings."[16]

Domination occurs in many arenas and is necessarily preceded by the acquisition of political power. Only through the garnering and abuse of such power can one group marginalize and subordinate another. Although these struggles can be societal (national or international), they also occur within sociopolitical subgroups. BGFs are one example of a terrain where such conflicts play out. After addressing the hegemonic struggle within BGFs, we shall examine a case that is clearly political in the traditional sense and utilize the argument to study black fraternities. In an unlikely comparison, it will become clear that the tactics employed by the American political Right to revive conservatism are very similar to the ones used to maintain the pledge process in contemporary BGFs, which seems unable to rid itself of violence.

EDUCATED GANGS? TO PLEDGE OR NOT TO PLEDGE

If everyday life is political, then the narrativity of everyday life is also political and possibly hegemonic. This is so because narrative as a contributor to identity serves as a powerful force in constructing an individual's reality. For instance, in *Metu Meter*, Ra Un Nefer Amen submits that myriad terms used in everyday life must be redefined to give existence greater meaning. Amen's work is largely religiospiritual in content, but some of his theories certainly apply here. One issue at the root of his construction of man as a spiritual being, for instance, is the difference between the *person* and the *Self*.[17] This differentiation is motivated by what he sees as a historical misunderstanding of what the ancient phrase, "Man, know thyself" actually means. He does not see the "person" as the true higher part of one's being. The person has ties to one's divine being, but it should not be confused with the Self. The Self, according to Amen, is the higher part of one's being—his true identity, which is capable of reunification with the Eternal Oneness of the Universe. The person, on the other hand, is only a temporary identity reference point. Amen's Ten-Stage Tree of Life Initiation system cites the second stage as centering on everyday language. He states:

> At this stage the teacher provides the initiate with a new set of definitions, descriptions, and explanations for what is life, what are emotions, etc. In short, the teacher redefines the basic ideas operating in the life of the student. Before this, all the individual's beliefs are based on the identification with the person (not the Self). We have already seen that up to this point the individual has been victimized by the host of illusions, segregative thinking, and rationalizations of emotions due to the operation of the lower faculties making up the person.[18]

Consequently, Amen argues that the individual must be taught to think in a different way about how he is situated in the universe. But there are barriers to accomplishing this task. He continues:

> This process of redefining the belief system of the student is made very difficult by the use of our everyday language. Most African societies of initiates possess "secret" languages for such purposes. One of the

reasons for this is that such languages create order in the thinking of the person through their semantical structures.[19]

Acceptance of Amen's argument concerning how the person and the Self should be regarded is not necessary to realize that narrative and language are political factors in everyday life. In *Afrocentricity*, Molefi Asante also notes the influence of these factors. He sees language as a "constituent of power," because it is "essentially the control of thought."[20]

Certainly, not physical force, but the exploitation of the desire to be a BGF member (largely engendered by narratives of members of the organizations) drives pledges' submission to acts condemned by organizational policy. Hazing's continuation is firmly locked in BGF narrative, and as we shall see, this is the reason for the failure of the groups' membership Intake Programs (MIPs), which were tailored to replace pledging. In BGFs, the language of domination centers around the concept of pledging, and it constructs criteria for acceptance. The greatest rift in BGFs to date may be the ongoing debate over whether the groups should reenact the traditional pledge process or continue to utilize MIPs to initiate members. The differences between traditional pledging and MIP are striking. The old process, which differed slightly from group to group, had five stages—the potential initiate (1) attended interest meetings or "smokers"; (2) submitted his application and, if it was deemed satisfactory, would be interviewed; (3) "made line" (was accepted as a member of the incoming pledge class); (4) pledged; and (5) was initiated.

Individual chapters routinely embedded particular criteria for "making line." For example, some chapters required potential pledges to "come around" before the official smoker. Quite often, this process could lead to men who "came around" participating in what was colloquially known as "prepledging"—taking part in pledge activities not officially condoned by the national organization. Such chapters would usually decide who was to make line even before the official smoker took place, and the smoker became nothing more than a facade for senior fraternity and school officials. Some argue that this trend afforded active members a better opportunity to test and become acquainted with the men who were to join their fold. Others contend that this practice led to the exclusion of quality candidates who refused to submit to non-fraternity-sanctioned activities and the extorting of money and servitude from those who would submit to them.

The MIP process, which also varies slightly across organizational lines, is different from the pledge process in that the steps consist of (1) attending an "interest meeting," (2) submitting an application and being interviewed, (3) acceptance, (4) initiation, and (5) participation in educational sessions. Noticeable is the absence of any mention of "pledging"—the educational sessions are used as substitutes. Beyond this and maybe more important, the candidate is carried through the initiation ritual before he goes through the pledging substitute. Beyond this, MIP educational sessions eradicate a number of traditional interactions. The candidates are no longer considered members of a "line," so they are not required to dress alike, walk in line, or learn fraternity history and lore in a confrontational manner. This process was constructed in an attempt to bring hazing to a halt, and its supporters contend that the eradication of pledging is the only way to eliminate hazing. This is so, on their view, because hazing has become such an integral part of the pledge process that the two cannot be divorced from one another. The core assumption involved in MIP is that men who are initiated first will not submit to hazing because they have obtained the object of their desire—membership.

Black Greek-letter fraternities initiated MIP after the spring of 1990 in most chapters, but it has failed in achieving its goal of discontinuing pledging and the violent hazing usually associated with it. A member of Kappa Alpha Psi addresses MIP:

> I am not the one who has made past tradition, those who came before us did. Knee-jerk responses to complicated issues [are] not advancement! I'm sure you would not deny that in many ways we were better off years ago. Sometimes when you advance too much you lose something important. In many ways, we have lost our identity. Intake was in effect in 1991, however my chapter pledged us the old way. If I had to do Membership Intake and not be able to pledge—hell no, you could keep it. Whoever said you need a fraternity to achieve or help mankind? My advice to any young men seeking such a thing would be to join an honor society, or the NAACP, or a church action committee. But if you're looking for brotherhood, find a fraternity chapter that has a pledge process. I would tell a young man not to fool himself, don't waste

that few hundred dollars that he will spend on membership. Send that money to a charity. You can't buy brotherhood. Frederick Douglass said, "If there is no struggle, there is no progress."

Soon after MIP began, John Anthony Williams Sr. completed a dissertation entitled "Perceptions of the No-Pledge Policy for New Member Intake by Undergraduate Members of Predominantly Black Fraternities and Sororities." Although Williams's study focused on undergraduates, I believe the results are also true of many graduate chapter members. Williams used a twenty-six-item original survey to access three scales: (1) the Policy Awareness Scale, (2) the Hazing Tolerance Scale, and (3) the Policy Endorsement Scale. He came to several conclusions concerning BGF members. Members felt that (1) the policy [MIP] was enacted too quickly with little input from members at large, (2) hazing definitions were too broad, (3) insufficient time was allowed by MIP to teach the history of the organizations, (4) bonding was lost, (5) lifelong commitment was jeopardized, (6) the policy promoted disunity in chapter ranks, and (7) new members felt they got no respect and acceptance from older members.[21]

Williams's findings indicate that many BGF members strongly oppose MIP. Subsequently, pledging and hazing persist. The refusal to embrace MIP occurs largely because there has been, and continues to be, a great emphasis on storytelling among members of BGFs. These narratives usually revolve around activities common to men in general (athletics, sexual conquests, and so forth). Unique to fraternities, however, is the "pledge story." A great factor that determines many members' sense of belonging or "bonding" is their ability to tell these pledge/war stories. To be able to say that one has engaged in the very same or similar rites of passage as the brothers in his company is somewhat comforting and, in theory, builds brotherhood and allegiance to the organization.

Regarding violence during this process as legitimating is pervasive among BGF members. In fact, the pressure to prove one's triumph over violent hazing and to engage in the "I pledged, too" discourse is so great in some circles that many members base a good deal of their fraternal worth on the abuse they received during the pledge period. This is so because many members are only slightly concerned with an individual's postpledge work and commitment to the organization. In one sense, this indicates that hazing and the unique fraternity narrative it brings is an attempt by BGF members to construct and maintain a collective memory and history distinct from that held by any other group. As Donald Polkinghorne states, "The stories we encounter carry the values of our culture by providing positive models to emulate and negative models to avoid."[22] A brother who has gone through the archaic pledge process that includes brutal hazing is looked on as a true or "real" member and accepted into the inner sanctum of a particular chapter, even if he makes no further substantive contributions to the organization scholastically, intellectually, and communally. Acceptance is extended to such a member much more readily than to one who does make these contributions, but who cannot attest to being abused during his sojourn into the fraternity.[23] This leads active members and candidates alike to strongly desire the right to say, "I pledged!" One BGF member comments:

> The ritualization of hazing baffles me. The *means* are what are important now. The means have superseded the ends of developing a good brother. It's almost like the question is, "Can you withstand this? You can be a pathological, deviant fool, but if you can withstand what we're going to put on you, you have proven your worthiness," which is really warped, but that kind of confusion pervades Greek life. There are some exceptions, but unfortunately it seems that the exceptions ultimately become alienated. They aren't "down." It's a shame, but stuff has become so topsy-turvy that abnormality has become the norm.

In this progression, even the word *pledge* has become nebulous since the formation of BGFs in the early years of the last century. Confusing *pledging* with *hazing* is problematic and helps prevent the discontinuance of violence in the groups. In one focus group, four undergraduate members of Kappa Alpha Psi were asked what they thought the differences were between pledging and hazing. To a man they all insisted the two were the same. One member strongly stated:

> I've been in the frat for three years and I've never been to a set [pledge session] where there was no wood [paddling] or something like it. That includes when I was coming in. Bruhs [brothers) were constantly housing us [beating]—night in and night out. There's no other way to instill discipline, respect, and love of the frat in a "G" [pledge].

Another added:

> I don't think anyone is going to appreciate something that they don't
> have to work for. Pledging makes you work for the frat and that includes
> some physical stuff. So yeah, I don't see how you can have pledging
> without hazing. Why don't you tell me the difference, because I don't
> think there is one.

A mix of undergraduate and graduate focus-group members at the
1995 National Pan-Hellenic Council (NPHC) Collegiate Leadership
Summit in Richmond, Virginia, articulated the same sentiment. BGF
members, along with their sorority counterparts, concluded that
pledging and hazing were synonymous—inextricably tied. Others,
however, contend that pledging is not synonymous with hazing at
all. In reality they are diametrically opposed. Their stance is based on
the belief that a pledge is simply a vow to uphold the ideals of the
organization one joins. When one makes this vow, he agrees to adhere
to the guiding principles of the organization. In this sense, anyone
who knowingly violates these principles breaks his pledge or vow; the
pledge process is merely an extension of the original pledge. What the
process seeks to do is prepare the potential initiate for a life guided by
the organization's principles. It, in effect, helps him to hold true to the
pledge.

One Phi Beta Sigma member asserted that pledging and hazing
conflict with one another, even though many BGF members do
not recognize this dynamic. He saw pledging as "a right of passage
that should developmentally enhance the individual intellectually,
physically, and spiritually. This should be exclusive of abuse. But, the
pledge process should somehow measure a person's commitment."
Interestingly, BGF members who support hazing also use "commitment"
rhetoric. This apparent similarity between the pro- and antipledge
camps must be examined by realizing that the overriding question
should not be whether the pledge process brings about commitment,
but what does it bring commitment to? A former Kappa Alpha Psi
chapter development specialist commented:

> Sometimes pledging the old way can almost make a brother less
> dedicated to working for the frat. I can't tell you how many brothers I

meet who feel that the frat owes them something because they "pledged hard." They feel like they paid their dues during the pledge process and then rest on that. On the other hand, brothers who go through MIP usually don't have that mentality. They still feel that they have to prove themselves, but they do it in a different way—by working for the frat after they are initiated.

An Alpha Phi Alpha member continued to differentiate pledging and hazing:

Hazing is a terrible distortion of pledging. The terms are often wrongfully used interchangeably, but hazing (unlike pledging) does not foster any real sense of bonding between individuals. It only leaves bitterness in its wake on many levels. From personal experience, I really didn't want anything to do with the guys who recklessly abused me just because they were in positions of power for that period. The men that I really had lasting relationships with were the ones that tried to save me from the abuse, even if on the "QT" [quiet tip—doing so without others knowing]. These guys sat us down and tried to give the whole thing meaning, you know? That's where I established my bonds, not with the crazies.

This member felt that discontinuing pledging, which he saw as a fruitful practice to stop hazing, was somewhat akin to "throwing the baby out with the bath water, but what else could be done?" Notably, he saw societal violence as the root of hazing, "You know, I think its just part of the culture. This society has historically been permeated with violence and no portion of it is immune to the effects of it." He also noted that a serious question of black machismo came into play. There was and is a "distorted sort of pride that comes from being able to survive the abuse of hazing." As another Alpha said in the *Wall Street Journal*, "It's a manhood thing."[24]

Some members believe hazing has always been a part of the organizations. Others believe it was an activity created to mimic white groups, and others contend it is a result of fraternity men going to World Wars I and II and bringing the hazing techniques of boot camp back to their fraternities. Although opinions vary on exactly when hazing rose to its present place in BGFs, many members acknowledge that it has grown, if not in brutality, in randomness. A member of Alpha Phi Alpha posits that even the threat of death has not stopped this progression:

The real question is, are we capable of coming up with a viable pledge process where there is no physical contact or mental denigration? Unfortunately, the very real answer is no! Brothers in my frat, as well as the others, have been doing these things long after they knew they were wrong. Death has not become an effective deterrent, neither has suspension or expulsion from the organizations. What we've reaped are vastly intertwined codes of silence that hamper all efforts to reach the truth. Why? Because the desire to belong is stronger than the will of the truth in our groups. Even good men sometimes succumb to the ways of their compatriots. It's sad, but this is what peer pressure can do.

Yet another member of Alpha Phi Alpha addresses this situation:

At one time when I would hear my cousins tell stories about pledging at places like Tennessee State and Fisk. . . . I mean it was bad in terms of what they would relate and they romanticized about it in terms of it being a macho thing, but somehow . . . I have to be careful saying this, it seemed to have some purpose to it. Yeah, they were paddled, but I never heard them talk about being seriously hurt or even feeling like their lives were in jeopardy or that they were being victimized by sadists. I don't want to in any way rationalize what happened there, but it seemed different from the stories I hear now where you've got horror story after horror story of young men being brutalized, subjected to all kinds of degradation, traumatized, humiliated—in some cases murdered. Somehow I got the sense that there used to be constraints on how far you could go. Somebody was going to check you if you got out of hand, but now there don't seem to be any constraints. I mean it's like Rodney King on a college campus, but we've changed roles and suddenly fraternity brothers have become the cops.

The societal implication brought to the fore by this member is insightful. As Deborah Prothrow-Stith notes, fraternities and sororities serve a purpose that organizations rarely associated with them also serve.[25] The obvious links between religious cults, secular secret societies, and Greek-letter organizations are often drawn. These comparisons disturb very few Greeks, in that these organizations are historically regarded as noble and positive in their own right. Mentioning black Greeks and street gangs in the same breath, however, occasions uneasiness. Prothrow-Stith ventures this observation, not in an effort to equate Greeks with gangs, but to position Greeks as models to which gangs should aspire. Ironically, her attempt to elucidate the deviancy of gangs by contrasting them with fraternities and sororities inadvertently brings to light an important similarity that could all but destroy her argument that Greeks are "prosocial." Prothrow-Stith begins her discussion by pointing out that both Greeks and gangs speak to members' personal needs:

> Gangs satisfy a whole range of normal adolescent needs. The most significant of these is the adolescent hunger for peer approval and acceptance. *But violent gangs are not normal.* When young people feel that their lives are knit into the fabric of the society at large and when they face the future knowing that a fair share awaits them, they do not form or join gangs, although they do form social clubs, fraternities, sororities, and other age-mate groups. Violent gangs arise when young people face a future of limited opportunity and despair, when for military, political, social, or economic reasons the life that awaits a young person has been stripped of meaning and validity.[26]

It is ironic that Prothrow-Stith does not also list disenfranchisement as an impetus for the formation of fraternities when, in actuality, it was an important factor leading to their founding. This point, though, is not where our attention will be focused, for she does realize that, practically and ritualistically, fraternities and gangs are not diametrically opposed:

> From a developmental perspective, however, anti-social groups such as youth gangs and pro-social groups such as fraternities have a great deal in common. Both kinds of associations exist to provide members with an interim emotional base, one that gives substance to the ambiguity the adolescent feels when he is between the dependency of childhood and the independence of adulthood. Pro-social and anti-social, they satisfy the adolescent need to belong to a group, separate from one's

family. Pro-social and anti-social, they provide young people with goals and objectives, a world view, and a place where they are valued. Group membership gives some purpose to life. The more adrift a young person feels, the more powerful the attraction of the peer group, but even well-adjusted young people need what groups offer.

Rituals are one way anti- and pro-social groups satisfy the developmental needs of adolescents. Interestingly, these rituals tend to be similar, whether adopted by adolescents operating inside or outside the law. The secrecy typical of youth gangs and of many sororities and fraternities suits teenagers trying to carve out areas in which they can be separate and distinct from their parents and siblings. The idea of wearing special clothing, "colors" that identify members, provides young adults an outlet for their narcissism. . . . Initiation rituals, common to adolescent groups the world over, speaks directly to the adolescent need to prove oneself. Usually prospective group members, be they sorority "pledges" or youth gang "wannabees," must undergo some sort of trial to prove their loyalty to the group. That's what pledge week, initiation rites, and hazing are all about. Once they pass, new members are allowed into the inner sanctum, where the affection and the loyalty of other insiders is guaranteed.[27]

Contesting Prothrow-Stith's stance that fraternities and gangs have similarities is difficult. But those who contemplate the link between black gangs and black Greeks often pose the question, "Outside of educational differentiation, murder, and drug trafficking, what makes fraternities different from gangs?" Prothrow-Stith answers that the use of violence is the difference. But, as we have seen, Greeks *are violent.* Violence is certainly not practiced to the same illegal degree in BGFs as in gangs, but initiatory violence is the same. To be sure, very little difference is found in the gang practice of "beating new members in" and the physical hazing employed by BGFs. Narratives from many members indicate that this hazing and this hazing alone guarantees "the affection and the loyalty of other insiders" to the neophyte. A Kappa Alpha Psi member addressed the nonhazing pledge process:

I was on line underground as an undergrad and was never initiated—you know how frat politics go, it just didn't work out. I later joined as a graduate member and the process at my chapter was totally different.

As an initiate who has endured both the new and old process I must say that I did not gain a sense of closeness or bonding in the Intake process the way I did during the pledge process. Not to say that my pledge process was perfect or even good, but it taught me many things, not the least among them being altruism and brotherly love. This whole idea of initiating somebody before they pledge is crazy. That's if they pledge at all. They can't appreciate it.

Another member of Kappa Alpha Psi commented:

There's just something different about people who don't pledge. I mean, they're still in the fraternity, but they're different. It's like having an adopted brother or sister. You still love them, but they aren't blood—so it's different.

This is another comment that supports the stance that the violence itself, the hazing of the pledge process, is what legitimates new members in the eyes of many of the already initiated. Some BGF members do not hesitate to openly admit this. For example, a member of Phi Beta Sigma remarks:

I'm pro-pledging and I don't mind saying that. I wholeheartedly disagree with the position that pledging is bad or purposeless. Yeah, bad things can happen to people who pledge and they often do, but the vehicle itself is not flawed or faulty—people are. Pledging and hazing aren't the same, but they help to reinforce one another. I mean, I'm not saying that anybody should be killed or anything, but I think the struggle in pledging has to stay in place for our organizations to remain viable as far as producing members who really love them.

From this perspective, pledging and hazing (at least in the contemporary sense) are inseparable as they relate to BGFs, and the melding of pledging and hazing is largely done with discourse.[28] This discourse is important, because the meaning that narrative conveys about human experience requires the use of discourse. To try to separate pledging and hazing is akin to attempting to get rid of a pesky problem by simply calling it something else. In BGFs, pledging and hazing are interlocked, and it is the discourse used within BGFs, not physical force, that convinces pledges not only to submit to, but to desire participation in, the violence of the BGF pledge process.

Discourse and narrative are powerful in BGFs, because they are used to differentiate and establish cleavages that separate members proper from perceived contagion. For example, one tool used to differentiate through discourse is the *challenge* or *charge*. The charge is a verbal tool used to identify a fraternity brother. One member asks a question that, on its face, may seem very common, and the other member properly responds. Supposedly, members who have not gone through a pledge process will not be able to effectively respond to charges, because they have inadequate exposure to the histories of the organizations and a good deal of unwritten traditional information.

Ironically, even members who have pledged often cannot respond to charges of members from different chapters and regions, because, as in gang "sets", a lack of cohesiveness exists in the fraternities' Intake processes (even pre-MIP) and localized or regionalized traditions. A member's allegiance to his particular chapter often supersedes his allegiance to the fraternity as a whole. Some members are at a loss when they are faced with regional, chapter, or personally constructed charges. The inability of members to respond to charges not sanctioned by the fraternity has led to intrafraternity violence in a number of instances, because one brother may feel that another, from a chapter he is unfamiliar with, is not "real."

The term "real" has very little to do with whether or not a member adheres to the ideals of, or actively participates in, his organization. In reality, it speaks to whether or not he was hazed. A member who does not go through the abuse of hazing is said to be "paper," in that he simply signed his name on paper and was allowed entrance into the organization without struggle. An Omega Psi Phi member addresses the respect that comes from hazing:

You take wood [beatings] to show your love for the frat. How else can you prove to brothers and yourself that you really want it? It's showing love, you know? If a brother doesn't want you in his frat, he won't even give you wood—he just won't f--- with you at all. On the for real tip, if you don't prove yourself nobody is going to respect you. You're going to be "cat" for the rest of your life. Tell me, would you rather get your ass kicked for six weeks or get it kicked for the rest of your life, because bruhs don't respect you?[29]

"Paper" or "cat" are tags most young black men interested in fraternities seek to avoid at all costs. The self-consciousness of pledges concerning how they will be viewed (and subsequently granted or denied acceptance by their potential fraternity brothers), and continued adherence to what are regarded as traditional ideas and practices by active members, continue to fuel the pledge/haze process. Some members assert that BGF men do not haze because they believe abuse will make better members, but because the practice is one of self-gratification and personal domination. One member stated, "Hey man, this process allows these people to have slaves and they refuse to let them go. These people do not even remain true to their own pledges to uphold the ideals and rules of the fraternities they claim to love so dearly, because they randomly break them by hazing." Other members sympathize, and the passages below relay only a sample of the panorama of arguments levied against pledging as it is traditionally carried out in BGFs:

- When I was on line, the phrase was "bump for your brother," which meant if he was to get a stroke, I asked for it instead. If he was getting beat down by visiting brothers, I was compelled to step up and take some heat. Looking back, would I do that again? Would I bump for my brother? Hell no! No, sir, I would not step in and take a paddle in the face, or let them put "Icy Hot" on my balls, or swallow an egg after it had been in three previous mouths—all for the sake of my line brother. No sir! It's nice to reminisce about the good old times and how we "grew" together, knew each other, loved each other, needed each other. But that line of BS is so played out it hurts even to say it. The truth is, we all wanted to be accepted by our fraternity so badly that we would have done just about anything they told us to do. We keep trying to make this a romantic experience, but we have forgotten that our big brothers would have hit us anyway, made us eat that rotten apple, drink that wine, skip class—regardless of whether we bumped for our brother or not.
- No matter what the fad is—gangsta rap, hip-hop, etc.—we should consider the type of individual we are attracting to our organizations.

As one brother said, "Trash in, trash out; trash out, trash in." People are even saying now that we seem to be portraying a "ganglike" image, which upsets some folks in our organizations, but what are we doing to make people say this, you know? It was pointed out to me that there was a time when being a part of the Elite Eight was something that was desired by many students, but only a few were accepted. These few tended to be those who were scholarly and upstanding members of the campus community—with exceptions, as in any case. However, this perpetuated the image of organizations being about scholarship and community service because these were emphasized during the pledge process and after. Now, the focus is solely on "How did you pledge?" As a result, you get a bunch of people who can take a beat-down, but can't put together a community service project. Thus, the campus community and the black community as a whole begin to question the purpose of our existence beyond pledging, hazing, and "kickin' it" at parties.[30]

- In academic terms, I guess the move from pledging to MIP could be considered a paradigm shift. However, in this case, as is the case with most drastic change, it has been rejected, and done so without being given full consideration. It is very popular today to look at pledging through rose-colored glasses. We all have an opinion of what pledging should be, and if it were a perfect world, we wouldn't be having this interview right now. But its not a perfect world and the very ugly reality of any pledge process has been and, it seems, will continue to be ignored. We've got brothers who advocate slapping and punching as positive motivation to remember inane facts. We have brothers who think the receipt of those occasional slaps or paddlings instilled a sense of pride, camaraderie, and esprit de corps, the level of which cannot be matched by any post-pledge experience. I sincerely do not agree with this reasoning.

To be fair, a counter-argument exists for every argument against pledging. These members are just as spirited as their brothers who argue against the continuation of the practice.

- Pledging as it was intended to be was never dangerous or bad. When pledging is conducted as a "rite of passage," wherein the big brothers or sisters act as mentors, trying to bring the neophyte pledgee into consciousness, the process indeed is positive.

- This Intake thing is so personal. I was one of eight, and even though it has only been three years, we are in different parts of the country, we still keep in touch and even came back this past December for our anniversary—all eight of us. Would we all have been there if we didn't pledge? I doubt it. The funny thing is that I did not know a single one of them before my process into this organization. Pledging may not be the thing that causes bonding, but if it doesn't, it sure does begin the process. In my case, who knows if I ever would have even met my seven sands. ["Sands" are men who were on the same "pledge line" and were initiated into their fraternities together.] We have cultivated a wonderful relationship that has grown since December 6, 1992, and are still cultivating it. Can brothers who do not pledge have the same kind of relationship—I don't think they can even comprehend it!

- Rituals are real valuable, particularly to us as Africans. We've always used rituals to reinforce our beliefs and our values, and when done properly, that can be achieved. Every society has these types of rituals. Why? As a biologist, I know that nothing useless is conserved in nature—so why are these rituals? Perhaps they are needed and perhaps desired by the youth as part of their process of growing up. So what happens if the rituals that have been developed and refined over years and years are suddenly taken away and replaced with nothing? I suggest that if it is indeed a necessary activity for fraternal and social development, the youth will start creating their own to fill the vacuum. If it is not needed, nothing will happen. As a test of my hypothesis, which do you see? What is this thing called "underground pledging?" Hmm.

CONSERVATISM AND DOMINATION

Pledging and hazing continue because they are the "popular" things to do within the structures of BGFs to gain acceptance. This unquestioned adherence to the popular is not unique to BGFs. Some believe the United States has become increasingly preoccupied with the popular, which has led to rising apathy, or even nihilism, where transformative political processes are concerned. The American populace has grown less and less concerned about being aware of why they do what they do in everyday life and political life. This is a necessary condition for hegemony. It is here, in the popular sphere, that hegemony must "take account of and even allow itself to be modified by its engagement with the fragmentary and contradictory terrain of common sense and popular culture."[31] Through these modifications, hegemony seeks to constantly reinvent the relations of state, economy, and culture. Lawrence Grossberg, with the help of Stuart Hall, summarizes the relationship of the popular to hegemonic struggles:

> This [the sphere of popular culture] is where the social imaginary is defined and changed; where people construct personal identifications, priorities and possibilities; where people form and formulate moral and political agendas for themselves and their societies. . . . Hall, following Gramsci, describes this as the need for any hegemonic struggle to ground itself in or pass through "the popular." The popular here is not a fixed set of texts or practices, nor a coherent ideology, nor some necessarily celebratory and subversive structure. It is the complex and contradictory terrain, the multidimensional context, within which people live out their daily lives.[32]

There is much support for what some perceive as an end of history as far as rational-critical discourse is concerned. Divisions along monolithic racial, gender, or class lines by themselves do not provide us with a substantive understanding of what is at work, although all of these factors help us understand the marginalization of particular subaltern groups. Although these cleavages can never be discarded, which one serves to marginalize most extremely or most often is debatable, and the answer changes from case to case. Closer examination reveals that largely anonymous factors are also at work to engineer social divisiveness and anxiety.

One of the most cogent examples of this anxiety and the political response to it is the United States congressional elections of 1994, in which the Republican Party seized the political reigns of America by a startling percentage of the vote. A common opinion articulated by many was that Americans were weary of Democratic rule and this wave of popular discontent swept the Democrats out of office. Certainly, discontent existed and remains to this day, but was it some type of a priori condition that manifested itself with no need of outside impetus, or were other factors at work? According to Grossberg, this state of discontent is not one that spontaneously rises from the masses. It is affectively and effectively engineered by what he calls *popular conservatism*.[33] Grossberg contends that the popular issues leading to public discontent are not the real factors driving the political machine of American society—they are only facades, and the masses fail to recognize the true culprits.

What is really at work is a combination of factors that brings about axial shifts in popular sentiment and subsequently provides a friendly environment for the growth of the popular conservative political machine. To say that politics drives culture or that culture drives politics is too simple (remember, many BGF members who support the pledge process defend it as a "cultural" phenomenon). The reality is that they are inextricably tied, and Grossberg seeks to show how. Popular conservatism is not a political rebellion, but a rebellion against politics. It is a rebellion that breeds adherence to cynicism, for cynicism is a necessary condition for popular conservatism to exist. Popular conservatism is a rebellion against politics because it continuously diverts attention away from the political and towards the social or cultural as reasons why discontent is present, and therefore it offers social or cultural solutions to alleviate suffering. The rise of the Tea Party movement after Barack Obama's election in 2008 is another example of this phenomenon.

Grossberg's engagement of the relationship between the political and the popular expands Gramsci's analysis of hegemony. Although Grossberg concedes that hegemony is based on both coercion and consent, he also posits that Gramsci's core/periphery model may not be dynamic enough to explain the modern American landscape. In an attempt to move away from a static engagement of U.S. hegemony, Grossberg partially rejects Gramsci's idea of the nonflexible core and replaces it with what he calls the *ruling bloc*.[34]

> In a hegemonic struggle . . . the social field cannot be easily divided into two competing groups. The diversity of "the people" confounds any such simple divisions; for while the masses appear to be undifferentiated, social differences actually proliferate. The difference between the subordinate and the dominant cannot be understood on a single dimension. Power has to be organized along many different, analytically equal axes: class, gender, ethnicity, rage, age, etc., each of which produces disturbances in the others. At the same time, those

seeking to hold the dominant position do not constitute a single coherent group or class. Instead, a specific alliance of class fractions, a "bloc" which must already have significant economic power, attempts to win a position of leadership by re-articulating the social and cultural landscape and their position within it. This re-articulation is never a single battle. It is a continuous "war of positions" dispersed across the entire terrain of social and cultural life. At each site, in each battle, the "ruling bloc" must re-articulate the possibilities and recreate a new alliance of support which places it in the leading position. It must win, not consensus, but consent.[35]

The ruling bloc, then, is not static, and realizes that it must constantly appeal to the popular by articulating and re-articulating as much as necessary that it is making a dynamic shift to some stable set of ideals—which are invariably past-oriented. Along these lines, Stuart Hall examines the advent of Thatcherism in Britain as reflective of this appeal to the popular where ideals, stability, and threat are concerned.[36] The driving force of Thatcherism was to identify an "enemy within" that threatened the very existence of good "Englishness."[37] Of course, to make this appeal to the society and cause lines of division that perpetuated Thatcher's political power in English society, she had to present what she felt this ideal "Englishness" was or had been to the public. What happened in reality was that Thatcher created an emotive or affective myth that appealed to the masses. This adherence to a false history of what engendered English greatness, stability, and morality produced paranoid side effects such as racism and classism along with it, because there must be reasons for the loss of the mythic state. This was the same strategy used by fascists in Germany, but with much more extreme results—the Holocaust.

This is also the case with American conservatism. The reasons for the loss of mythic America are largely temporal. They shift from external (the Russian threat, Gaddafi, Hussein, Osama bin Laden, or Middle Eastern terrorists in general) to internal (affirmative action, welfare policy, the deviancy of homosexuals, Obama's "socialism") depending on the national crisis at hand. The progression of the popular conservative strategy, however, does not change. The conservatives move forward around the notion of a *postmodern frontier.* That is, they must put into place parameters that define when "America was what it should be" and when "America became what it is." This involves the historical designation of a period that marks the "fall of America."[38] Like Thatcherism and fascism, popular conservativism must construct a glorious past that did not suffer from postmodern problems. The problems that did exist supposedly could be handled in a quick, effective manner that was agreeable to the majority of this mythic America's populace. The dividing line for this frontier is usually placed somewhere around the Vietnam years—the late 1960s or early to mid-1970s. It casts the America of the 1950s and early 1960s as what the country should be, and the post-1960s period as the time of the "fall" into degeneration.

Certainly the United States of the 1950s and 1960s was quite different from the one we know today. Some of these differences, especially the cultural ones, are not the reasons America's "place" has changed on the global terrain. Popular conservatism, however, engenders the belief that these are precisely the changes that have led to the continued demise of country. This is the realm that not only allows the existence of racism, classism, ethnic conflict, sexism, and other myopic divisions, but helps to create and cultivate them. Whether the popular conservatives believe their rhetoric is really not the point. The point is that past-oriented discourse is an essential tool of domination, because it serves to actuate the next stage in the process—what Grossberg calls *affective epidemics*.

These epidemics usually function in a diversionary manner. For example, one of the very real problems driving the condition of United States and the world is the growth in power of disembodied multinational corporations mandating the existence of Hannah Arendt's *animal laborens*.[39] No longer is the oppressed/oppressor dichotomy limited to the space of individual states. The economic pursuits of the multinationals are quickly turning the world into one that houses invisible economic giants and subaltern laborers. The focus of popular conservatism does not allow for the engagement of politics on this level. Popular conservatives push the reification of a totally different set of concerns. Although the problems of race, ethnicity, class, and gender are quite real, the new global economy may be more relevant today in that it mixes all these ingredients into a particularly explosive, fetishized, paranoid brew in postmodern America. Xenophobic cleavages, more than anything, present issues (largely mythic) that popular conservatives can seize and use to create misleading affective epidemics. We must not forget that cynicism is necessary for this dumbing of the masses. A general disinterest in alternate perspectives on the epidemics and a willingness to be lied to must exist:

> The apparent success of such manipulation cannot be explained by falling back on images of the masses as intrinsically manipulatable, as cultural and ideological dopes. In fact, vast numbers know or assume that they are being lied to, or else they seem not to care. . . . This is precisely the paradox at the heart of contemporary U.S. politics and of the new conservatism's success. A large proportion of the population is outraged by at least some of what is going on, yet they remain inactive and uncommitted. There is a feeling of helplessness: what can anyone do?[40]

Consequently, some thinkers believe the United States, without a doubt, has become a "cynical society."[41] Stuart Ewen asserts that Americans are far less concerned with substantive political matters that dominate everyday life and are more consumed with the notion that their existence is defined by the image (false or not) that they are able to present to their fellows. Because of a preoccupation with the anti-intellectual and nonpolitical, popular conservative discourse becomes a tool capable of defining reality for a good percentage of the populace.[42] The preoccupation with image is intimately tied to Paulo Freire's evaluation of the oppressor's psychology in *Pedagogy of the Oppressed*, which carries over to the oppressed. In the Marxist tradition, Freire realizes that the oppressed can easily buy into a system he cannot define independent of the oppressor. Both suffer from false consciousness in that the oppressor feels "to have is to be" and the oppressed feels "to be is to be like the oppressor."[43]

Eventually, the construction of the postmodern frontier and the use of affective epidemics leads to the phenomenon of *disciplined mobilization.* The nonagents who arise from the popular conservative progression are eventually caught in a cycle of conceptual movement that Grossberg says is the psychological equivalent of "spaces without places."[44] Ultimately, consumers of popular conservatism are constantly led along by the ruling bloc—blind, with no sense of direction or critical engagement of the very realities contributing to their oppression.

BGF RULING BLOCS AND THE MEMBERSHIP INTAKE EPIDEMIC

An examination of the internal BGF debate over the pledge process makes it clear that a paradigm shift from pledging to MIP has not occurred. Finding members of the groups initiated after the implementation of the various MIPs who did pledge is much easier than finding ones who did not. Only 2 of the more than 170 men interviewed for this study admitted to having properly gone through MIP, even though a good number of them were initiated after pledging was outlawed. When we compare the identity narrative of propledge BGF members (who seem to be winning the battle thus far when the groups' practices are studied) to that of popular conservatives, we come full circle and see striking similarities in the tools used to maintain adherence to their agendas.

Hegemony, and in this case domination, always involves a struggle to define and rearticulate the popular or even the essential. As we have seen, simple membership does not necessarily lead to reification of the programs or practices espoused by organizational leadership. To the contrary, members' approaches are often defined by the very contexts and practices of which the national organizations disapprove. This is so because speaking the language of the popular is more important to many than remaining true to regulations of an organization whose purpose has already been altered by the progression of time. It is ironic that one member commented, "Whoever said you need a fraternity to achieve or help mankind?" He goes on to advise any young man seeking these goals to join an "honor society, the NAACP, or a church action committee." This is ironic because BGFs were founded for these very reasons—achieving and helping mankind in their own particular way. The search for some elusive brotherhood notwithstanding, what other real purpose can the organizations serve?

Historically, these groups have raged against labels branding them as "social." They fancy themselves as community service organizations whose mission is to better the life chances of the entire African American community. However, a contingent of members obviously exists to which this purpose is secondary—if not forgotten. If the perceived purposes of the organizations have indeed shifted in the minds of the members, then stated fraternity policy is for all intents and purposes inconsequential. With the progressive loss of memory concerning the macropolitical roots of BGFs as sociopolitical movements, attention can easily be shifted from the political to the popular. This is so because the concept of pledging has moved from its place as sacrificial ritual with clear purposes in the Girardian sense to one of simple popular ideology. When positioned as such an ideology, it becomes unclear whether many members know why they continue to hold on to the process when it does not accomplish its intended task. How this can be empirically proven or disproven, though, is not important to BGF members. What is important is that, beyond anything else, pledging is a celebration of the pleasures of social differentiation. The rejection of MIP is an attempt to maintain the dividing line by maintaining the practice.

Just as hegemony in the popular conservative sense is organized around an explicitly defined national project of structuring social and political formations to define and mobilize the struggles of everyday life, the project of pledging speaks to the same mission within BGFs. In the BGF case, brothers who have been hazed (be it before or after 1990) form a powerful ruling bloc. This bloc of "real brothers" engages in a struggle with antipledge movements for the hearts, minds, and bodies of entering members. Like the popular conservatives, they are winning. They win because this is not a struggle that speaks to logic or critical thinking, and maybe not even to "achievement," "scholarship," or "altruism" of any recognizable sort. It is one that speaks to actives' and potentials' moods, passions, desires, and volitions.

To aid in its struggle against antipledge movements, the BGF ruling bloc must (like popular conservatives) establish the frontier that marked a decline in BGF strength of membership and purpose. This decline in fraternity viability, for these men, is marked by the adoption of MIP. Consequently, the MIP frontier is the enemy, because it is defined as the moment when "unhealthy" individuals gained entrance into the fraternity and infected its body. All propledge rhetoric invokes this belief in one way or another, and BGF affective epidemics are numerous. They purport that MIP members do not know history, have no or questionable love for the organization, did not work to join, are uncomfortable with "real" brothers, cannot handle challenges, have no respect for tradition, will not actively participate beyond the trivial aspects of the groups, and so forth. The list goes on; whether the assertions are true is not the issue. The fact of the matter is BGFs now have a population of "illegitimate sons" who are targeted as reasons to maintain the violent pledge process. The MIP frontier, as with all postmodern frontiers and the affective epidemics that accompany them, "distributes people and practices (and the investments that connect them) in a specific way."[45] Participation in pledging divides BGF populations by identifications and processes rather than identities and contributions.

If the products of the MIP process are not considered enemies, they certainly exist on the other side of the frontier and are excluded from certain relations, for they are plagued with "otherness." Little fraternal space is set aside for these men, who are located outside of the popular conception of what entrance should entail. They are subsequently relegated to a netherworld in which they are simultaneously members and nonmembers of the organization. The struggle in BGFs then is one that is very much concerned with defining what "matters." This is more than a philosophical question, because it involves a very real struggle to define the nature of authority in BGFs. The fact that national policies change but chapter practices remain constant brings Hobbes to mind: "He is the ruler who rules." Clearly, the national organizations are not the sovereign; they do not rule—the violently initiated ruling bloc does. Here we find those who construct various crises in the organizations and use them to determine why, where, and when fraternal benefits are bestowed on other members. This political process does not work in one direction. Not only does the ruling bloc define parameters of acceptance, but parameters of acceptance also define members of the ruling bloc, for they are mobilized in a very disciplined manner that eventually seizes control of many of their identities.

The assertion that pledging is a "cultural" construct that cannot be understood by outsiders may or may not be true, but there is also the possibility that it is not understood by insiders either. Either way, insiders are continuously moved by the project because of its emotive and social appeal. Undoubtedly, pledging produces a common experience on some levels. Whether the experience is necessary, positive, or negative is debatable. But it is clear that once people enter this field of experience, they quite often "find themselves almost uncontrollably situated on or at least pulled toward 'the right' regardless of their ideological relations (or lack of relations) with the Right."[46] Those who wish to maintain pledging must be considered the

Right, for thcy espouse the conservative ideal of never letting go of the past, because to "let go" opens the door to destructive consequences. These conservatives, like all conservatives, strive to establish substance and meaning where individuals are concerned based on an idyllic (or even mythic) past resting on a perception of "when fraternities were what they ought to be." The invocation of affective epidemics has far-reaching ramifications, as Grossberg indicates:

> Affective epidemics define empty sites which, as they travel, can be contextually re-articulated. These mobile sites are constantly fetishized, invested with values disproportionate to their actual worth. Their most important function is to proliferate wildly so that, like a moral panic, once an affective epidemic is put into place, it is seen everywhere, displacing every other possible investment. But unlike moral panics, such epidemics are not always negatively charged and they have no specific focal point of identity, working instead through structures of identification and belonging. Mattering places are transformed into vectors so that the concerns and investments of real social history become the ruins of a displaced, perhaps even misplaced, paranoia. In response to a condition that has been often characterized as "cultural weightlessness," the new conservatism establishes a daily economy of saturated panics. This leaves only two possibilities: either fanaticism or sentimentality, both struggling to make a difference within a condition of affective excess.[47]

Whether pledging is driven by fanaticism or sentimentality is not certain. More than likely, it is both. What Grossberg speaks to is the important invention and reinvention of fetishization and misplaced paranoia. Is it really possible that MIP, in and of itself, has or even *could* destroy the very fabric of black fraternities, as some members purport? Conversely, is pledging the tool that can really deliver fraternities to and beyond old heights of success? Whether it can or cannot accomplish such a task, a number of pledging's features offer perplexing quandaries. The most obvious issue is the contradiction between the fraternities' stated rejection of pledging and members' actions that continue to perpetuate it.

The reality is, regardless of whether the process is coveted or condemned by national officers or philosophers, its appeal continues to mobilize men. It not only mobilizes them, but mobilizes them with such force that it has all but closed off the possibility of a sustained, organized movement to dethrone it. In most circles, it has all but erased those fractions of the fraternities' populations that have not received its stamp of authenticity. These "paper" or "cat" individuals are not embraced, because they carry the contagion perceived as having the potential of unraveling the fabric of the fraternal orders. These MIP initiates are viewed as infectious because their initiation experiences cannot compare to those of duly pledged members.

Engaging BGFs as having ruling blocs, a pledge frontier, and epidemics established through narratives that mobilize potential initiates is telling, because these are the very factors that ultimately substitute a mechanical discursive tradition that locates blame for BGF shortcomings elsewhere instead of attempting to find viable oppositional practices that would help eradicate the deficiencies. Clearly, many members do not remember the original purposes or adhere to the founding ideals of their organizations. This lack of memory does not matter to them, however, because the acceptance that comes with submission to violence is defined by powerful affective lines and practices, not by logical reasoning. If this political memory were left intact or reconstructed, it would be here that we could locate a key to resistance to modern ritualization of random violence in BGFs. This is not to say there is any single or simple conspiracy in BGFs to maintain pledging. Perhaps members are involved in a complex conspiracy, but conspire without knowing they conspire. This unconscious conspiracy can be located in narrative, which is one of the most powerful tools of domination used to maintain any conservative structure.

Such structures often effectively cause the realm of the Self to collapse into everyday fraternal life. As a result, the life-world of the individual is increasingly politicized on the fraternities' contested terrain and loses sight of societies' topography. Subsequently, these men become increasingly vulnerable. They are vulnerable because individuals desire acceptance by the fraternal body, but can easily be rejected if correct avenues are not followed. This rejection (or maybe more importantly, the threat of it) continuously subjects potential and active members to the surveillance of the accepted other. Individuals on this ruling bloc's mobile terrain make every effort to compensate for perceived shortcomings so as not to be denied acceptance or expelled from the space reserved for "real" members. It follows that examination of narrative, hegemony, and domination help explain *how* the violence of pledging is maintained, but the deeper and even more telling question as to *why* it survives speaks directly to the issues of black male identity.

6

Acceptance, Freedom, and Identity Construction in Black Greek-Letter Fraternities

The interaction of black men within their group and in American society brings us to the core question of violence and how it relates to black male identity. This is where I believe the most cogent answers to our questions concerning violence in BGFs can be found. The violence in BGFs occurs in a historical and contemporary context. We have seen that definitions of violence have been historically imprecise among academicians. Be this as it may, the sociopolitical acclimation of blacks in America is deeply woven into the fabric of the five BGFs. This acclimation has certainly been violent and, at some points, brutally inhuman. Black fraternity hazing is but another manifestation of violence and sacrifice, whether it is realized or not. This violence and sacrifice are solidly political, because they connect processes of interpersonal and societal socialization to the predicaments arising from cultural and political power discrepancies between ruling blocs and marginalized groups, and ultimately, to issues of construction of the black male Self.

FORMATIONS OF THE BLACK MALE SELF

The crisis of identity, or the Self, speaks to problems concerning how the black male is physically and psychologically situated within public and private space. Many factors contribute to the formation of the Self. We must address issues of race, class, and society that act to construct black male Selves and the environments in which they dwell. The formation of identities is a complicated matter, and the factors presented here are by no means exhaustive. Although no effort is made here to produce an ultimate checklist of identity contributors, I do illustrate that identity contributes to violence (and vice versa) and is not intrinsic, but is a social construct largely external to individuals.

Economic Anxiety

The modern economic landscape forces the serious researcher to note that the social and moral ecology of the phenomena with which this study is concerned increasingly finds its boundaries in national and global political economy. Economic restructuring, in its most carnal sense, threatens to transform the world into collections of wandering, working or nonworking) bodies. The objectification of these bodies crosses lines of race and class in its dehumanization of nomadic populations. Many global factors, as Homi Bhabha notes, fuel anxiety on the national as well as personal level.[1] All social and political problems posed cannot be explained away by probing the global or national economic situation, but the colonization and massification of individual and group life-worlds affects all identities—the black male's included.

The ramifications of changing economic and labor structures are strong. The current economic reality, which started on a different level decades ago, is one that combines corporate power, economic globalization, and conservative politics to dominate the life of U.S. and international labor. What workers "see" from this lethal mixture is downsizing, which, as writers such as Bob Herbert note, affects both the "governmental and corporate workplace."[2] Jeremy Brecher and Tim Costello comment that "corporate downsizing" is done in an attempt to "become more lean and mean [in the face of global competition]."[3] The appearance of the "stateless" corporation with no ties to nations, but only to money, makes it all too clear that gone are the days when "what is good for GM is good for America." Now, if countries fail to provide labor, social, economic, and regulatory conditions to corporations' liking, they simply move elsewhere—leaving economic devastation in their wake.

The United States is forced to compete in this economic reality of falling wages, increased job loss, and decreased job security. Brutally, the phenomenon of downsizing is one that many see as positive. For example, in the mid-1990s Mobil Corporation announced it was slashing its Fairfax, Virginia, workforce by one-third, eliminating 1,250 jobs. When the announcement was made, Mobil's stock hit a new high. The same happened with corporations such as AT&T, Digital, IBM, and Scott. Ford Motor Company also levied massive cuts at the turn of the current century. Herbert believes this process is nothing more than "an extremely efficient way to suck money up from the middle classes to the elite."[4] If the middle class is hit this hard, what happens to the lower class?

The onslaught of automation, which has its roots in Taylorism and Fordism, is another factor contributing to modern economic, psychological, and sociopolitical stress. Jeremy Rifkin sees this situation as one influencing black American males in a unique way. Rifkin's *The End of Work* revolves around a notion advanced by Sidney Willhelm in *Who Needs the Negro?* two-and-a-half decades earlier. Rifkin believes the African American labor plight is important because it not only speaks to blacks, but serves as a lesson for what may lie ahead for young white males. According to Rifkin, automation, which started with the Fordist revolution, began to have a visible impact on the nation's manufacturing sector in the 1950s, and unskilled jobs manned by black workers were the hardest hit.

By 1964, the black unemployment rate reached an unprecedented 12 percent (before then it had never exceeded 8.5 percent), compared to a 5.9 percent rate for whites. Plainly stated, the Taylorist drive to create a "trained gorilla worker" reached a point where there was no longer any need for the gorilla. Willhelm probably stated it best when he wrote, "With the onset of automation, the Negro moves out of his historical state of oppression into one of uselessness. Increasingly, he is not so much economically exploited as he is irrelevant. . . . The dominant whites no longer need to exploit the black minority. As automation proceeds, it will be easier for the former to disregard the latter."[5]

The results of this progression are enormous. Increased economic pressure, which adversely affects whites as well as blacks, helps fuel axial shifts in American culture. These shifts, which Lawrence Grossberg calls *affective epidemics*, have heavy impacts on American race relations and to a large extent also help define mainstream politics. Herbert reports that this economic phenomenon "is a recipe for anger and anxiety. . . . But when the anger is expressed, it is seldom directed towards the corporate elites or the politicians who do their bidding . . . . When it comes time to rage, they [American workers] find something or someone else to rage at."[6] The ongoing vehement attacks on affirmative action and other safety-net programs from America's political Right are examples of this rage, which certainly widens the ideological gulf between whites and people of color. This situation contributes mightily to the black male's feeling of isolation, alienation, and non-self-identification.

Black Identity Fragmentation

Economic factors fuel anxiety, discontent, and suffering, but they do not stand alone. Although they are undoubtedly pieces of the puzzle, the ability to construct the big picture lies in the realization of the possibility that what Emile Durkheim called national "social facts" always dominate the culture of individuals and groups. Bhabha adds to this view in "Anxious Nations, Nervous States." Black fraternity men, in the Bhabhan sense, are quite possibly embroiled in a sea of hegemony along with other subaltern groups:

> What if the nature of historical experience produces tiles that have incommensurable, jagged dimensions? What if different social experiences occupy disjunct spaces and divergent time-lines? What if the "big picture" has always dominated and silenced the anxious, split truths and double destinies of those who are minoritized and marginalized by the inequities of modern society?[7]

If the answer to Bhabha's query is in the affirmative and the "big picture" really does dominate the "anxious," then very disturbing possibilities are brought to bear. This is so because no Self, ego, or "I," the black American male's included, is manufactured autonomously, and the impact of modern society must be greater than we have traditionally assumed. Hence, through incoherent interpersonal and societal socialization, black male identity is often fragmented. Du Bois spoke powerfully to this fragmentation when he posited that blacks in the United States suffer from "double consciousness."

> After the Egyptian and Indian, the Greek and Roman, the Teuton and Mongolian, the Negro is a sort of seventh son, born with a veil, and gifted with second-sight in this American world—a world which yields him no true self-consciousness, but only lets him see himself through the revelation of the other world. It is a peculiar sensation, this double consciousness, this sense of always looking at one's self through the eyes of others, of measuring one's soul by the tape of a world that

looks on in amused contempt and pity. One ever feels his two-ness—an American, a Negro; two souls, two thoughts, two unreconciled strivings; two warring ideals in one dark body, whose dogged strength alone keeps it from being torn asunder.

The history of the American Negro is the history of this strife—this longing to attain self-conscious manhood, to merge his double self into a better and truer self. In this merging he wishes neither of the older selves to be lost. He would not Africanize America, for America has too much to teach the world and Africa. He would not bleach his Negro soul in a flood of white Americanism, for he knows that Negro blood has a message for the world. He simply wishes to make it possible for a man to be both a Negro and an American, without being cursed and spit upon by his fellows, without having the doors of Opportunity closed roughly in his face.[8]

As part of the larger black freedom struggle of the early twentieth century, one of black fraternities' original goals was to contribute to the construction of Du Bois's "better and truer" black male Self that could positively influence black struggle on the American landscape as a whole. This could possibly be done by somehow reworking subjects' cognitive recognition of opposing factors within the interpersonal and societal realm to arm them with tools of resistance in the construction and reconstruction of the I. One persistent problem, however, is the reality (as Du Bois noted) of the African American male being undeniably *American*. In the American case, the subject is possibly never unified. Harold Cruse commented almost a half-century ago:

In liberal and radical circles it is often said that New York City is not truly representative of what America is, deep in its hinterlands. It has been said that it is a mistake to confuse the cosmopolitanism of New York with the outlook of the Midwest, the Deep South, the North and Far West, the state of Texas or even Maine. This would seem to raise the question: Where is the "real" America to be found? Or who is the "typical" American and from what region in the United States does he come?[9]

In many ways, we have constructed a national life-world populated by hyphenated beings. This stance in no way embraces the separatist belief found in some sects that the answer for the African American is to somehow secede from the United States and therefore discover his "true" Self. I also do not believe African Americans will alleviate any internal or external pressures by denying their Americanness. Beyond this, I am concerned, not with answering Cruse's question of where we can locate the "real American" (for such an animal may not exist), but with discovering cleavages that define which Americans are more fragmented than others. This fragmentation may be so extreme in some arenas that it serves to confuse hyphenated dwellers on the issue of identity or construction of the Self.

THE SELF, SELVES, AND THE VICTORY OF CONSENT

Our engagement of violence in black fraternities inevitably forces us to face the brute fact that hazing would end immediately if potential members simply refused to be hazed. Admittedly, this process, as with all hegemonic interactions, involves coercion and consent. Without the consent of the violated subject, this particular type of victimage could not occur. The fact of the matter is, some black males desire to be hazed. As we shall see, this is because the construction of a Self has much to do with a societal and personal dialectic. This type of struggle is seen as a way to prove one's manhood. The attainment of masculinity in the United States speaks to a perennial quest among American males to have access to certain realms of the capitalist landscape. The traditional Anglo American definition of a viable man often includes being a "responsible, good provider for self and family."[10] This definition has historically placed most black American males on the margins of manhood, because most outlets for achieving masculine pride and identity in political, economic, educational, and social circles have been more readily available to white men.

Restrictions placed on many black men naturally hamper their ability to achieve in family systems—to take care of a wife and children, or be effective fathers according to traditional standards. Noel Cazenave asks an important question in *Black Men in America*, "What happens to black men who accept society's notions of what it takes to be a man but are denied the resources to 'earn' their masculinity through traditional channels?"[11] Black men try to alleviate this pressure through various avenues—even fraternities. Many men who pledge BGFs say they do so, not only for the social outlets they afford, but access to "a network of fiercely loyal alumni who can be counted on for introductions, jobs, favors and contracts."[12] These benefits, ideally, create a mechanism that enables black men to help one another survive in economic, social, and political structures that have largely ignored and oppressed them. Understanding the predicament of disenfranchisement, the double consciousness of black men, and the ways these men seek to remedy these problems cogently helps us understand black male identity.

Our current national ideas surrounding decency and propriety must be considered here. Modern America has constructed a culture that places inordinate value on materialism, prestige, personal possessions, and wealth. The dominance of these values intensifies the black male's identity problems along with his fellow Americans'. In our modern environment of conspicuous consumption, envy, and greed, the very core of who we are as Americans and people, black and white, has changed. People are only rarely concerned with being moral or pursuing some Platonic "virtue." Most no longer have a preoccupation with being "good"; we only wish to bathe in the warm glow of popularity, acceptance, and success. The impact of this is evident nowhere more than in U.S. political life. Ironically, cynicism regarding the good (or even anomie related uncertainty as to what the good *is*) simultaneously accounts for the success of conservatives in 1994 congressional elections and the failure of their 1992 and 1996 attacks on Bill Clinton's character in their unsuccessful impeachment attempt of 2000. The fact of the matter is that many Americans did not care that Bill Clinton avoided Vietnam or was something of a womanizer. They feel that all politicians do this, so why should they hold it against Clinton? "I like him—he eats at McDonalds." The same holds true for the reelection of Marion Barry as mayor of Washington, DC, even though he was a convicted crack user, and George W. Bush's presidential election despite his history of alcohol abuse.

Unvirtuous, anxious, racist, classist, sexist postmodern America inevitably brings a different, brutal, selfish, greedy, uncivil, xenophobic American Self into existence. This is so because we all are products of society—no one can be a Self on one's own. We are who we are only as we relate to others. We are, therefore, always conscious of others in the affirmative (those we wish to accept us) and in the negative (those we are not accepted by who we wish to accept us, and subsequently those we do not wish to join or become). Craig Calhoun notes, "Problems involving recognition—or nonrecognition—by others are integrally related to issues of personal self-recognition, [because] identity turns on the interrelated problems of self-recognition and recognition by others."[13] Dialectically, one must always deal with the intersubjectivity of the "I" and the "me" when forming identity in that we all ask the questions, "What do I think of myself? And, what do others think of me?" Identity and recognition are intimately tied to multileveled sociopolitical interactions because "socially sustained discourses about who it is possible or appropriate or valuable to be inevitably shape the way we look at and constitute ourselves, with varying degrees of agonism and tension."[14] Harry Frankfurt speaks to this issue in "Identification and Wholeheartedness":

> It is a salient characteristic of human beings, one which affects our lives in deep and innumerable ways, that we care about what we are. This is closely connected both as cause and as effect to our enormous preoccupation with what other people think of us. *We are ceaselessly alert to the danger that there may be discrepancies between what we wish to be (or what we wish to seem to be) and how we actually appear to others and to ourselves.* (emphasis added)[15]

The black male Self, like all American Selves, is caught up in the upheavals of the modernized United States. Old problems (racism, classism, sexism, etc.) remain and new ones (intensified economic anxiety) brought on by modernization and economic globalization intensify them. By changing the terrain of the Self, modernity has mandated distinctively modern discourses and approaches to the problems of identity. Although questions of identity are not locked within the modern era, they are certainly of a different sort than identity questions posed in the past. Calhoun notes:

> That this morally charged subjectivity [of identity] is not in all respects uniquely modern does not stop it from being distinctively modern. The discourse of self is distinctively modern, and modernity is distinctively linked to the discourse of self, not just because of the cognitive and moral weight attached to selves and self-identity. Modern concerns with identity stem also from ways in which modernity has made

identity distinctively problematic. It is not simply—or even clearly the case—that it matters more to us than to our forebearers to be who we are. Rather, it is much harder for us to establish who we are and maintain this own identity satisfactorily in our lives and the recognition of others.[16]

The identity problems brought on by modernity are not simply resolved. "The sheer scope and complexity of recognizable identities and competing social projects and identity-schemes makes recognition problematic and in need of specific establishment of various institutional and interactional settings."[17] Considering this supposition, let us return to the case of BGF hazing. BGFs serve as a setting to help solve the identity problem, and hazing is an avenue to recognition in this setting. Most potential BGF initiates are probably not sadomasochists, but consent to hazing because they do not want to be considered the negative "other." But beyond fraternal association, what do these black men really want? Simply joining a fraternity is probably not their core desire. This is where historic societal disenfranchisement comes to bear. It may be that black men constantly seek alternative zones of power and intimacy denied to them in the larger national life-world.

In *Secret Ritual and Manhood in Victorian America*, Mark Carnes makes a case that many men were and are attracted to ritualistic processes that mandate ordeal and provide the symbolic threat of death. Carnes rejects Lionel Tiger's hypothesis that men are biologically compelled to take part in initiation rituals and asserts that the reasons for taking part are very much external to the individual.[18] Carnes hypothesizes that fraternity initiation ritual is the product of Victorian social structures, because capitalism mandated familial interaction in which fathers were away earning a living and mothers were left to rear their sons. Eventually, this caused an identity crisis in males, and they sought avenues to affirm their masculinity. Carnes applies his theory to the work of J. M. Whiting when he remarks:

The most important work in this field was the cross-cultural study of cultural anthropologist John Whiting and his associates. They determined that male initiation ceremonies were most commonly found in societies where women exerted almost exclusive control over male infants and boys, and men controlled the economic and political resources. Whiting subsequently hypothesized that in societies where the father is absent or plays a minor role in child rearing, the male infant perceives the mother as all-powerful and comes to envy her role. Yet when that boy begins to notice the world outside the home, perhaps around the age of five, he becomes aware that men control resources and clearly occupy an enviable position. A secondary identification with the masculine role thus becomes superimposed on the female identification. Male initiation ceremonies "serve psychologically to brainwash the primary feminine identity and to establish firmly the secondary male identity." In societies where this "cross-sex identity conflict" becomes sufficiently widespread, initiation rituals will emerge in response to this psychological need. The rituals, by resolving these emotional conflicts, promote the well-being of young men and, presumably, of society itself.[19]

In the modern black case, the father may be away from home in the workplace, but he is often absent from the life of his son altogether. This phenomenon is largely a result of the historical attack on black family structures. Whether or not there is a trend toward recovery in contemporary America is questionable. Considering that the absent father exists in many instances in the black case (and even if he is not absent, rarely does he control the economic and political resources that his white male counterpart does), the crisis of identity is, once again, intensified in the black male subject. Clearly related to Du Bois's "double consciousness" is Richard Majors and Janet Billson's assertion that the black male's unavoidable search for manhood is "lined with pitfalls of racism and discrimination, negative self image, guilt, shame, and fear."

He struggles toward manhood with a sense that he lacks something; he is *manqué.* His schools place him in lower achievement groups; teachers speak of language deficits; economists call him disadvantaged; and psychologists refer to him as disordered. Keil believes that, "Having been denied a natural development of his sense of manliness, he must constantly prove to himself that he is a man." This "masculine protest" can become the constant thread woven throughout the black male's daily interaction: "I am worthy, I am powerful, I am a man." . . . The humiliating double bind of having to prove manhood while being denied access to the legitimate tools with which to do so creates emotional drudgery for black males. Like other men, black males want to be productive and responsible citizens—but can they? Do they have real choices? Sitting on the margins of American society makes those choices distressingly narrow.[20]

Akrasia and Choice

The quest for affirmation of black manhood is obviously challenging because of the ever-present Du Boisian duality brought on by the black male's marginalized existence. The notion of manliness itself affects individual choices to such an extent that we need to examine the psychological makeup of all individuals on the macro level and then move to black men on the micro level in an attempt to explain decisions to participate in violence of the type with which we are concerned. In considering the makeup of any individual and his individual freedom, we would be wise to consider studies of *akrasia*, or freedom of the will, by Alfred Mele and Harry Frankfurt.[21]

Let us again return to the Michael Davis case and the question of blameworthiness. In the conventional sense of the conceptualization of freedom, which simply means if an agent wants to do some X and that agent is allowed to do that X, then he is free, Davis was certainly free, and is therefore blameworthy along with his tormentors. I, however, submit that a more rigorous engagement of the psychological factors driving Davis's behavior proves that he (in one sense) was not free at all, but suffered from weakness of the will, or *akrasia.* According to Mele, weakness of the will is not a type of action per se, but a trait of character. He sees it as "a lack of, or deficiency in, a certain kind of power or strength (*kratos*)."[22] *Akratic* action is thus viewed as an intentional action contrary to an agent's better judgment. Mele believes that the earliest philosophical treatment of *akrasia* is found in Plato's *Protagoras*, where Socrates submits the thesis "no one willingly does wrong." Although Mele attributes this philosophical honor to Plato, he forwards that the notion of *akrasia* earlier found its way into Euripides's *Hippolytus* and *Medea* and even into the writings of Homer.

As we shall see directly, Mele would probably conclude that Michael Davis and others like him suffer from incontinence and are, therefore, not necessarily blameworthy for their participation in illegal pledging.

Frankfurt's work helps clarify Mele's stance by speaking to the following questions: (1) What is it to be conscious? (2) What is this consciousness for? (3) What role does self-consciousness play in human interaction? and finally (4) What are desiring, valuing, and freedom in light of *akrasia*? I hope to use the answers to these queries to explain Davis's behavior as *akratic* and nonfree.

First of all, let us consider the first and second questions. Frankfurt does not see consciousness as the state in which an agent is simply awake and able to differentiate stimuli. Being conscious entails the agent being aware not only of the stimuli, but aware of its responses to the stimuli. This statement can be somewhat unclear, but Frankfurt employs the nifty example of a piece of metal to elucidate his point. Metal differentiates between physical stimuli just as a human agent does. For example, it expands when heated and contracts when cooled. But is the metal conscious? Surely it is not, for it is not aware of its responses. It simply responds. To be conscious, an agent must be "aware of its responses and, therefore have the feature of reflexivity in its interaction with its environment."[23] The purpose of this consciousness is simply so that a creature can monitor its own condition and effectively respond to circumstances in which its interests are adversely affected.

Beyond the question of consciousness, and more important for the purpose of this study, is the reflexivity of self-consciousness. As noted, we as humans are very concerned with what others think of us. When Frankfurt states, "We are ceaselessly alert to the danger that there may be discrepancies between what we wish to be (or what we wish to seem to be) and how we actually appear to others and ourselves," he intimates that we are concerned with our motives to do the things we do. An agent deliberates over whether his motives move him because he wants them to be effective in moving him, or whether they move him regardless of, or even in spite of, himself. The latter case denotes a lack of self-control. Frankfurt feels that if the latter moves an agent, then he does not act "wholeheartedly" because he does not totally endorse his motive, in that it is not something he really wants or values. What the agent wants is simply the object of his motivating desire.

Obviously, the desired object for Michael Davis was to be a respected member of a BGF. The same was true of Joel Harris five years earlier.

Within black fraternities' subculture (be it acknowledged or not on the national level), members have been traditionally hazed as a rite of passage to gain a sense of fraternal viability and respect. These conceptualizations of respect, manhood, and worth are more external to the agent than internal, because respect is given or denied by one's fraternity brothers. This worth is what members refer to when they say a member is "real." In truth, they mean that he was physically beaten to join the fraternity. Davis and Harris wanted to be "real" because only "real" brothers are respected and accepted. So the role of self-consciousness is clear in submission to hazing. The problem of freedom runs deeper, for it involves questions centered on the will.

Frankfurt's "Freedom of the Will and the Concept of a Person" and "Identification and Wholeheartedness" both center on hierarchically ordered desires to argue for the notion of freedom that I contend proves Davis was not free. Frankfurt asserts the essence of a person is found in the structure of the will. A person is an agent with first- and second-order desires and volitions. Desires are simple passions. Volitions, however, go beyond the passion stage. They are "decisions made" that are powerful enough to be acted on. Frankfurt summarizes, "According to this schema, there are at the lowest level first-order desires to perform one or another action. Whichever of these first-order desires actually leads to action is, by virtue of that effectiveness, designated the will of the individual whose desire it is. In addition, people characteristically have second-order desires concerning what first-order desires they want; and they have second-order volitions concerning which first-order desires they want to be their will."[24]

An agent without the faculties of first- and second-order desires and volitions is seen as not having the power of reflection and reason. He is, subsequently, not considered a person at all, but a "wanton." As Frankfurt states in "Identification and Wholeheartedness," "The deliberate use of reason (which enables an agent to decide) necessarily has a hierarchical structure requiring higher-order elements that are unavailable to a genuine wanton."[25] Importantly, in this formulation of freedom, a distinct difference exists between "freedom of action" and "freedom of will"; this difference considers the presence of *incoherence*. Eleonore Stump summarizes Frankfurt's criteria for an individual to have freedom of will:

1. The agent has second-order volitions.
2. The agent does not have first-order volitions that are discordant with those second-order volitions.
3. The agent has the first-order volitions *because* of his second-order volitions (his second-order volitions have, directly or indirectly, produced his first-order volitions; and if his second-order volitions had been different, he would have had different first-order volitions).[26]

One must understand that a distinct difference exists between an agent acting freely and having freedom of will when he acts. Let us consider the example of a reluctant smoker. The smoker's first-order desire is that he wants to smoke (possibly because of the pleasure the nicotine gives him or because he feels it makes him popular with a certain group of people). His second-order desire and volition, however, is that he wishes he were not the kind of person who wants to smoke. Let us say the first-order desire to smoke subsequently becomes a volition, and the person smokes. His ultimate volition and second-order volition are now in a state of incoherence. This agent is, however, *acting* freely.

Freedom of action merely requires the absence of obstacles to doing what one wants to do. The action may very well involve incoherence. The smoker in this example does not have freedom of will because this involves the absence of obstacles to *willing* what one wants to will. He is suffering from *akrasia* because his will is not strong enough for him to will what he wants to will and turn it into a first-order volition instead of a desire. He desires to smoke, but he does not value it. Valuing is more than a brute desire. It involves reflection and coming to an opinion that can be maintained. The smoker cannot make manifest his second-order volition to be the kind of person who does not want to smoke, so he smokes.

Obstacles to freedom in general may be internal (psychoses) or external (social, political institutions, manipulators, etc.). There are four basic obstacles to what one wants and four basic modes of freedom with respect to these obstacles:

1. having no external obstacles to doing what one wants to do,
2. having no internal obstacles to doing what one wants to do,

3. having no external obstacles to willing what one wants to will, and

4. having no internal obstacles to willing what one wants to will.[27]

Only someone who has freedom in the fourth sense has freedom of will. Young men who allow themselves to be hazed are not free because they do not value this violence. They face psychological dilemmas that prompt them to believe it somehow enhances their fraternal worth, social worth, and masculinity. Certainly Michael Davis suffered from the same incoherence as the smoker. On one level he wanted to be hazed, because he did not feel he would be respected by his potential fraternity brothers if he was not. On the second-order level, however, surely he wished he were not so self-conscious as to want to be beaten to gain respect. Hence the incoherence and presence of *akrasia*. If he did, in fact, want to be beaten on the second-order level (such cases do exist, of course, such as with masochistic behavior), then he suffered from even greater psychosis. The same can be said of black men in other social arenas who engage in violent acts. Surely, most of them do not, at least on the second-order level, wish to be the violent sort.

Admittedly, Frankfurt's notion of free will is strict, but it carries us to the heart of the matter where black men and violence is concerned. It provides an effective schema for analyzing the strange phenomenon of black men desiring to be hazed and aids in understanding black male violence in other arenas. Although it can be legitimately argued that fraternity men act freely when they submit to brutal pledge beatings, they certainly do not, by and large, submit with freedom of the will. Surprisingly, the hazing is not even desired solely for the sake of being accepted by fraternities. This leads us to one of the most powerful factors at work when considering black male violence: the fact that American society has not provided many black males with "legitimate" channels for developing a sense of masculinity, status, success, and respect that are acceptable in American ruling blocs. From chattel slavery through the twentieth century, black males have been historically attacked physically in the United States through lashings, dismemberments, hobblings, lynchings, burnings, and police brutality. This has created a being who, *akratically*, sees infliction of violence as power and the ability to withstand it as manly. Subsequently, "a potpourri of violence, toughness, and symbolic control over others constitutes a prime means through which black men can demonstrate masculinity."[28]

SUBSTITUTION OF THE FRATERNAL SELF

For the black man, violence and struggle have been reified as tools for acquiring critical social rewards. They have become achievements in and of themselves, because everything else seems to have failed. So here he stands—the black male—a man who often lacks, or perceives that there is a great possibility that he lacks, the means to attain or maintain his position as the traditional head of his family, acquire a "good" education, get or move up in a "good" job, or have the respect of his fellows as well as the ever-watchful "other." He subsequently seeks to maintain some semblance of these proper, manly achievements by traveling alternate paths. These paths often include the use of physical force, for the "language of violence is one way to write a more dominative script":[29] "Many black males have attempted to assert themselves by adopting a defiant, confrontational style known in black folklore as the 'bad nigga' or 'badman' who 'refuses to accept the subservient position allocated to blacks.' Badmen such as John Henry Stagalee [Railroad Bill], Shine, and boxer Jack Johnson had one thing in common: they used a conscious show of some type of physical force to prove themselves.[30]This obsession crosses over into many spheres of American life that receive the black male. Here we find the socially unaccepted (the gang member and the wife beater) as well as the accepted (the high-risk, front-line military volunteer and yes—the fraternity man).[31] It is violence itself that makes these men "cool," "hard," "down" . . . "real."

The case of fraternities and black male identity brings a number of intriguing questions to bear. To begin with, as we have seen, the special attraction of the fraternity can be found in its historic implementation of ritualized ordeal and initiation. The loss of memory and depoliticalization of the organizations has replaced the historic purpose of ordeal and initiation with the pursuit of a rather different, almost unrecognizable sort of manhood. The practice of branding probably should be engaged here. We must ask questions concerning this tradition of searing the flesh with fraternal symbols. Does this historically dehumanizing practice somehow become one of honor, love, and fidelity when it is voluntarily adopted and incorporated into the rituals of one's organization? Or, in the modern sense, is this simply a carry-over from American slave socialization and therefore a dysfunctional, oppressive tradition that members cannot come to grips with because of false or even double consciousness? Or could it possibly even be just another crass display of machismo and lack of sense of Self?

Bobby McMinn would probably say this is nothing more than a reproduction of ritual scarring practices of ancient rituals, and many black Greeks would agree. Beyond branding and maybe more importantly, in *Men and the Water of Life* Michael Meade argues that ordeal, initiation, wounds, and scars make men mysterious, and in every ritual death there is an opening and the possibility (or even expectation) of rebirth.[32] Unfortunately, after a ritual death, whether or not the new male is going to be reborn as a mensch is not certain. He may, in fact, be just the opposite in many respects.

Practically speaking, neither fraternities nor any other organizational constructs seem to be up to the task of cleansing the black male subject of deeply encoded social debris. Such expectations from both potential and active members are simply too high. Admittedly, we all wear different masks and necessarily have different "selves." Though many selves exist, the two of concern with respect to BGFs are the *authentic* (or *the* "Self" in contrast to *a* "self") and the *fraternal*. The *authentic self* speaks to who we are at our core, and it is constructed by our interpersonal and societal socializations over long periods of time and through diverse successes and failures. The authentic self is overarching, and all other selves are really nothing more than subsidiaries or tributaries. Though the *fraternal self* (or any other self) is nothing more than a tributary, many fraternity members mistakenly see it as the authentic. No organization can construct an authentic self on its own.

If this is not realized and the fraternal is seen *as* the authentic, insidious behaviors from the larger life-world are transferred to the fraternal. Hazing is the result of the illusion that the power of the authentic "I" is brought into being and continuously reaffirmed through the dehumanization of the other (in this case, the pledge). The perception is that the infliction of unchecked violence and pain on another is a victory for the "I" because a world is brought into existence in which he is truly master. This belief is embraced without realizing individuation and socialization are forever interdependent, and fraternal orders are really helpless to counter this "social fact" on their own. This is why the continuity of the Self that BGFs seem to construct is inconsistent over time. In reality, the BGFs are not autonomous builders of the Self at all. The black male Self to date is (independent of fraternities) a decentered, fragmented, sociopolitical construct acted on by societal forces. It seems all too appropriate at this juncture to once again look to Du Bois, who possibly more than any other thinker down to today had his finger on the pulse of black America. His evaluation is long, but well worth quoting.

> He [the black man] felt his poverty; without a cent, without a home, without land, tools, or savings, he had entered into competition with the rich, landed skilled neighbors. To be a poor man is hard, but to be a poor race in a land of dollars is the very bottom of hardships. He felt the weight of his ignorance,—not simply of letters, but of life, of business, of the humanities; the accumulated sloth and shirking and awkwardness of decades and centuries shackled his hands and feet. Nor was his burden all poverty and ignorance. The red stain of bastardy, which two centuries of systemic legal defilement of Negro women had stamped upon his race, meant not only the loss of ancient African chastity, but also the hereditary weight of a mass of corruption from white adulterers, threatening almost the obliteration of the Negro home.
>
> A people thus handicapped ought not to be asked to race with the world, but rather allowed to give all its time and thought to its own social problems. But alas! while sociologists gleefully count his bastards and his prostitutes, the very soil of the toiling, sweating black man is darkened by the shadow of a vast despair. Men call the shadow prejudice, and learnedly explain it as the natural defence of culture against barbarism, learning against ignorance, purity against crime, the "higher" against the "lower" races. To which the Negro cries Amen! and swears that to so much of this strange prejudice as is founded on just homage to civilization, culture, righteousness, and progress, he humbly bows and meekly does obeisance. But before that nameless prejudice that leaps beyond all this he stands helpless, dismayed, and well-nigh speechless; before that personal disrespect and mockery, the ridicule and systematic humiliation, the distortion of fact and wanton license of

fancy, the cynical ignorance of the better and the boisterous welcoming of the worse, the all-pervading desire to inculcate disdain for everything black, from Toussaint to the devil,—before this there rises a sickening despair that would disarm and discourage any nation save that black host to whom "discouragement" is an unwritten word.

But the facing of so vast a prejudice could not but bring the inevitable self-questioning, self-disparagement, and lowering of ideals which ever accompany repression and breed in an atmosphere of contempt and hate. Whisperings and portents came borne upon the four winds: Lo! we are diseased and dying, cried the dark hosts; we cannot write, our voting is vain; what need of education, since we must always cook and serve? And the Nation echoed and enforced this self-criticism saying: Be content to be servants, and nothing more; what need of higher culture for half-men? Away with the black man's ballot, by force or fraud,—and behold the suicide of a race![33]

Hence, most (not all) black males are victims to some extent. They are not victims in the felonious sense, but in the fact that they are *akratic* identities and bodies immersed in social currents with little ability to build life-worlds for the true "I" outside the whims of the "other." We, therefore, must continue to look beyond the atomistic and obvious to locate sources of violence and struggles for identity among black males. Violence is a major problem that must be remedied, but it is not alone. Neither is violence a victory for the "I," but a victory for hegemonic consent with respect to the violator and the violated. Historical and contemporary racial, economic, social, and political systemic agents partner with BGFs to create a maddeningly noxious mixture. Their damage is not limited to the evident (injuries and death), but psychically engulfs all concerned black subjects involved—and ripples.

7

Beyond the Fraternal Self

As we conclude our inquiry into violence in black Greek-letter fraternities, we are faced with the reality that this study has carried us down a path of explanation that, in some ways, has little to do with fraternities. In one sense, this becomes readily apparent when one notes the major intellectual influences for this book. To be sure, neither Antonio Gramsci nor René Girard, Lawrence Grossberg, Mark Carnes, or Harry Frankfurt had BGFs in mind when they penned their works on hegemony, sacrifice, or manhood. The blame many observers rightfully heap on BGFs is complicated a bit by searching for explanations in these philosophical interrogations. That violence occurs in the groups (especially during the pledge process) cannot be denied, but to assert that these organizations independently cause this violence is too simplistic.

More importantly than being an investigation into black Greek life, this study has been an inquiry into the American political, economic, social, and moral landscape. That being the case, this work is important not only for black men, but for all people concerned with the resituation of American men as a whole. Currently, we see a crisis of identity among men in general. The remedies to this identity crisis suggested by the actions of black men are important, because they are the group of American men that felt threatened and vulnerable long before the "fall of America" or the tragedies of September 11, 2001. It follows that black male intragroup interaction may foreshadow things to come for other American men as they continue to embrace the perception (or reality) that they are becoming more marginalized and subsequently more anxious.

Without a doubt, in some quarters of America today there exists what many call a "men's movement." Whether this movement is a response to feminism, to new levels of female independence, or to the natural deterioration of male privilege in a modern society is

129

debatable. Either way, many men in the United States across lines of race clearly feel threatened. In his 1995 book, *A Man's World*, Ellis Cose comments, "many men feel anything but powerful. . . . Instead, they feel vulnerable, off balance, and in need of assistance to help them redefine their place in a newly confusing world."[1] Cose reflects that many white men responded to his earlier work, *Rage of a Privileged Class*, with the sentiment that whatever the problems of racial minorities, women, or gays—white men "also needed sympathy."

If white men need sympathy and analysis, then black men probably need a bit more. This is so because although the plight of white males needs to be taken into account and some sympathy extended for their struggle—they are, as a group, already on top in America and have been since the founding of the country: "No one is denying them intellectual affirmation or demanding that they sacrifice their ambitions to a life of homebound drudgery. . . . The most that is being asked (or so we are led to believe) is that they share what they already have. . . . And why in the world shouldn't they be willing to divvy up the power and the perquisites that men have hoarded so long?"[2]

Yet, far beyond the fraternal realm—black or white—men suffer still and seek avenues for comfort. In the main, the modern men's movement is but another attempt by white men to alleviate their identity sufferings in much the same way as black men have done in their fraternities since the early years of the twentieth century. If we can find one man who has set many participants in the modern men's movement in motion, it would probably be Robert Bly and his rather strange work, *Iron John: A Book About Men*.[3]

Just as it is a discussion of violence, this work has also been an inquiry into manhood. Analyses of manhood have seldom been of interest to the general American public. *Iron John*, a strange mix of poetry, philosophy, and pseudopsychology, all tied to a little-known Grimm Brothers' myth, seemed an unlikely work to change this reality. The book, however, bolted to the best-seller list and stayed there for more than a year. The book's success and the subsequent activities of its readers seem to confirm the belief that there is indeed a crisis of identity among many American males.

Bly's core supposition is that many American men, some of whom renounced the Vietnam War and embraced feminism, fear that they have become too soft. These men have drifted too far from traditional manhood and need help relocating it. These men are drawn to the notion of Iron John—a character described as a "Wild Man" who led boys from the suffocating confines of childhood into the liberating expanses of manhood. Bly believes the story of Iron John outlines the initiatory process by which boys become men in most societies.

Through Bly we once again arrive in familiar territory—the one in which we locate initiation, ritual, and the manhood they supposedly bring. These are the factors Bly feels are at the heart of American male discontent, and he actually formed groups across the country to encourage men to get in touch with the Wild Man at the heart of their masculinity. These gatherings are essential because, in Bly's opinion, American males are damaged by the lack of initiation rites and older male mentors to guide them. But Bly exclaims that men need not worry, because initiatory rituals are too embedded in the male psyche to be lost—they are still very much alive in their genetic structure. Although this notion may be appealing to some, until some test is devised to genetically locate such tendencies in men, its appeal will probably be limited to the already convinced. Whether the observer is convinced or not, sacrificial rituals (past and present) are not without effect. Bly's man camp participants, like newly initiated fraternity men, are commonly beset with intense sobs of joy and accomplishment on entrance into their respective folds. This moaning and weeping is no gag or folly, but quite authentic.

This authenticity makes it is clear that men seek rites of passage in many societies in attempts to develop or reaffirm a sense of manhood, and often feel they work. Realizing this, the BGF members who assert that the pledge process is an historical, cultural construct that should not be tampered with are partially right. These sacrificial rituals definitely have historical origins, and they, then as now, sought to develop boys into men. What should probably be asked concerning ritual, then, is not whether ritual has significance, but which rituals are destructive and which ones are constructive in the development of male identity? The answer to this is important for BGFs because black fraternities have historically attempted to help develop the authentic black male Self by first constructing the fraternal self. This effort has failed in many cases, because the fraternal has often become identified as the authentic in the confusion of modern American society. There are several reasons for this, including but not limited to the preoccupation with popular culture and the neglect of things political (do fraternity members want to be gangsters or do gangsters pattern themselves after fraternity members?). A more telling reason may lie in the issue of mentors raised by Bly.

The importance of the "father figure" is omnipresent in fraternal orders, Bly's men's groups, and life. The central drama of fraternal rituals displayed Greeks, sachems, or some other noble, powerful authority figure as presenting the standard to which—in the black instance—"Sphinxmen," "Scrollers," "Lamps," and "Crescents" should aspire.[4] In every case, tension between the symbolic father and son steadily rose to a climax, and on completion of the son's symbolic journey, the father embraces him. Father and son become one in a bond—brothers.

The premise of these dramas and journeys is that even in life, fathers discipline their sons to "show them the correct way to live." Fraternities attempt to recreate this dynamic. The fatherly discipline often becomes physically violent in the black case because, as we have seen, this is the only way many black men have felt they could assert some measure of power and prove themselves as men. This carries over to fraternal interaction and is intensified because, over the years, it came to be regarded as the only legitimate way to mold an appreciative, knowledgeable, full-fledged brother. Bly feels that modern men suffer because they have no idea what being a man means. They do not know because their "enfeebled, dejected, paltry" or absent fathers have failed to teach them.

Some of Bly's men's groups even place an empty "Spirit Chair" at the front of the room to symbolize (or indict) the missing fathers. The problem of the castigated or absent "father" is doubled for black men in America. As noted, the fact that the BGF pledge process has historical and cultural significance cannot be denied, but there seems to be a shortcoming in today's chapters. Elders always directed traditional rites of passage. There was no case of a twenty-year-old carrying an eighteen-year-old through the rites on his own. This is hardly more than boys attempting to teach boys to be men—an overwhelming endeavor indeed.

For its part, this work has engaged the pledge processes of BGFs as attempts to recreate ancient sacrificial crises and subsequently maintain community (organizational) stability through the use of ritualized violence. Clearly, the fact that BGF physical violence has risen to inordinate levels relative to other Greek-letter fraternities causes distress. This violence is nothing more than the use of different tactics during an initiate's symbolic journey to achieve liminality. The very real threat to black life that comes along with these out-of-control tactics, however, mandates that we not only understand BGF violence, but eradicate it. Curbing hazing in BGFs will be no easy task.

The reality is that, in many instances, BGF pledge ritual today is random, aimless, and degenerative. This is so because of the loss of memory (or complete absence of knowledge) by members concerning the original purposes and tactics involved in fraternity ritual. It cannot be overemphasized that with regular repetition and perceptions of success, sacrificial rites are gradually transformed into simple tests or trials that become increasingly symbolic and formulaic. With this progression, the sacrificial nature of the process tends to become obscured, until finally it is hard to say what the symbols are intended to symbolize. What members often do not understand is the fact that they participate in a process that has historical roots, and that its purpose has been to channel otherwise random violence in controllable, purposeful directions.

Those concerned with combating black Greek violence must insist that the long practice of ignoring BGF violence by college and university administrators cease. This neglect has not only added to hazing's intensity, because there are few (or no) institutional checks placed on black fraternal organizations (especially at predominantly white universities), it has strengthened the feeling among many BGF members that what they do to their pledges is "nobody's business." The general neglect of some institutions where the problems of BGFs are concerned can possibly be examined from a societal perspective. If it is possible that an individual can be collectivized, then it is also possible that groups can be individuated. That is, members of the dominant American core group who believe that many (or even most) black males resemble the stereotypical violent, thuggish, underachieving black man will have little problem with the presence of violence in this "sacrificeable" group as long as it does not spill over into the core. In actuality, spillover has not affected educational institutions by having the particular violence of BGFs infect white groups. More disturbingly for the institutions, the violence has begun to bring legal concerns of liability to the fore, because there is, after all, "a direct correlation between the elimination of sacrificial practices and the establishment of a judicial system."[5]

When issues of violent hazing and injuries present themselves, educational institutions usually mete out suspensions and expulsions of students and chapters rather than initiating serious attempts to study, understand, and prevent the occurrences. This reliance on punishment instead of prevention must be eradicated. One way to move toward prevention is to end administrative neglect. This reality does not absolve members of responsibility for their behavior. Contrarily, it is a clarion call that universities need to start taking very seriously the danger BGFs may consistently present to interested students.

Membership intake programs have failed. It should be noted that every injury and death (with the exception of Joel Harris) mentioned at the outset of this study happened *after* MIP was introduced. Without a doubt, initiates and members continue to be drawn to ritualized pledging and hazing and the acceptance they bring. Unfortunately, only time and the legal system may present serious challenges to hazing in the end. Four of the five major BGFs have been or are embroiled in legal battles stemming from hazing abuses.

On one level, BGF violence is an attempt by a fragmented, victimized, and marginalized group to seize agency, create space, and become men . . . even to become human. These men are acted on by all the ills of modernized society that affect other men, *and more.* This study will not compel many to excuse fraternities for their shortcomings, nor should it, for it is not intended to evoke such a response. In fact, after we consider all the complications covered in this book we still come back to the fact that BGFs are dangerous and they show no signs of changing their ways. That reality is not only troubling; it should mobilize us. Regrettably, the organizations themselves are the inescapable primary targets of that mobilization.

Afterword:
Reflections On Failure

If you were there, I don't need to explain it to you. If you weren't there,
I *can't* explain it to you.

> —Marine Corps saying, according to former Marine,
> Secretary of the Navy, and United States
> Senator James Webb[1]

The first edition of *Black Haze* drilled deeply into scarcely discussed issues impacting the identities of black men in myriad ways. At the end of the day, it was a hopeful book that saw BGFs as troubled but salvageable. A revisitation of this work, crafted in my late twenties and early thirties, forced me to realize I was not a "detached observer." Ultimately, the conclusions did not subject the organizations to stern-enough condemnation. In fact, the book endeavored to move blameworthiness from individuals and organizations and place it squarely on the shoulders of society and institutions at multiple junctures.

Admittedly, I am in no hurry to completely dismiss painstaking research conducted at the beginning of my career. In fact, I believe much of the identity theory remains sound. That said, I am also not so stubborn as to entrap myself in a Freirean "circle of certainty" that prevents me from modifying other theories and positions that were flawed. Presently, I still believe American society deeply impacts the identities of black males in unique ways. The problem with the initial version of *Black Haze*, though, is that it was encased in a bifurcated philosophical paradigm seeking to condemn or exonerate BGFs. Even though the groups were certainly taken to task, my youthful romantic notions led me to ultimately shoehorn conclusions into the latter formulation that absolved them of as much culpability as possible. Despite my attempts at balance, there was always an ideological "shadow program" running in my mental background.

I was all too eager to push for extra-organizational solutions, such as mandatory seminars and workshops, full-time university advisers, pledge windows, more "caring" administrators, and initiatives constructed in concert with BGF general memberships. This all flowed back to my belief (no matter how subconscious) that the organizations bore a modicum of the burden, but the majority of it rested with society and negligent educational institutions. I was wrong. To be sure, colleges and universities have their failures. Nowhere has this been more evident over the last few years than in the sad examples set by Florida A&M (FAMU) and Penn State.

FOR REPUTATION AND REVENUE:
THE CHAMPION AND SANDUSKY FAILURES

FAMU entered the national spotlight for all the wrong reasons when drum major Robert Champion was beaten to death on a band bus after a football game in late November 2011. Asking how a band hazing is related to Greek-letter organizations is a legitimate question, in that the two types of groups seem worlds apart to the casual observer. Those more familiar with historically black college and university (HCBU) culture, however, understand that many HBCU bands, band fraternities, and instrument sectional organizations are eerily similar to BGLOs in their propensity to violently haze.

This is especially true at schools with more elite bands (for example, FAMU, Jackson State University, Howard University, Southern University, Grambling State University, Tuskegee University, and a few others). In fact, the allure of the bands often outweighs that of athletic teams at these schools. Since the 1970s, the trend for top-tier athletes to increasingly choose to hone their crafts at higher-profile predominantly white universities has woefully diminished the talent level of HBCU sports. The same is not true of the bands. As a result, HBCUs have created a sort of "Bizarro World" in which fans are often more interested in band performances than in the second-rate athletics. Indeed, the number of spectators in football stands frequently decreases after the band's halftime shows end. FAMU's Marching 100 is arguably the most exclusive band in this pantheon. As a result, the demands it has historically placed on its members for acceptance have been as great as those in any BGF.

Atlanta native Robert Champion was not only talented enough to join the Marching 100, he rose to the coveted rank of drum major—which made his death all the more puzzling. The reasons behind what was eventually ruled a homicide were initially unclear. Some speculated that Champion's beating was internal discipline because of mistakes he made during the band's performance. His parents believed he was assaulted because he opposed hazing. Still others argued that he was targeted because he was gay. All these theories were erroneous or incomplete.

As the story unfolded, it was revealed Champion was beaten because he was seeking membership in the band's "Bus C" clique—a group that rode a charter bus reserved for percussionists and their initiates on band road trips. A ritual called "Crossing Bus C"—considered the most brutal of all FAMU band-hazing processes—led to his death. Crossing Bus C required the supplicant to fight his way from the front to the rear of the bus while being struck by fists, drumsticks, mallets, and other objects. It was widely believed that Champion had to endure Crossing Bus C or his fellow bandmates would refuse to follow him once he became a principal drum major (FAMU uses multiple drum majors, who apparently hold different ranks). CNN reported, "Champion's roommate Keon Hollis told police that the initiation process went against everything that the drum major believed in. Champion didn't want to go through with it, but decided he had to in order to earn respect (from fellow members). 'If you want to *be somebody* you have to do it,' said band member Ryan Dean." (emphasis mine) [2]

In the aftermath of his death, Champion's fellow band members proclaimed there was no intention to injure him. As in all hazing cases, however, intent mattered little—the drum major did not live to enjoy the "respect" he so desperately sought. He was not the first to endure such abuse at FAMU. The school has a terrible track record of such mistreatment inside and outside the band. After Champion's death, *USA Today* reported, "In 1998, former clarinet player Ivery Luckey was struck some 300 times with a wooden paddle and required hospitalization. In 2001, Marcus Parker, a member of the band's trumpet section, sued FAMU and individual band members separately, alleging that he was beaten so badly one of his kidneys shut down. The university settled with Parker and he won a $1.8 million judgment against several individual defendants." [3]

The school's black Greeks also have a tradition of cruelty, which engulfed young Marcus Jones as he attempted to join the FAMU chapter of Kappa Alpha Psi in 2006. Jones was beaten so badly by the Kappas that he required surgery on his buttocks. Allegedly, he and other pledges were literally knocked out at one point, revived, and hazed more. A number of Kappas were eventually jailed for short periods as a result. FAMU's culture of hazing did not discriminate based on gender. FAMU band member Bria Hunter was hazed so badly that she suffered severe bruising, blood clots, and an injured thigh less than a month before Champion's death. As a result of this and other allegations, band director Julian White suspended more than a score of band members.

In response to the Hunter case and continuing violations, a number of FAMU administrators met three days before Champion was beaten to death. The *Orlando Sentinel* reported that a document, later released by FAMU, stated that now-retired campus police chief Calvin Ross suggested that the entire band be suspended because of out-of-control hazing. Dean of Students Henry Kirby, band director Julian White, police lieutenant Angela Kirkland, Vice President William Hudson Jr., and Provost Cynthia Hughes Harris joined Chief Ross at the meeting.[4]

According to the report, Ross recommended that either the entire band be suspended, or minimally, that the suspension of all upperclassmen was warranted. Kirby claimed that he supported the long-term suspension of the band in hopes of "scaring straight" other campus organizations that hazed. Band director White allegedly rejected the police chief's suggestion. White's attorney later contradicted this account of the events in the meeting, saying his client actually agreed that the band should be suspended. Inconsistencies abounded, and they did not end there. Even though he was the university's chief executive, President James Ammons said in a statement that it was not him but the group present at the meeting that decided that the police chief, dean of students, and band director should only *talk* to the band about hazing rather than suspend.[5]

Ultimately, White retired (after Ammons unsuccessfully attempted to fire him). The Florida A&M board of trustees issued a vote of no confidence against Ammons (but did not demand his dismissal). The marching band was suspended—but only for a year. Ammons eventually resigned on the same day that Champion's family brought suit against the University.

Abuse and administrative malfeasance are definitely not limited to FAMU, Greeks, or bands. The Champion case happened concurrently with the even more high-profile Gerry Sandusky scandal at the Pennsylvania State University. The initial allegations that former Penn State football assistant coach Sandusky molested a string of children over more than a decade and a half surfaced in March 2011. He was formally indicted on November 4 of that year—fifteen days before Robert Champion was killed. The Penn State case created a cauldron of controversy that engulfed not only Sandusky but legendary coach Joe Paterno and a host of university administrators. Sandusky was eventually convicted of abusing ten boys over fifteen years.

An independent investigation led by former FBI director Louis Freeh released in July 2012 yielded a damning report on how upper-level Penn State officials handled Sandusky. The "Freeh Report" opined that Penn State was entrenched in a retrograde culture tightly controlled by four men: President Graham Spanier, head football coach Paterno, athletic director Tim Curley, and Vice President Gary Schultz. The blistering 267-page document asserted that even though they had known about Sandusky's behavior for years, the quartet did nothing substantive to protect the children, and the case showed "a striking lack of empathy for child abuse victims by the most senior leaders of the University."[6]

Freeh concluded that the four men repeatedly failed to seriously deal with the troubling Sandusky dilemma because of one overarching goal: to avoid the consequences of bad publicity. Outside of certain insular Penn State circles, reasonable people considered the alleged negligence of these men troubling. The story ended well for no one in the Penn State case. Sandusky will probably die in prison, but his victims bear lifelong scars. Penn State's board of trustees dismissed Paterno four days after Sandusky's indictment on November 8, 2011. Spanier—who had been considered a model university president—left his post a day after Paterno's firing. Children were damaged, Sandusky was incarcerated, Spanier was professionally ruined, and a little over two months later, the eighty-five-year-old Paterno was dead from lung cancer complications.

In both the Penn State and FAMU cases, leadership seemingly made decisions based on reputation and money rather than propriety and decency. For Penn State, the football program is a legendary revenue-generating engine. In black college circles, FAMU's band is just as iconic as Penn State football, and it is also a cash cow for the school. As a result of the seemingly misplaced priorities of two university administrations, several young people are psychologically scarred for life or, in FAMU's case, dead.

There is great controversy regarding what administrators knew and did not know in both the FAMU and Penn State cases. Unfortunately for FAMU, it is probably more reasonable to believe that Paterno, Spanier, and their colleagues did not know the full extent of Gerry Sandusky's abuse than to believe that FAMU personnel did not know hazing was a deep-seated problem across a number of organizations at their university. Though different in key respects, both cases show glaring examples of leadership missteps and outright institutional failures. All that being acknowledged in these two extreme cases suggests that the most intractable problems for BGFs are not rooted in institutional, but in organizational culture.

THE ORGANIZATIONAL BOTTOM LINE

Casual, scholarly, and cinematic critique of black Greek-letter organizations is not completely new.[7] Mainstream America's initial theatrical exposure to the groups was filmmaker Spike Lee's *School Daze* in 1988. Lee levied numerous critiques in the film. He railed against inept black college administrators, black-middle-class selfishness, and intraracial color complexes. Lee, who has admitted he is no fan of black Greeks, took the organizations to task in a story thread that spoke to their cultural shallowness, retrograde apoliticism, and unchecked misogyny. Even though he intended *School Daze* to, at least in part, chastise and even condemn black Greeks, Lee failed to effectively demonize the groups' greatest problem—ubiquitous, life-threatening hazing. In fact, to an extent, *School Daze* unintentionally popularized the groups and their practices. In fairness to Lee, the film was released in 1989, a year before Joel Harris died attempting to join Alpha Phi Alpha at the filmmaker's alma mater, Morehouse College.

Decades later, two other theatrical representations of black Greek life entered America's public sphere. Unlike *School Daze*, 2007's *Stomp the Yard* and it's 2010 sequel, *Stomp the Yard II: Homecoming*, did little to address some of the troubling issues Lee touched on. Contrarily, these films (both produced by members of Alpha Phi Alpha) largely played like "brag pieces" centered on formulaic romantic story lines and one of the most superficial but popularized aspects of black Greekdom—stepping. Both *Stomp the Yard* movies emphasized the often-trumpeted benefits of membership—selflessness, purpose, unity, sacrifice, teamwork, and love. Unlike Lee's movie, the *Stomp the Yard* endeavors (outside of a scene or two) made little effort to substantively speak to the deeper sociopolitical quandaries faced by black folk. Where *School Daze* sought to educate, the *Stomp the Yard* series largely served only to entertain.

As readers of this volume know, black Greek-letter organizations are almost exclusively populated by college-educated African Americans. Hence, one would expect them to be in the vanguard of the struggle for an egalitarian society. This, however, is usually not the case. Even though they dispute it, with few exceptions, black Greek organizational voices are mostly absent from discussions of today's pressing issues of black poverty, political disempowerment, disproportionate incarceration, recidivism, police brutality, educational achievement gaps, unemployment and underemployment, health disparities, violence, and so forth. This is not to say black Greeks do *no* good. This stance does argue, however, that they often overstate their organizational contributions to society. Make no mistake, the intentional or unintentional simultaneous glorification of certain aspects of black Greekdom coupled with the refusal or inability to consistently speak to its underbelly literally has deadly consequences.

At various speaking engagements on campuses around the country I have talked about students being abused, injured, or killed while pledging. Non-Greeks in the audiences often sit with mouths open—aghast. Greeks, however, are unflinching—emotionless. Enthusiasm only emerges when a bold few openly defend the pledge process and its benefits in spite of the cruelties recounted during our sessions. Much of their defense circles back to a variation of James Webb's "If you weren't there, I can't explain it to you" argument. In effect, non-Greeks cannot cross the "great impassable divide" separating Greeks from the rest of the world.[8] According to their logic, something is also terribly flawed in fellow members who oppose them. More than likely, they were "made wrong" and are subsequently subjected to vehement ad hominem attacks. This scene is repeated again and again.

Eventually, I was forced to bow before a number of stark and disturbing realities. In a supposed effort to eradicate hazing, black

Greeks have constructed various membership intake programs that, in many respects, created more problems than they solved. Pledging did not die, it simply moved underground. Many chapters have augmented illegal underground pledging to the point that it is now the norm instead of the exception. There is no avoiding the fact that a good percentage of the organizations' memberships see their traditional processes, no matter how dangerous, as positive rather than negative and are willing to go to extraordinary lengths to preserve them. Members often actually argue that the solution is bringing the traditional process back "above ground" by reinstating pledging as an organizationally and institutionally acceptable public rite of passage. They conveniently forget that the "old process" was publicly abandoned because of its long history of abuse.

Others allege racism in higher education by proclaiming that black Greeks are disproportionately targeted even though "white Greeks haze, too." National organizations continue to refuse to admit that hazing is not limited to small groups of "renegade" members. In fact, it is deeply rooted in the cultures of the groups, and it occurs in every region of the country where they have chapters. Little has been done to curb it, which indicates that the groups' leaders have largely lost control of their memberships. Consequently, they have resorted to rule changes and public stances that they hope will shield them from legal attack but have little or no effect in stopping the dangerous behavior of their members. Honest, reasonable conversation with Greeks, individually and organizationally, is almost impossible. So, what is to be done?

As the first decade of the twenty-first century ended, I arrived at a more somber place marked by the belief that Greek leadership, like alcoholics, needs to publicly admit they have a serious problem embedded in their organizational cultures that they have little idea how to solve. To date, they have proven they cannot, or do not want to, stop hazing on their own. Certainly there is also the possibility that pledging—and the hazing that invariably accompanies it—cannot be stopped at all. If stopping it is impossible as long as the orders exist then increasingly drastic steps are mandated. Either way, Greeks must organizationally accept full responsibility for each and every injury and death resulting from hazing in their groups.

Minimally, national organizations must immediately adopt a real zero-tolerance policy on hazing. Any chapter involved in such activities should not be suspended—it must be closed forever. There are too many instances of the same chapters incurring suspension after suspension without end. In fact, some see frequent suspension as a badge of honor rather than a mark of shame. If Greek leadership is serious about stopping hazing, these chapters must simply cease to exist. Black Greek leadership should also proactively seek legislators in every state who will sponsor bills to make hazing a felony instead of a misdemeanor. They should then join in the prosecution of hazers to the fullest extent of the law. If none of these things work—they must go even further.

THE *IF* INDICTMENT

In the wake of yet another injury at Fisk University involving my own fraternity, in 2007 I penned, "Is it Time to Disband Black Greek-letter Fraternities and Sororities?" for *Diverse* (then *Black Issues in Higher Education*).[9] The very title of this short piece ignited a firestorm such as *Black Haze* never did. The reason was simple. Even though I had not arrived at the point where I openly pushed for the dissolution of black Greek fraternities and sororities, I certainly posed the question of whether they should be dissolved. I absolutely refused to seriously consider the idea that the only way to stop Greek hazing would be to eradicate the organizations for a very long time. Over the years, black Greeks themselves forced me to reexamine that commitment.

Black Greek national organizations repeatedly prove that they are primarily concerned with protecting their organizations from legal entanglement. Contrarily, people of good conscience must concern themselves with the lives put at risk by seemingly immortal pledge processes. Where should the line be drawn on lives lost before something radical is done? One more? Two? Five? Twenty? Fifty? These interests have been at loggerheads for some time and have brought us to a nihilistic place where Greeks and hazing are concerned. For years I joined a small cadre of scholars in arguing that hazers would cease their abuse if they understood what was at its heart. Greeks (and their copycat organizations) have disabused some of us of that notion.

A serious reading of the original edition of *Black Haze* reveals that, at its core, it was an exploration. Unfortunately, the current edition ends as an indictment. The closing charge should be read very carefully. **IF** no internal or external measures can stop hazing in

Greek-letter organizations and they continue to psychologically harm, physically injure, or kill prospective members, they should disband. This is a difficult proposition. Like many black Greeks, I believe in the organizations' ideals and possibilities. Unfortunately, there is a yawning gap between stated purposes and reality. This is not a bifurcated argument. Greeks are not all bad. As this book has shown, they have very rich histories, and undeniably make some contributions to their communities to this day. These realities complicate the matter. The loss of black Greeks and their potential on our campuses and in our communities would be notable.

No matter what pain it causes, we must now at least consider the option of eradicating these groups if they will not cease their destructive behavior. If they are humane, Greek-letter organizations should voluntarily cease operations (minimally on college and university campuses) if they cannot remedy their hazing ill. If they will not (and I do not believe they will), colleges and universities should mobilize their in-house counsels to seek legal redress and have them forcibly removed. From an administrator's point of view, these groups are risk-management nightmares and should no longer be recognized as registered student organizations in their present incarnations. From a concerned citizen's point of view, they offer a continuous threat to life and mental health that can no longer be tolerated. A number of schools, including Williams, Colby, Harvard, Princeton, Georgetown, Notre Dame, Rice, Boston College, and others, have already dispensed with traditional Greek systems over time.

We must remember that, by all accounts, Gerry Sandusky was an outstanding football coach. Despite this talent, he had a fatal flaw. Anyone who believed his football acumen outweighed his propensity to abuse children might turn a blind eye to his wickedness. Like Sandusky, black Greeks are impressive in many ways. But also like him, they have a fatal flaw—they are wedded to a process that periodically injures and kills people. In no way should this analogy be read as comparing hazing to pedophilia. That is not the point. The point is that neither individual nor organizational "good" excuses or minimizes unacceptable evil.

The first version of this book ended with the sentiment that the roots of violent hazing in BGFs were knowable and correctable. That was only half right. Ultimately, in its original incarnation, *Black Haze* was so immersed in cloudy epistemological exploration that it ignored clear ontological fact. No matter how they arrived in that place, Greeks are what they are—dangerous and unrepentant. Indeed, the reasons behind their abuse are knowable. Unfortunately, the maltreatment itself does not seem correctable. Contrarily, the groups are sending a clear message that no policy or procedural changes, revolving suspensions, or even incarceration will stop them as their injury tolls rise year after year. They unapologetically state through their actions, "We value pledging and hazing so much that we will not stop. We don't care if someone dies from time to time. This is the way we've always done things, the way we do things, and the way we will continue to do them." There is no evidence this will change. The only question remaining is, what can and should be done to stop them?

Acknowledgments

I often tell people that I am just a "poor ol' boy from the projects of Atlanta" at my core. I am well aware that any success I have enjoyed over the years during my sojourn from Carver Homes to this point in life has not been achieved alone. I have been blessed to have a large cadre of family, friends, and supporters who I do not take for granted. A dear friend once told me, "You take family where you find it." She was right. So, I want to take a moment to acknowledge members of my "family"—blood and beyond—who have contributed not only to *Black Haze*, but to my life.

Despite the trials and tribulations that all families endure, many of my relatives have always been there when the smoke cleared. The wisdom of my late grandmother, Linnie Mae Jones, continues to illuminate my path. My mother and sister, Betty and Amanda Jones, should never doubt how much I cherish them. My uncle Eddie Dean Ashley (alias John Henry) has also been a great source of joy and laughter. June—it's gonna get better. Hang in there, buddy. My extended family has also been a great source of support and love, especially since my grandmother passed away in 2009. Shouts to Pumpkin, Shake, Otha, Faye, Dee, Bessie, Kathy, Karen, Gwen, Jackie, and all the rest. Particular love to my baby cousins O.J. and Mike. I'm sure the three of us will argue about the mishaps of the Atlanta Falcons every Sunday for the rest of our lives.

A special thanks to my daughter, Jordan, who has sacrificed a ton of daddy-daughter time so I could finish this project. You've been a gem of a kid. Thank you for being so sweet and understanding.

My oldest friends, Kerry and Rashida, have been indispensable. Kerry "The Big Ol' Pimp" Norwood has been a great friend since we were twelve years old. Thank you for providing an example of what true bravery looks like. I have seen you deal with pain and struggle all your life. Your spirit of survival has been an inspiration. Rashida "Ra" Owens-Oliver is the epitome of balance, positivity, and class. Thank you for loving me even when I did not deserve it.

I am eternally appreciative of Tonja Edmond for invaluable support during the formative stages of the original version of this project many years ago. You took time to read choppy first drafts, provided a peaceful environment to write, and even offered financial support when I was a dirt-poor graduate student. Maybe most importantly, you took the initiative to track my father down and twisted my arm to meet him. That helped me put demons to rest that would not have otherwise been conquered.

I came into manhood with the "S1 members"—my classmates at the Naval Academy. They form a powerful crew of men I have loved and respected since we were teenagers. Much love to Mawuli Mel "Tricks" Davis, Jason "J Double" Pace, Paul "Hostile" Hogue, Neil "Books" Williams, Marc "Hawthorne" Davis, Ken "Dean" Finley, Daron "Fleet Admiral" Fullwood, Gary "Mac" McIntosh, Jay "Master" Harrell, Leon "Easy Lee" Wilson, DuJuan "Gunny" Graham, Torrence "T" Simmons, and Chris "Faulty" Frye. A special shout to my high school classmate and Academy road-dog, Eugene Malveaux. Maintain, boy!

I am thankful to the educational "guides" placed in my path over the years. Brother James R. Terry is still the greatest example of black manhood and decency I have ever seen. Two of my teachers at Northside High School—Jaye Guy and Arnold Heller—knew my potential long before I did. My time at Morehouse College exposed me to a set of outstanding men who brought the best out of me. Sterling Hudson, Tobe Johnson, Abraham Davis, and the late Robert Brisbane were instrumental in setting me on course to become a serious thinker.

I was fortunate to have access to an incredible group of scholars at the University of Kentucky who helped mold me into a viable intellectual—rather than just an angry young dilettante who thought he knew everything, but actually knew very little. Herbert Reid was an ideal advisor and has become an even better friend. Thank you for your patience. Ernest Yanarella helped Herb in getting me through. I am also grateful to Gerald Smith and Cynthia Irvin for your sternness and encouragement. Chester Grundy, George Brown, and Emmett "Buzz"

Burnam were the greatest campus allies a young fellow away from home could hope for.

I knew no one other than the man who recruited me from Morehouse College when I moved to Lexington, Kentucky for graduate school. My fraternity brothers there became my family, friends, and foundation. I am particularly indebted to the Lexington Alumni and Kappa Tau chapters of Kappa Alpha Psi. Both adopted me and provided unparalleled levels of affection and protection. Special thanks to Stewart "Peace" Peoples, Kim "Justice" Clay, and the late Sherman "Power" Fields. Rest easy, Sherm. I hope you finally found your "Eve." I also want to remember older brothers who took care of me when I was much younger and far dumber. The late Willie Edwards, Eugene Ballentine, and Eugene Shaw are all missed. Sammie Brooks, Earl Wright, Wil James, and a host of other Nupes provided a lot of love as well.

A very, very special thanks to my big brother, Keith "Bogey" Jackson. You have been one of the best human beings I have ever met. Thank you for being there through every valley for over twenty years. Keep 'em off your back, bruh! The mighty, mighty Brian Edwards has also been a steadfast brother and friend throughout.

To the "Drapetomania Society"—Jelani Cobb, Peniel Joseph, Jeremy Levitt, Matthew Whitaker, Rhonda Williams, and Yohuru Williams. These are all relatively new friends but just as valuable as any others. Thank you for reigniting a scholarly fire that life can sometimes snuff out. My colleagues in the Department of Pan-African Studies (PAS) at the University of Louisville have been a godsend. They continue to make work fun. Forty-plus years of PAS and going strong! My former graduate assistant, Shelby Pumphrey, also contributed a great deal to updating this volume.

Finally, this book would never have seen the light of day without the enthusiasm of the folks at SUNY. Thanks to Ryan Morris for her masterful production work. Kate Seburyamo publicized this edition early and often. The greatest thanks go to Charles Jones, Terry Kershaw, and the eminent Robert C. Smith and Michael Rinella. My longtime mentors Charles and Terry introduced me to Robert Smith well over a decade ago. He was gracious enough to take a serious look at *Black Haze* when a number of other publishers had turned it away. Robert read the manuscript, offered a critique, and passed it on to SUNY editor Michael

Rinella. Since then, Michael has easily been the most important person in the evolution of this work. He has always believed in it. He pushed the original edition and never let go. It was his idea (not mine) to do an anniversary volume. He then stayed on me after 1 missed deadline after deadline to get a new manuscript going. I'm glad he did. You're the man, Michael! Thank you!

Appendix

This appendix gives readers actual examples of hazing and violent incidents involving BGFs and other black collegiate organizations from the 1970s until today. In light of the Robert Champion case, a number of band hazings not included in the first edition are noted. No sorority cases are included, though they are numerous and growing.

A few other observations about this list should be noted. First, it is not comprehensive. Fewer than 10 percent of hazing cases are reported. Therefore, for every hazing violation reported, many more happen, but they are kept within the ranks of the organization or institution. Second, there are few reports of hazing in BGFs before the 1970s. This is possibly due to a dearth of media attention, a basic lack of concern about the activities of these organizations at predominantly white institutions, and a tacit condoning of the practices at predominantly black schools where many administrators and professors were members of the fraternities.

Parts of this list are exact reproductions of the work of Hank Nuwer, who has contributed more to tracking hazing cases than anyone else. Many of the cases before 1999 can be found in the appendix of his masterful book *Broken Pledges*. Nuwer has done yeoman's work in compiling later occurrences and deaths on his website—www. hanknuwer.com. The remainder of the cases are from news reports and personal tracking. The list of cases simply grows too fast for one book to document. To be sure, there will have been additions by the time this volume is published.

1970s

Alpha Phi Alpha (1977)
Bradley University (Peoria, Illinois)
A pledge claimed he had been beaten with fists and paddles. He was treated for acute kidney failure. Twelve active members pled guilty to hazing charges.

Omega Psi Phi (1977)
North Carolina Central University (Durham, North Carolina)
A pledge dropped dead after calisthenics. This chapter was not officially recognized by the national chapter of Omega Psi Phi.

Omega Psi Phi (1977)
University of Pennsylvania (Philadelphia, Pennsylvania)
Robert Bazile died of a heart attack after pledge-session activities. This chapter was not recognized by the University of Pennsylvania as an official student organization.

Omega Psi Phi (1979)
University of Florida (Gainesville, Florida)
Eighteen pledges were violently hazed, resulting in a one-year suspension of the fraternity. "You name it, I got it," pledge Michael Lawrence told reporters, "They had a heyday with us." One pledge spent the night in a psychiatric ward. Other pledges charged that they were forced to consume large amounts of marijuana and alcohol.

1980s

Kappa Alpha Psi (1980)
Virginia State University (Ettrick, Virginia)
The Alpha Psi chapter was suspended for infractions of rules, and its adviser dismissed. The group was investigated because hazing charges were brought against the chapter by a concerned student. VSU officials denied that hazing was a factor in their decision to suspend the chapter.

Omega Psi Phi and Phi Beta Sigma (1981)
State University of New York (Old Westbury, New York)

During an investigation, a district attorney found several examples of what he called "sadistic and dangerous hazing." Practices included branding with hangers while pledges were involuntarily restrained, forced eating of dog food and laxatives, and sleep deprivation. Some pledges were not allowed to bathe for up to a month. "There is a possible handful of students involved in the hazing," claimed the school's president.

Alpha Phi Alpha and Omega Psi Phi (1981)
North Carolina Central University (Durham, North Carolina)
The university temporarily suspended pledging after an Alpha pledge was twice hospitalized because of an "extreme illness." An Omega pledge, identified only as "Number 8," was hospitalized with a groin injury. Pledging was allowed to resume even before the initiation was concluded, according to the student newspaper.

Alpha Phi Alpha (1981)
University of Pittsburgh (Pittsburgh, Pennsylvania)
Two students were hospitalized in hazing incidents, one after being paddled.

Omega Psi Phi (1982)
Alabama A&M University (Normal, Alabama)
The university banned the fraternity for multiple offenses. One report said that members abducted one student and threatened to throw him over a cliff.

Kappa Alpha Psi (1982)
Rider College (Lawrenceville, New Jersey)
Rider students pledging at nearby Trenton State College were injured in an unspecified hazing incident. A security director said that the injuries to one pledge were "substantial."

Omega Psi Phi (1983)
East Carolina University (Greenville, North Carolina)
A judge dismissed hazing charges against three fraternity members, claiming the statute against hazing was too vague. A pledge had been knocked unconscious during his initiation and was hospitalized.

Omega Psi Phi (1983)
University of Maryland (College Park, Maryland)
According to a pledge, an active member struck him for being too clumsy while doing a "step" (a choreographed dance that has become an integral part of BGFs popularity). The pledge suffered a ruptured eardrum. Other pledges claim they were beaten with table legs.

Omega Psi Phi (1983)
Tennessee State University (Nashville, Tennessee)
Pledge Vann Watts and eight others were badly beaten with switches and forced to consume incredible amounts of alcohol. Watts died with a blood alcohol level of 0.52 percent; he had switch marks on his body. The fraternity was given a five-year suspension after one pledge admitted he'd been hazed. The remaining pledges stuck to their stories that no hazing had occurred.

Omega Psi Phi (1983)
West Georgia College (Carrollton, Georgia)
An associate professor charged that pledges of the fraternity were required to be branded as part of their initiation ceremony. Advisers denied the charges, saying that branding was voluntary.

Kappa Kappa Psi Band Fraternity (1984)
University of Akron (Akron, Ohio)
The Associated Student Government Supreme Court heard a petition charging the fraternity with hazing.

Kappa Alpha Psi (1984)
Ball State University (Muncie, Indiana)
School officials suspended the fraternity for three years after determining that brothers violently hazed pledges and forced them to consume alcohol.

Kappa Alpha Psi (1985)
California University of Pennsylvania (California, Pennsylvania)
A pledge charged that he had been beaten repeatedly by members, including his roommate.

Kappa Alpha Psi (1985)
Michigan State University (East Lansing, Michigan)
Michigan State suspended the chapter after two students suffered severely burned feet in an incident at Porter Park.

Phi Beta Sigma (1986)
Long Island University (C. W. Post Campus, Brookville, New York)
Five pledges who had complained to university officials about being beaten changed their stories and said they had not been beaten.

Kappa Alpha Psi (1986)
State University of New York (Old Westbury, New York)
Two pledges were rendered unconscious after a "slamming"—a chapter ritual in which pledges were hung upside down, beaten, and dropped on their heads. Two members of Kappa Alpha Psi were expelled, two suspended, and one reprimanded.

Omega Psi Phi (1986)
North Carolina A&T State University (Greensboro, North Carolina)
Eight Omega pledges were beaten, including seven who were hit on the head with a two-by-four. One student was hospitalized with a blood clot to the brain. Fraternity member Steven Jones was sentenced to jail on hazing and miscellaneous charges.

Omega Psi Phi (1986)
University of South Carolina (Colombia, South Carolina)
A student reported that he had been slapped and punched while pledging Omega Psi Phi.

Phi Beta Sigma (1987)
Morehouse College (Atlanta, Georgia)
A "blackballed" pledge of Phi Beta Sigma sued members for damages, alleging he had suffered a concussion from being struck on the head with "unknown objects" while trying "to crawl on hands and knees up a hill against the force of fraternity members."

Omega Psi Phi (1987)
Seton Hall University (South Orange, New Jersey)
An outsider was bitten when he tried touching the collar of a pledge who was walking on his leash for Omega Psi Phi.

Alpha Phi Alpha (1988)
University of Houston (Houston, Texas)
A member was fined $500 for hazing a blindfolded pledge by striking him in the chest.

Omega Psi Phi (1988)
Norfolk State University (Norfolk, Virginia)
During a so-called "inspiration session," pledge Christopher Peace suffered a broken jaw. He charged that he and other pledges had been slapped, punched, and beaten with paddles.

Kappa Alpha Psi (1989)
Fort Valley State College (Fort Valley, Georgia)
A twenty-one-year-old pledge was dehydrated and suffered kidney dysfunction after members paddled him, drubbed him with canes, and battered him with their fists. "It was like being in hell," the pledge said. Another pledge was hospitalized with a sprained back.

Alpha Phi Alpha (1989)
Morehouse College (Atlanta, Georgia)
Joel Harris, eighteen, collapsed and died during a three-hour pledge session. The medical examiner said that pledges were struck if they were unable to recite historical facts.

Kappa Alpha Psi (1989)
State University of New York (Stony Brook, New York)
A Kappa pledge filed hazing charges against three fraternity brothers he said beat him and others during pledging. During the beating, the pledge blacked out. The university suspended the fraternity indefinitely from on-campus activities. The university suspended the hazers for one year. The national fraternity denied responsibility, claiming this was a renegade group whose activities were not sanctioned.

Alpha Phi Alpha (1989)
Purdue University (West Lafayette, Indiana)
Purdue University officials suspended privileges of the local chapter for a minimum of three years for mentally and physically hazing a pledge the previous fall.

1990s

Kappa Alpha Psi (1990)
Northwestern State University (Natchitoches, Louisiana)
The university suspended the chapter for two years after a pledge reported he had been hazed.

Phi Beta Sigma (1991)
Clark Atlanta University (Atlanta, Georgia)
The fraternity was suspended pending an investigation of the alleged hazing of twenty-one-year-old sophomore Roderick Green and twenty-year-old Willie Mingo. Each contended that he was beaten with a wooden paddle about the buttocks and kidney areas, resulting in kidney damage to both.

Omega Psi Phi (1991)
Clark Atlanta University (Atlanta, Georgia)
Ten student members of Omega Psi Phi fraternity were arrested on charges of hazing after beating James Albert Bush, twenty, with their hands, fists, rubber tires, and a wooden paddle, resulting in severe kidney damage as well as bruises to his calves and arms.

Phi Beta Sigma (1991)
University of Missouri (Columbia, Missouri)
The fraternity was suspended after a student was "hit over the head" while pledging.

Omega Psi Phi (1992)
Norfolk State University (Norfolk, Virginia)
A student pledging Omega Psi Phi fraternity complained about both sides of his jaw being broken, and the chapter was banned from campus.

The university suspended all of its fraternities and sororities after widespread reports of hazing continued.

Phi Beta Sigma (1992)
Southern University (Baton Rouge, Louisiana)
During the initiation of prospective members, a big brother hit twenty-three-year-old Derone Walker over the head with a frying pan, blinding him. At the time of the incident doctors were unsure whether Walker would ever regain his sight.

Kappa Alpha Psi (1993)
University of Georgia (Athens, Georgia)
Christopher Allen Powell was hospitalized with infected buttocks after being repeatedly paddled during hazing.

Omega Psi Phi (1993)
University of Maryland (College Park, Maryland)
Twenty-four members of the Omega Psi Phi fraternity were arrested and charged with hazing after six pledges are brutalized in a rite of initiation. Police accounts revealed that the would-be members were kicked, punched, beaten, and whipped over a two-month period, resulting in serious injuries requiring hospitalization for all of them. The most seriously injured pledge suffered a ruptured spleen and a collapsed lung; another was treated for liver damage, cracked ribs, and a punctured eardrum resulting in a 70 percent hearing loss. Other reported injuries among the six young men included a fractured ankle and a concussion. The fraternity lost the court case and paid out $375,000.

Kappa Alpha Psi (1994)
Southeast Missouri State University (Cape Giradeau, Missouri)
Kappa pledge Michael Davis died after an intense night of hazing.

Kappa Alpha Psi (1994)
Tennessee State University (Nashville, Tennessee)
Suspended Kappa Alpha Psi member Wardell Pride sued Kappa Alpha Psi for damages sustained during his pledge process three years earlier. The fraternity settled out of court.

Kappa Alpha Psi (1994)
Southern College of Technology (Marietta, Georgia)
Steven Otey Jr. was hospitalized after members of Kappa Alpha Psi stood on his abdomen and beat him repeatedly during a three-hour hazing session.

Omega Psi Phi (1994)
Indiana University (Bloomington, Indiana)
Pledge Kevin Nash was hospitalized after being struck more than 100 times during an Omega hazing session. Three Omegas, including the chapter's adviser, were arrested. The fraternity eventually paid $774,500 in damages.

Omega Psi Phi (1994)
Paine College (Augusta, Georgia)
Gary Ross was partly paralyzed after being hit on the head while pledging.

Phi Beta Sigma (1994)
University of Southern Mississippi (Hattiesburg, Mississippi)
Five members of the fraternity were arrested for hazing.

Kappa Alpha Psi (1994)
Georgia Institute of Technology (Atlanta, Georgia)
Seven Kappas were arrested after a pledge suffered abdominal injuries.

Alpha Phi Alpha (1995)
Purdue University (West Lafayette, Indiana)
Ten undergraduates and two alumni members of the fraternity are arrested as a result of hazing.

Kappa Alpha Psi (1996)
University of Pittsburgh (Pittsburgh, Pennsylvania)
Santana Kenner-Henderson was beaten so badly that he suffered kidney damage and had to be placed on a dialysis machine. Another pledge, Byron Woodson, was beaten for about an hour by other members of the chapter. The active members were charged with aggravated assault, reckless endangerment, and conspiracy.

Omega Psi Phi (1996)
University of West Virginia (Morgantown, West Virginia)
An Omega pledge was hospitalized with kidney damage.

Phi Beta Sigma (1996)
University of Georgia (Athens, Georgia)
A pledge was allegedly paddled more than seventy times. He suffered bruises to his buttocks and torn blood vessels. Three Sigmas were arrested, including their adviser.

Kappa Alpha Psi (1996)
Northern Illinois University (Dekalb, Illinois)
A pledge alleged that hazing caused kidney damage and a concussion.

Omega Psi Phi (1997)
University of Louisville (Louisville, Kentucky)
Shawn Blackston almost died from kidney damage. He successfully sued the fraternity for close to $1 million.

Phi Beta Sigma (1997)
Georgia State University (Atlanta, Georgia)
Among other abuses, a pledge was pushed through a wall. The chapter was suspended and the student body president, a Sigma, resigned under pressure.

Kappa Alpha Psi (1998)
University of Maryland, Eastern Shore (Princess Anne, Maryland)
Five pledges were hospitalized. Treatments include surgery for cuts and buttock infection.

Kappa Alpha Psi (1998)
Kansas State University (Manhattan, Kansas)
A pledge was hospitalized with kidney damage.

Phi Beta Sigma (1998)
Southern Illinois University (Carbondale, Illinois)
A pledge was hospitalized with chest injuries.

Kappa Alpha Psi, Omega Psi Phi, and Phi Beta Sigma (1998)
Kent State University (Kent, Ohio)
The institution banned black fraternity- and sorority-sponsored dances and parties because of a series of fights involving members of the three fraternities.

Phi Beta Sigma (1999)
Michigan State University (East Lansing, Michigan)
A Phi Beta Sigma pledge suffered kidney damage after being paddled. According to the Associated Press, to avoid accusations of hazing, the chapter's president claimed that the pledge was already a member and had been voluntarily "trading wood" in a hitting contest to see who was toughest.

Kappa Alpha Psi (1999)
Georgia State University (Atlanta, Georgia)
Five Kappas were arrested after beating a pledge and sending him to the hospital with "serious injuries to his buttocks, stomach, and legs." The injured pledge also had blood in his urine.

Phi Beta Sigma (1999)
West Virginia University (Morgantown, West Virginia)
A Sigma pledge received medical treatment in May after being beaten at West Virginia University, where another fraternity, Omega Phi Psi, had been banned for hazing in 1996. Seven Sigmas were arrested in the case.

Alpha Phi Alpha (1999)
Lincoln University (Lincoln University, Pennsylvania)
An Alpha pledge was hospitalized and needed a colostomy. The chapter had already received a five-year suspension for beating a student in 1994. It was later discovered that the brothers running the process were from an entirely different campus and had never sent the pledges' dues to Alpha headquarters.

Kappa Alpha Psi (1999)
Grambling State University (Grambling, Louisiana)
A pledge was treated for injuries resulting from paddling and cane beatings. Three Kappas were arrested.

Omega Psi Phi (1999)
Mississippi State (Starkville, Mississippi)
An Omega pledge was hospitalized after being beaten during pledging.

Kappa Alpha Psi (1999)
Bowie State University (Bowie, Maryland)
Kappa officials— investigated charges of hazing and closed down the chapter at the University of Maryland at Eastern Shore.

Alpha Phi Alpha (1999)
The University of Florida (Gainesville, Florida)
The fraternity was suspended for hazing. Abuses included extensive paddling.

Kappa Alpha Psi (1999)
Illinois State University (Normal, Illinois)
Kappa Alpha Psi was suspended after members were photographed hazing pledges.

Omega Psi Phi (1999)
University of Georgia (Athens, Georgia)
The chapter was suspended for hazing three students.

Kappa Alpha Psi (1999)
Georgia Institute of Technology (Atlanta, Georgia)
The chapter was found guilty of minor physical abuses and personal servitude. It was placed on "suspended suspension"—meaning Kappas would serve a one-year probation. If they committed further violations they would be suspended for no fewer than five years.

Omega Psi Phi (1999)
Northern Illinois University (Dekalb, Illinois)
Three members were arrested for hazing. Offenses included forcing others to eat dog food and run barefoot in the snow.

2000s

Phi Beta Sigma (2000)
University of Arkansas, Monticello (Monticello, Arkansas)
A pledge suffered broken ribs and internal bleeding and lost consciousness.

Phi Beta Sigma (2000)
Norfolk State University (Norfolk, Virginia)
A pledge spent two weeks in the hospital. Three members were expelled and the fraternity was sued for $500,000.

Kappa Alpha Psi (2001)
Louisiana State University (Baton Rouge, Louisiana)
A pledge was paddled so severely that blood seeped through his jeans. A circular seven-inch-around, two-inch-deep wound required two surgeries.

Kappa Alpha Psi (2001)
Old Dominion University (Norfolk, Virginia)
As a result of hazing that inflicted numerous bruises to a student's hands and buttocks, two members were expelled, four suspended for a semester, and one suspended for two semesters.

Omega Psi Phi (2001)
Tennessee State University (Nashville, Tennessee)
Joseph T. Green, a pledge, died of an exercise activity suggested by members of the fraternity during an unofficial pledging session.

Alpha Phi Alpha (2001)
Ohio State University (Columbus, Ohio)
The chapter was suspended on January 1, 2001, after rumors of hazing and inappropriate intake practices began to circulate. The chapter was suspended for two years and on probationary status for one year.

Kappa Alpha Psi (2001)
Western Kentucky University (Bowling Green, Kentucky)
The chapter was suspended for five years and fined $1,000 because of hazing.

Alpha Phi Alpha (2001)
University of Texas (Austin, Texas)
In spite of fraternity denials, the university found evidence that the chapter had engaged in hazing and suspended it for three years.

Kappa Alpha Psi (2001)
Ball State University (Muncie, Indiana)
The chapter was suspended after investigation of a hazing case. A victim filed a civil suit against the chapter.

Phi Beta Sigma (2002)
Southern Illinois University, Edwardsville (Edwardsville, Illinois)
Prentice Motley was hospitalized after a hazing session where he was beaten hard enough to rupture a kidney. Every member of the six-man chapter was arrested and charged with hazing as well as perjury.

Alpha Phi Alpha (2003)
Southern Methodist University (Dallas, Texas)
Braylon Curry was hospitalized for nine days and suffered from pulmonary edema and a sodium imbalance due to the pledging process he underwent.

Kappa Alpha Psi (2004)
Emory University (Atlanta, Georgia)
Raymond McCoy filed a civil lawsuit against Kappa Alpha Psi and some its former members for the psychological and physical abuse he sustained throughout the pledging process the year before.

Kappa Alpha Psi (2005)
Fisk University (Nashville, Tennessee)
Akeem Alexander reported that he was ordered to bend over and receive beatings from fraternity members with canes and paddles, and that he was beaten with fists and slammed into the ground. Alexander reportedly left the university after he was admitted to the hospital for his injuries, and he filed a civil suit against the fraternity for $4 million.

Alpha Phi Alpha (2005)
University of Pennsylvania (Philadelphia, Pennsylvania)
E. Martyn Griffen, a pledge, sued Alpha Phi Alpha after claiming he had

been punched in the thighs and repeatedly popped in the arms with rubber bands by fraternity members. The chapter was suspended on grounds of violating the antihazing regulations of the university.

Kappa Alpha Psi (2006)
Florida A&M University (Tallahassee, Florida)
Marcus Jones, a pledge, was beaten with wooden canes and hospitalized for two days due to a ruptured eardrum, a lost half-pint of blood, and an injured right buttock that required a drainage tube and twenty-five stitches. Five members of the fraternity faced felony charges.

Alpha Phi Alpha (2007)
Oklahoma State University, Stillwater (Stillwater, Oklahoma)
Pledges complained of sleep deprivation, having to do sit-ups while members of the fraternity were sitting on top of them, and being beaten repeatedly with fists at an off-campus fraternity house. One pledge was reportedly beaten so badly that muscle tissue was exposed.

Phi Beta Sigma (2008)
Mansfield University (Mansfield, Pennsylvania)
Five members of Phi Beta Sigma were arrested in relation to a hazing incident where victim Jessie D. Wilson, a pledge, was beaten and required hospitalization for several days.

Alpha Phi Alpha (2009)
Fort Valley State University (Fort Valley, Georgia)
Brian Tukes, a pledge, was hospitalized after complaining of chills, back pain, and nausea and was diagnosed with acute renal failure.

Phi Beta Sigma (2009)
Prairie View A&M University (Prairie View, Texas)
Donnie Wade II, a pledge, died as a result of "acute exertional rhabdo-myolysis" from fraternity members requiring him and other pledges to perform trials called the "Indian Run," "Snake," and "Six inches." The pledge's family sued the fraternity for $97 million dollars.

Kappa Alpha Psi (2009)
Eastern Kentucky University (Richmond, Kentucky)
Three members of Kappa Alpha Psi pleaded guilty to fourth-degree

assault charges after a pledge, Brent Whiteside, was hospitalized with kidney failure.

Omega Psi Phi (2009)
University of Houston (Houston, Texas)
Pledges Jermel Kyle and Lee West III were beaten across their torsos, buttocks, and calves with a two-by-six-inch wooden board wrapped in duct tape. They were also beaten with an aluminum baseball bat and a TV antenna. One pledge reported that he struggled to remain conscious as he was repeatedly punched in the stomach. According to West, multiple hazings occurred at the private residences of Omega Psi Phi fraternity members and alumni. During one such session, West said, a broomstick snapped in two across the backside of a fellow pledge.

2010s

Alpha Phi Alpha (2010)
Mercer University (Macon, Georgia)
The Mercer University chapter was suspended by the university administration for three years. Pledges accused the chapter of forced sleep deprivation and dietary restrictions.

Alpha Phi Alpha (2010)
Citing flawed membership intake processes at chapters across the country, Alpha Phi Alpha halted new membership processes nationwide.

Kappa Alpha Psi (2010)
University of Central Florida (Orlando, Florida)
An official cease-and-desist order was issued to the UCF chapter of Kappa Alpha Psi after reports surfaced that fraternity members were beating pledges with canes.

Omega Psi Phi (2010)
University of South Florida (Tampa, Florida)
The chapter was suspended while detectives investigated allegations of two nights of off-campus hazing.

Kappa Alpha Psi (2010)
Wayne State University (Detroit, Michigan)
Eric Walker claimed he was hazed for thirty-two days; he was hospi-
talized as a result of being repeatedly beaten with canes. Wayne State
University suspended the chapter.

Kappa Alpha Psi (2011)
University of Maryland (Baltimore, Maryland)
The chapter was suspended indefinitely by the University of Maryland
once the administration heard allegations of hazing.

Kappa Alpha Psi (2011)
California State University, Bakersfield (Bakersfield, California)
Five students and alumni were arrested for hazing four Kappa pledges
by beating them with paddles, canes, and whips, and shooting them
with a pellet gun.

Phi Beta Sigma (2011)
Francis Marion University (Florence, South Carolina)
Nine members of Phi Beta Sigma were arrested in connection with a
hazing incident where a pledge was beaten and paddled. Pledge Daniel
McElveen sued and won a $1,600,000 verdict in 2014.

The "Marching 100" (2011)
Florida A&M University (Tallahassee, Florida)
FAMU student and band member Robert Champion died from a band-
hazing ritual called "Crossing Bus C" (walking from the front to the
back of the bus while being beaten). The band was suspended for a year
and multiple members served jail time (none for more than a year).

Kappa Alpha Psi (2012)
Youngstown State University (Youngstown, Ohio)
Kappa Alpha Psi, Beta Pi chapter, was suspended for fifteen years and
nine members were indicted on two counts of felonious assault each
after two pledges, Resean Yancey and Breylon Stubbs, were beaten in
off-campus rituals.

Kappa Alpha Psi (2012)
Arkansas Tech (Russellville, Arkansas)
Kappa Alpha Psi, Pi Upsilon chapter, was permanently suspended from Arkansas Tech after pledge Dashawn Scoggins was beaten with wooden paddles and canes and hospitalized after a Kappa Alpha Psi ritual. Three members faced battery charges.

Alpha Phi Alpha (2012)
University of Florida (Gainesville, Florida)
Nine members of Alpha Phi Alpha faced first-degree misdemeanor charges after being accused of paddling the buttocks of five pledges and "thunder slapping" them in the chest during a fraternity ritual.

Kappa Alpha Psi (2012)
University of Florida (Gainesville, Florida)
Members of Kappa Alpha Psi faced first-degree misdemeanor charges after five pledges complained that they had been beaten with wooden canes from 30 to 150 times a day on six occasions.

The "Mighty Marching Panthers" (2012)
Clark Atlanta University (Atlanta, Georgia)
The "Mighty Marching Panthers" were temporarily suspended for hazing allegations, but were later reinstated.

The "Marching Sound Machine" (2012)
North Carolina Central University (Durham, North Carolina)
All thirty-six members of the drumline of the "Marching Sound Machine" band were temporarily suspended after hazing allegations, but were later reinstated. Campus officials mandated that members of the drumline attend a hazing workshop and perform ten hours of community service. They received no other punishment.

"Men of Honor" (2013)
Virginia State University (Petersburg, Virginia)
Nineteen-year-olds Marvell Edmondson and Jauwan M. Holmes drowned after an initiation similar to one that in 1979 took two lives at historically black Virginia State. Four Men of Honor members were charged with hazing: James A. Mackey, thirty-five, freshman Cory D.

Baytop, twenty-six, freshman Eriq K. Benson, nineteen, and Charles E. Zollicoffer, twenty-nine.

Alpha Phi Alpha (2013)
Virginia State University (Petersburg, Virginia)
Four members of the fraternity were formally charged with causing bodily injury to another student at multiple off-campus fraternity events between August and November, 2012.

Alpha Phi Alpha (2013)
Jacksonville State University (Jacksonville, Alabama)
Alpha Phi Alpha members Justavious Quintae Johnson, Juston Eugene Thomas, Mikel Deloch Whittier, and Varian May pleaded guilty to hazing. In total, eighteen people were arrested in connection with a case reaching back to 2011. Pledge Jason Horton spent two weeks in the hospital due to injuries from repeated beatings. As a result of the hazing, his liver was enlarged and his kidneys were functioning at 50 percent.

Kappa Alpha Psi (2014)
University of Central Arkansas (Conway, Arkansas)
According to police, four victims came forward with formal complaints. One was listed as receiving a "major injury." The prosecuting attorney's form affidavit listed the injuries and claimed they resulted from the victims being paddled on the buttocks repeatedly, assuming a "plank position" while being slapped in the face, and being pelted with raw eggs while kneeling on uncooked rice.

Alpha Phi Alpha (2014)
University of Akron (Akron, Ohio)
University of Akron police issued warrants for six members of the fraternity for allegedly hazing at least one of five pledges over the course of three weeks. University police had previously investigated the fraternity after receiving tips about hazing in 2007 and 2008, but no charges were filed. One victim told campus police that he had been admitted to the hospital after sustaining bloody injuries to his backside. Afraid that hospital staff would notify authorities, he initially said the injuries were from sledding. The pledge, whose father and brother were members of

the fraternity, told police in the interview that he still wanted to be part of Alpha Phi Alpha, even after the chapter president had to intervene when the paddling got out of control on a day after he had already bled through his pants.

Kappa Alpha Psi (2014)
University of Memphis (Memphis, Tennessee)
Thirty-nine-year-old Kappa and real estate broker Adrian Bond is accused of using a wooden stick to beat a new member on the butt and punching him in the chest. Police say Bond directed a group of fraternity brothers in the beating as a way to repledge a current member from the University of Memphis. Bond's attorney, fellow Kappa Alpha Psi member Arther Horne, proclaimed that Kappa may have practiced hazing when he pledged in 1989, but not anymore.

Kappa Alpha Psi (2014)
University of Georgia (Athens, Georgia)
As a result of physically striking pledges, eleven fraternity members were arrested and charged with hazing as well as one misdemeanor of a high and aggravated nature. Under Georgia law the charge carries a maximum penalty of twelve months in jail and a $5,000 fine.

Alpha Phi Alpha (2014)
University of Tennessee (Knoxville, Tennessee)
The university suspended its chapter of Alpha Phi Alpha after members admitted to hazing. The school's investigation began with a complaint from a parent. The hazing allegations involved hitting pledges with a paddle as well as pouring hot sauce on their genitals.

Kappa Alpha Psi (2014)
In the wake of continued hazing incidents, Kappa's international headquarters issued an indefinite fraternity-wide moratorium on all membership intake in September 2014.

Notes

PREFACE

1. Martin Luther King Jr. was himself a member of Alpha Phi Alpha.

2. J. P. Olsen, "Blood Brothers," *Swing* (February 1995): 49.

3. Robert Harris, "Grand Polemarch's Message," *Kappa Alpha Psi Journal* (December 1994).

4. Hank Nuwer delivers a good account of Harris's death in *Broken Pledges: The Deadly Rite of Hazing* (Marietta, GA: Longstreet Press, 1990).

5. Paul Ruffins, "Are the Black Fraternities Beating Themselves to Death?" *Black Issues in Higher Education* (June 12, 1997): 25.

CHAPTER 1: HAZING THEN AND NOW

1. Several articles by journalist Christopher Shea illustrate this trend. In 1994 alone, Shea wrote "Two More Alumni in Fraternity Charged in Hazing Death" for the *New York Times* (February 24, 1994) and two pieces for the *Chronicle of Higher Education*: "Brutal Hazing Death Shocks Missouri Campus" in March and "Wall of Silence" in June. The fraternity pledge process and the hazing that usually accompanies it are not new phenomena. For partial historical documentation of "reported" hazing incidents, injuries, and deaths see Nuwer, *Broken Pledges*, as well as the appendix of this book. Public concern with the brutality of the BGF pledge process increased after Joel Harris was killed in 1989, and as already mentioned, it intensified after Michael Davis's death at Southeast Missouri State University. For another account of the Davis case, see William Cox, "Joining a Fraternity Should Not Result in Death," *Black Issues in Higher Education* (March 1, 1994). The finest recounting of the Davis case is probably Olsen's "Blood Brothers."

2. Nuwer, *Broken Pledges.*

3. Ibid., 62.

4. Ibid., 63.

5. Ibid., 63.

6. To preserve anonymity, BGF members are not referenced by name, but by fraternal affiliation. Anonymity was guaranteed to interviewees and

focus-group participants in an effort to prompt as much honesty as possible about their views on their organizations and behavior.

7. Allan Feldman, *Formations of Violence: The Narrative of the Body and Political Terror in Northern Ireland* (Chicago: University of Chicago Press, 1991), 258.

8. Louis Knowles and Kenneth Prewitt, *Institutional Racism in America* (Englewood Cliffs, NJ: Prentice Hall, 1969).

9. This is what I see as a broad and powerful definition of politics advanced by Harold Lasswell in *Politics: Who Gets What, When, How* (Cleveland, OH: Meridian Books, 1958).

CHAPTER 2: MEN, MEDIA, AND MOVEMENTS

1. Deborah Prothrow-Stith, *Deadly Consequences: How Violence Is Destroying Our Teenage Population and a Plan to Begin Solving the Problem* (New York: Harper Collins, 1993).

2. Emile Durkheim, "Social Facts," in *Readings in the Philosophy of Social Science,* ed. M. Broadbeck (New York: MacMillan, 1968), 247.

3. Ibid., 248.

4. Earl Ofari Hutchinson, *The Assassination of the Black Male Image* (Los Angeles: Middle Passage Press, 1994).

5. See James Carey, "Abolishing the Old Spirit World," *Critical Studies in Mass Communications* 12.1 (March 1, 1995), and Christopher Sharrett, "Movies vs. the Media," *USA Today* (March 25, 1995).

6. Jürgen Habermas, *The Structural Transformation of the Public Sphere* (Boston: MIT Press, 1991).

7. Many examinations of Habermas are available to those interested in such engagements. It is impossible to cite every study or even most of them, but two that were quite beneficial for the purposes of this piece were Craig Calhoun's *Habermas and the Public Sphere* (Cambridge, MA: MIT Press, 1992) and Maeve Cook's *Language and Reason: A Study of Habermas's Pragmatics* (Cambridge, MA: MIT Press, 1994). Joan Alway's *Critical Theory and Political Possibilities* (Westport, CT: Greenwood Press, 1995), Jay Bernstein's *Recovering Ethical Life: Jürgen Habermas and the Future of Critical Theory* (New York: Routledge, 1995), and Jane Braaten's *Habermas's Critical Theory of Society* (Albany: SUNY Press, 1991) are also fine reads.

8. The meteoric rise of the Internet has complicated this issue exponentially.

9. Lawrence Grossberg, *We Gotta Get Outta This Place* (New York: Routledge, 1992), 217.

10. Examples include Johanna Meehan, *Feminists Read Habermas: Gendering the Subject of Discourse* (New York: Routledge, 1995).

11. Studies that engage the theme of historical black alienation are widespread. For example, see Albert Boime, *The Art of Exclusion: Representing*

Blacks in the Nineteenth Century (Washington, DC: Smithsonian Institute Press, 1990), Price Cobbs and William Grier, *Black Rage* (New York: Basic Books, 1968), George Fredrickson, *The Black Image in the White Mind: Character and Destiny, 1817–1914* (Middletown, CT: University Press of New England, 1971), and Haki Madhubuti, *Black Men: Obsolete, Single, Dangerous?* (Chicago: Third World Press, 1990).

12. Craig Calhoun, *Critical Social Theory* (Cambridge, MA: Blackwell, 1995), 215.

13. Ibid., 215–216.

14. Lisa Hoshmand gives a fine synopsis of ethnographic research techniques in "Alternate Research Paradigms: A Review and Teaching Proposal," *Counseling Psychologist* 17.1 (1989): 3–79.

15. See Norman Denzin and Yvonna Lincoln, *Handbook of Qualitative Research* (Thousand Oaks, CA: Sage, 1994).

16. Donald Polkinghourne, *Narrative Knowing and the Human Sciences* (Albany: SUNY Press, 1988), 14.

17. Ibid., 14.

18. Ibid., 14.

19. Michael Carpini and Bruce Williams, "The Method Is the Message: Focus Groups as a Means of Examining the Uses of Television in Political Discourse," paper presented to the International Society of Political Psychology, Washington, DC, July 1990.

20. Richard Krueger, *Focus Groups: A Practical Guide for Applied Research* (Newbury Park, CA: Sage, 1988), 18.

2. Lawrence Ross, *The Divine Nine: The History of African-American Fraternities and Sororities* (New York: Kensington, 2000).

22. Walter Kimbrough is a member of Alpha Phi Alpha who pledged at the University of Georgia in the mid-1980s. While I was completing graduate study at Kentucky, Kimbrough was earning the PhD at Georgia State University. Both of us were interested in black Greek issues, but we took different paths in academia. Walter became a student affairs administrator at several universities and eventually president of Philander Smith College. He currently serves as president of Dillard University in New Orleans. He was kind enough to give me an interview as well as a few unpublished papers on black Greeks that helped greatly with my research. As noted earlier, Kimbrough published *Black Greek 101* in 2003.

CHAPTER 3: THE HISTORY
OF BLACK GREEK-LETTER FRATERNITIES

1. Ellis Cose, *A Man's World: How Real Is Male Privilege and How High Is Its Price?* (New York: Harper Collins, 1995), 51.

2. Joy James, *Transcending the Talented Tenth: Black Leaders and American Intellectuals* (New York: Routledge, 1997).

3. In certain instances, Phi Beta Sigma has initiated men who have not attended college but have outstanding credentials in other areas of life. To my knowledge, no other BGF offers this opportunity. Three of the other four groups have provisions for honorary membership that incorporate postsecondary educational requirements. Kappa Alpha Psi is the only BGF that does not allow honorary membership under any circumstances.

4. Lawrence Otis Graham, *Our Kind of People: Inside America's Black Upper Class* (New York: Harper Perennial, 2000), 86.

5. The National Pan-Hellenic Council is the umbrella organization for the nine largest historically black Greek-letter fraternities and sororities: Alpha Phi Alpha, Kappa Alpha Psi, Omega Psi Phi, Phi Beta Sigma, Iota Phi Theta, Alpha Kappa Alpha, Delta Sigma Theta, Zeta Phi Beta, and Sigma Gamma Rho.

6. Graham, *Our Kind of People*, 89.

7. Ironically, even Howard University—the location of most black Greek-letter organizations' Alpha (first) chapters (Alpha Phi Alpha, Alpha Kappa Alpha, Omega Psi Phi, Delta Sigma Theta, Phi Beta Sigma, and Zeta Phi Beta were all founded at Howard)—was not initially positive about the presence of black fraternities and sororities on its campus. Elite women's colleges such as Bennett and Spelman banned Greekdom until well into the twentieth century. One Spelman graduate who joined Delta after college in the late 1940s commented in *Our Kind of People*, "Our President, Florence Read, felt sororities would distract us from our work and create divisions and cliques" (p. 90). In many respects, it cannot be denied that—to a serious degree—Read has been proven correct.

8. Bruce Barnes does a fine job of distinguishing between Era I, II, and III fraternities in his paper "Our Common Bonds," presented at the Southeastern Intra-fraternity Conference, Atlanta, 1994.

9. Francis Shepardson, *Baird's Manual: American College Fraternities* (Menasha, WI: The Collegiate Press & George Banta, 1930), 1-10.

10. James Brunson, *Frat and Soror: The African Origins of Greek Lettered Organizations* (Cleage Group, 1991), 47.

11. Frank Bowles and Frank Decosta's *Between Two Worlds: A Profile of Negro Higher Education* (New York: McGraw-Hill, 1971) was an indispensable work in tracing the history of blacks at American colleges and universities. I owe a great debt to Walter Kimbrough for introducing me to this book. Kimbrough also did a masterful job of condensing information on early black college graduates in a paper entitled, "Founding of Black Fraternities and Sororities" while he was completing graduate study at Georgia State University. A special thanks is extended to Dr. Kimbrough for giving me a copy of this unpublished paper while I was doing research for this book.

12. Alfred Lee, *Fraternities Without Brotherhood* (Boston: Beacon Press, 1955), 24.

13. Ibid.

14. Ibid., 6.

15. Ibid., 14.

16. Graham, *Our Kind of People*, 87.

17. M. G. Lord, "The Greek Rites of Exclusion," *The Nation* (July 4–11, 1987): 10.

18. Ibid.

19. Ibid.

20. Shaft was portrayed as a pimp, even though the popular black cinematic character was actually a detective.

21. Erik Lords, "Outrage Continues over Fraternities' Racially Offensive Costumes," *Black Issues in Higher Education* (December 6, 2001): 10.

22. Charles Wesley, *The History of Alpha Phi Alpha: A Development in College Life* (Chicago: Foundation Publishers, 1961), xx.

23. Kimbrough, "Founding of Black Fraternities and Sororities."

24. See William Crump, *The Story of Kappa Alpha Psi* (Philadelphia: Kappa Alpha Psi Fraternity, Inc., 1991) and Thomas Clark, *Indiana University: Midwestern Pioneer*, vol. 2 (Bloomington: Indiana University, 1973).

25. Karen Bates, "Elite Fraternity Widens Agenda for Black Men," *Los Angeles Times* (July 18, 1990): E1.

26. Ibid., E2.

27. Ibid.

28. Ibid.

29. Graham, *Our Kind of People*, 92.

30. Kimbrough, "Founding of Black Fraternities and Sororities," 5.

31. Wesley, *History of Alpha Phi Alpha*, 60.

32. Crump, *The Story of Kappa Alpha Psi*, xxi.

33. The fraternity changed its name to Kappa Alpha Psi in 1915.

34. Although these groups are often identified with one another, only Phi Beta Sigma and Zeta Phi Beta are constitutionally linked.

35. Graham, *Our Kind of People*, 93.

36. This claim, which is a not-so-subtle indictment of blacks who historically, individually and organizationally, cultivated intraracial color stratification, is boldly put forward on the Sigma's national website (www. pbs1914.org/main.htm).

37. After sometimes-contentious debate among the eight older black Greek-letter organizations, Iota Phi Theta was admitted as an NPHC member group in the late 1990s.

38. Iota Phi Theta Fraternity, Inc. national website (www.iotaphitheta. org).

39. Crump, *The Story of Kappa Alpha Psi*, 37.

40. Ibid.

41. Ibid., 41.

42. Maulana Karenga, *Introduction to Black Studies* (Los Angeles: Sankore, 2002), 169–170.

43. Graham, *Our Kind of People,* 85.

44. William Henry, "Pride and Prejudice," *Time* (June 27, 1994): 20.

45. Brunson, *Frat and Soror,* 13.

CHAPTER 4: THE PLEDGE PROCESS AS SACRIFICE

1. Several works seek to explain ritualistic ordeals by placing them in a social context. Notable among these are Hans-Gunter Heimbrock and H. Barbara Boudewijnse's edited volume, *Current Studies in Rituals: Perspectives for the Psychology of Religion* (Atlanta, GA: Rodopi, 1990) and M. Edem, *Confused Values in Nigerian Context: Rituals Reveal Mythology* (Lagos: Jeromelaiho & Associates, Ltd., 1993). This chapter primarily engages René Girard's *Violence and the Sacred* (Baltimore: Johns Hopkins University Press, 1989).

2. BGF's reluctance to cease participation in activities they regard as "traditional" is examined to a degree in Peter Applebome, "Lawsuit Shatters Code of Silence Over Hazing at Black Fraternities," *New York Times* (December 21, 1994) and Eleena DeLisser, "Violent Hazing Threatens Black Fraternities," *Wall Street Journal* (November 18, 1994).

3. Girard has no such self-imposed limitation where the incorporation of religious values is concerned. His work, in fact, revolves around religion in that he uses religious parables and myths from numerous societies. Ultimately, he goes so far as to assert that we find the very roots of ritual in religion.

4. Girard, *Violence and the Sacred,* 3–4.

5. Various Afrocentric texts assert that African secret societies are the true sources of similar orders found in the Western world. Among these works are Ra Un Nefer Amen, *Metu Neter* (Bronx, NY: Khamit Corporation, 1990); Brunson, *Frat and Soror;* and George G. M. James, *Stolen Legacy* (Newport News, VA: United Brothers Communications Systems, 1989).

6. James, *Stolen Legacy:* 27. An in-depth (though highly disputed) account of the Egyptian Mysteries System and the grades of initiation can be found in chapter 3.

7. Even though Leftkowitz denies the very existence of the Egyptian Mysteries System, she does assert that the *myth* of the Mysteries System among Europeans was integral in the formation of Freemasonry. Certainly, one must ask a number of questions here: Why would Europeans create a myth of an African-dominated Mysteries System? Even if this system is, in fact, a myth—does not the fact that the myth *exists* and has had such heavy historical consequences mandate that we engage it as historically important?

8. An outstanding condensation of commonalities among fraternal and historical ritualistic systems can be found in Bobby McMinn, *A Content Analysis of the Esoteric Ritual Manuals of National College Social Fraternities* (PhD diss., University of Mississippi, 1979; Ann Arbor, MI: University

Microfilms International, 1979). Even though McMinn does not adequately deal with BGFs in his work, the very important sections of this chapter that address the commonalities of fraternity ritual borrow heavily from him.

9. Many representations of the Greek god Dionysus suggest a fusion or confusion of the sexes. He is also associated with newborn or youthful things, vegetation, the phallus, and masks. A very important element of Dionysus is that he calls for abandonment of the ego. According to Greek myth, Dionysus appears among the mortals of Thebes and eventually causes the death of the ruler Pentheus because the Thebans, egotistically, do not acknowledge Dionysus's divinity. Pentheus is induced with amnesia and subsequently led through a series of identity crises by Dionysus. The power of forgetfulness is induced among the citizens of Thebes by wine and enchantment from Dionysus, and they eventually kill Pentheus without realizing what they are doing. Some see this story as an examination of ego and identity that makes use of the concept of memory. The theme of forgetfulness or memory is found extensively in literature. Two examples of engagements of such a theme are Robert Luyster, "Dionysus: The Masks of Madness," *Parabola* 20.4 (Winter 1995); and Alexander Tulin, "A Note on Euripides' *Bacchae*," *Mnemosyne* 47.2 (April 1994).

10. For more readings on the spread of Mithraism see Oliver Nicholson, "The End of Mithraism," *Antiquity* 69 (June 1995); and Alan Schofield, "The Search for Iconographic Variation in Roman Mithraism," *Religion* 25.1 (January 1995).

11. For readings on Freemason ritual see the Freemason publication, *Ceremonials for the Use of the W. M. Grand Lodge of Ancient, Free, and Accepted Masons of the State of Illinois and Its Constituent Lodges* (Bloomington, IL: Panograph Printing & Stationary Co., 1931).

12. Crump, *The Story of Kappa Alpha Psi.*

13. McMinn, *Content Analysis.*

14. Mark Carnes, *Ritual and Manhood in Victorian America* (New Haven, CT: Yale University Press, 1989).

15. Ibid., 39.

16. Ibid., 40.

17. Ibid., 41–42.

18. Ibid., 44.

19. Michael Gordon, personal interview.

20. Nuwer, *Broken Pledges*, 53.

21. Ibid., 54.

22. Ibid., 26.

23. Girard, *Violence and the Sacred*, 281.

24. Roberto Calasso's *The Ruin of Kasch* (Cambridge, MA: Belknap Press of Harvard University, 1994) supports the stance that Girard presents in *Violence and the Sacred* on the historical importance of ritual.

25. Arnold Van Gennep, *Rites of Passage* (Paris: Norry, 1909).

26. Girard, *Violence and the Sacred*, 281.

27. Ibid.

28. Ibid., 282.

29. Ibid., 283.

30. Brunson, *Frat and Soror*, 86.

31. Asa Hilliard, "Pedagogy in Ancient Kemet," in *Kemet and the African Worldview*, eds. Maulana Karenga and Jacob Carruthers (Los Angeles: University of Sankore Press, 1985).

32. Brunson, *Frat and Soror*, 93–96.

33. As noted in chapter 3, Omega Psi Phi's international headquarters does not now, nor has it ever, condoned the use of canine references by members of the organization. Although the use of the reference is not universal among members of the fraternity, it is widespread.

34. Thomas Hobbes, *Leviathan* (New York: Penguin Classics, 1982; orig. pub. 1651).

35. Walter Kimbrough, personal interview.

CHAPTER 5: THE HEGEMONIC STRUGGLE AND DOMINATION IN BLACK GREEK-LETTER FRATERNITIES

1. Allen Feldman, *Formations of Violence: The Narrative of the Body and Political Terror in Northern Ireland* (Chicago: University of Chicago Press, 1991), 13.

2. *Intake* is the modified initiation process adopted by BGFs in the early 1990s to curtail hazing. This process will be discussed in depth later.

3. Graeme Newman, *Understanding Violence* (New York: Lippincott, 1972), 2.

4. Hussein Abdilahi Bulhan, *Frantz Fanon and the Psychology of Oppression* (Boston, MA: Boston University Press, 1985), 18.

5. Richard Gelles and Murray Straus, "Determinants of Violence in the Family: Toward a Theoretical Investigation," in *Contemporary Theories About the Family*, eds. Wesley Burr et al. (New York: Free Press, 1979), 554.

6. Hannah Arendt provided such a rearticulation in her classic, *On Violence* (New York: Harcourt Brace Jovanovich, 1970).

7. Bulhan, *Frantz Fanon*, 18.

8. Harold Laswell, *Politics: Who Gets What, When, How* (Cleveland, OH: Meridian, 1958).

9. Karenga, *Introduction to Black Studies*, 359.

10. Harold Cruse, *The Crisis of the Negro Intellectual* (New York: Quill, 1967).

11. Hanes Walton Jr., *Invisible Politics: Black Political Behavior* (Albany: SUNY Press, 1985).

12. Gramsci provides extensive (and sometimes confusing) engagements of his conceptualization of hegemony in *Selections from the Prison Notebooks* (New York: International Publishers, 1971).

13. Fine examinations of consensus formation can be found in Todd Gitlin, *The Whole World Is Watching: Mass Media and the Making and Unmaking of the New Left* (Berkeley: University of California, 1980); Jeffery Goldfarb, *The Cynical Society: The Culture of Politics and the Politics of Culture in American Life* (Chicago: University of Chicago Press, 1991); and Grossberg, *We Gotta Get Outta This Place.*

14. Valentino Gerratana, *Antonio Gramsci: Quaderni del carcere* (Turin, Italy: Einaudi, 1975), 130.

15. Marx engages this progression and its consequences in *Capital* (New York: The Modern Library, 1936) as well as the classic *Manifesto of the Communist Party* (Garden City, NY: Doubleday Anchor, 1959); coauthored with Friedrich Engels.

16. Bernard Susser, *Political Ideology in the Modern World* (Boston: Allyn and Bacon, 1995), 121.

17. Many engagements of this dynamic exist. One of the better ones is David Mann's *A Simple Theory of the Self* (New York: Norton, 1994). Interested readers may also examine Jane Kopas's *Sacred Identity: Exploring the Theology of the Person* (Mahwah, NJ: Paulist Press, 1994) and Geoffrey Madell's *The Identity of the Self* (Edinburgh, Scotland: Edinburgh University Press, 1981).

18. Amen, *Metu Neter*, vol. I, 142.

19. Ibid., 143.

20. Molefi Kete Asante, *Afrocentricity* (Trenton, NJ: Africa World Press, 1988), 31.

21. John A. Williams, "Perceptions of the No-Pledge Policy for New Member Intake by Undergraduate Members of Predominantly Black Fraternities and Sororities," PhD diss., Kansas State University, 1992. Dissertation Abstracts International, vol. 53-09, Sec. A, 1992).

22. Donald Polkinghorne, *Narrative Knowing and the Human Sciences.* Albany, NY: SUNY Press, 1998, 14.

23. This reality produces a relatively new but now often-encountered quandary in BGFs concerning men who have never been officially initiated into the fraternities, but were pledged by local chapters. The perennial question is, "Should we regard this man as a brother?" even if duly initiated members who followed the guidelines of MIP are marginalized. Quite often the answer is yes, which supports the view that it is not legitimate membership by the guidelines of the national offices that gains acceptance, but pledging itself.

24. Eleena DeLisser, "Violent Hazing Threatens Black Fraternities," *Wall Street Journal,* November 18, 1994: B1.

25. Prothrow-Stith, *Deadly Consequences.* 26. Ibid., 96–97.

27. Ibid., 97.

28. For clarity's sake, and with the realization that for many BGF members there is no clear distinction (at least in practice) between pledging and hazing, the reader should regard any mention of pledging from this point

forward as including hazing. This is not to say that I feel that hazing and pledging are synonymous; it is to say that, for all intents and purposes, when BGF members speak of pledging, they are usually speaking of a practice that includes hazing.

29. *Cat* is another term of disrespect used among some black Greeks (particularly members of Omega Psi Phi) to denote a person who did not pledge properly.

30. *Elite Eight* refers to the four major BGFs (Alpha Phi Alpha, Kappa Alpha Psi, Omega Psi Phi, and Phi Beta Sigma)—along with Alpha Kappa Alpha, Delta Sigma Theta, Zeta Phi Beta, and Sigma Gamma Rho—the four major historically black sororities. With the addition of Iota Phi Theta to the National Pan-Hellenic Council, the group changed this moniker to "The Divine Nine."

31. Grossberg, *We Gotta Get Outta This Place*, 246.

32. Ibid., 246–247.

33. Grossberg's *popular conservatism* does not necessarily refer to the American Republican Party, though the Republicans often utilize popular conservative tactics.

34. Grossberg's assessment of Gramsci's idea of the "core" as nonflexible may be somewhat inaccurate. It stands to reason, in fact, that Gramsci's idea of an *historical block* goes toward Grossberg's *ruling bloc*, though Gramsci can be said to run aground on the issue of class essentialism. This too is debatable, for Gramsci's overall arguments move well beyond issues of class.

35. Grossberg, *We Gotta Get Outta This Place*, 245.

36. Hall addresses the effects of Thatcherism in a number of works, including *The Hard Road to Renewal: Thatcherism and the Crisis of the Left* (London: Verso, 1988) and "The Toad in the Garden: Thatcherism among the Theorists," in *Marxism and the Interpretation of Culture,* eds. C. Nelson and L. Grossberg (Urbana: University of Illinois, 1988).

37. Grossberg, *We Gotta Get Outta This Place*, 249.

38. Ibid., 267.

39. See Hannah Arendt, *The Human Condition* (Chicago: University of Chicago Press, 1958).

40. Grossberg, *We Gotta Get Outta This Place*, 258.

4. Jeffery Goldfarb believed this so strongly that he entitled a treatise on the subject very simply, *The Cynical Society: The Culture of Politics and the Politics of Culture in American Life* (Chicago: University of Chicago Press, 1991).

42. Stuart Ewen, *All Consuming Images: The Politics of Style in Contemporary Culture* (New York: Basic Books, 1998).

43. In the black case, as with any study of marginalization, the temptation is to quickly accept the notion of false consciousness to explain the dilemma. Although this is somewhat appropriate, it brings with it the Marxist tendency to reduce the argument to material concerns. Material concerns are not to be discarded, but they do not provide a full picture in and of

themselves. Considering this, Du Bois's idea of double consciousness should also be considered here. The Marxist analysis is essential, but I believe Du Bois's paradigm is also necessary to provide a more complete understanding.

44. Grossberg, *We Gotta Get Outta This Place*, 296.

45. Ibid., 260.

46. Ibid., 283.

47. Ibid., 284.

CHAPTER 6: ACCEPTANCE, FREEDOM, AND IDENTITY CONSTRUCTION IN BLACK GREEK-LETTER FRATERNITIES

1. Homi Bhabha, "Anxious Nations, Nervous States," in *Supposing the Subject*, ed. J. Copjec (London: Verso, 1994).

2. Bob Herbert, "The Issue Is Jobs," *New York Times* (May 6, 1995): 15N.

3. Jeremy Brecher and Tim Costello, *Global Village or Global Pillage: Economic Restructuring from the Bottom Up* (Boston: South End Press, 1994).

4. Herbert, "The Issue Is Jobs," 19.

5. Sidney Willhelm, *Who Needs the Negro?* (Cambridge, MA: Schenkman, 1970), 13.

6. Herbert, "The Issue Is Jobs," 19.

7. Bhabha, "Anxious Nations, Nervous States," 216.

8. W. E. B. Du Bois, *The Souls of Black Folk* (New York: Library of America, 1986 printing), 8–9.

9. Cruse, *Crisis of the Negro Intellectual*, 11.

10. Richard Majors and Janet Billson, *Cool Pose: The Dilemma of Black Manhood in America* (New York: Simon & Schuster, 1992), 30.

11. Noel Cazenave, "Black Men in America: The Quest for Manhood," in *Black Families*, ed. H. P. McAdoo (Beverly Hills, CA: Sage, 1981), 176.

12. DeLisser, "Violent Hazing," B1.

13. Calhoun, *Critical Social Theory*, 213.

14. Ibid.

15. Harry Frankfurt, "Identification and Wholeheartedness," in *Perspectives on Moral Responsibility*, eds. John Martin Fischer and Mark Ravizza (Ithaca, NY: Cornell University Press), 174.

16. Calhoun, *Critical Social Theory*, 194.

17. Ibid., 213.

18. Tiger advanced his position in *Men in Groups* (New York: Random House, 1969).

19. Mark Carnes, *Secret Ritual and Manhood in Victorian America* (New Haven, CT: Yale University Press, 1989), 46.

20. Majors and Billson, *Cool Pose*, 31.

21. Frankfurt's work in this area has already been noted. Alfred Mele's *Irrationality: An Essay on Akrasia, Self-Deception, and Self-Control* (New York: Oxford University Press, 1987) is also an important contribution.

22. Mele, *Irrationality*, 3.

23. Frankfurt, "Identification and Wholeheartedness," 174.

24. Ibid., 175.

25. Ibid.

26. Elenore Stump, "Sanctification, Hardening of the Heart, and Frankfurt's Concept of Free Will," in *Perspectives on Moral Responsibility*, eds. John Martin Fischer and Mark Ravizza (Ithaca, NY: Cornell University Press, 1993).

27. Ibid.

28. Cazenave, "Black Men in America," 177.

29. Majors and Billson, *Cool Pose*, 33.

30. Ibid.

31. If the American playing field was indeed level, then one could argue that the percentage of blacks in the military should not exceed the percentage of blacks in American society as a whole, which would be 12 percent to 13 percent. To the contrary, at the advent of America's self-proclaimed "war on terror" in 2001, blacks accounted for 21 percent of all branches of the military (this is greater in some branches, particularly the U.S. Army, where a full third of the enlisted corps is black). There is, however, a large discrepancy in numbers between officers and enlisted men; a higher proportion of officers are white, despite the disproportionate number of black enlisted men. During the Gulf War, blacks made up 20 percent of the deployment. Fifty percent of the women serving in the Gulf War were black. Beyond this, an inordinate number of black men serve in comparatively dangerous military units such as paratroopers and various special forces units (Army Rangers and Green Berets, Navy SEALs, etc.). Robert Staples noticed this trend developing over four decades ago in his book *Black Masculinity* (San Francisco: The Black Scholars Press, 1972) and attributed it to black males' need to prove their manhood, the military being a readily available option.

32. Michael Meade, *Men and the Water of Life: Initiation and the Tempering of Men* (San Francisco: Harper, 1994).

33. Du Bois, *Souls of Black Folk*, 12–13.

CHAPTER 7: BEYOND THE FRATERNAL SELF

1. Ellis Cose, *A Man's World: How Real Is Male Privilege and How High Is Its Price?* (New York: Harper Collins, 1995), 2.

2. Ibid., 1.

3. Robert Bly, *Iron John: A Book about Men* (Reading, MA: Addison-Wesley, 1990). Mark Carnes rendered a fine analysis of Bly and the phenomena that contributed to the wave of male studies at the end of the twentieth century in "Iron John in the Gilded Age," *American Heritage* 44.5 (September, 1993).

4. These are the traditional names for members of Alpha Phi Alpha's,

Kappa Alpha Psi's, Omega Psi Phi's, and Phi Beta Sigma's pledge lines, respectively.

5. Girard, *Violence and the Sacred*, 297.

AFTERWORD: REFLECTIONS ON FAILURE

1. *CBS News Sunday Morning*, May 25, 2014.

2. Mallory Simon, "Witnesses: FAMU Drum Major Beaten with Drum Mallets in Hazing Gauntlet," CNN, May 25, 2012.

3. Larry Copeland and Yamiche Alcindor, "Hazing Culture Mars Marching Band's Glamour," *USA Today*, December 16, 2011.

4. George Howell and Mariano Castillo, "Recommendations for Suspension Preceded FAMU Band Death," CNN, July 6, 2012.

5. Ibid.

6. Louis Freeh, "Report of the Special Investigative Counsel Regarding the Actions of the Pennsylvania State University Related to the Child Abuse Committed by Gerald Sandusky," Freeh, Sporkin, & Sullivan, LLP, July 12, 2012: 16. The full report is available online from Penn State at http://progress.psu.edu/the-freeh-report.

7. Much of what follows is largely a restatement of important points made in two articles written as my perspective on BGLOs evolved: Ricky L. Jones, "Is It Time to Disband Black Fraternities and Sororities?" *Black Issues in Higher Education* (October 21, 2004) and Ricky L. Jones, "From *School Days* to *Stomp the Yard*: Why Black Greeks Must Go," *Diverse* (February 7, 2007).

8. Webb commented on a passage from his memoir—*I Heard My Country Calling* (New York: Simon and Schuster, 2014) on *CBS News Sunday Morning*, May 25, 2014. The quote from the book was, "I and my fellow combat veterans stand on one side of a great impassable divide, with the rest of the world on the other." When questioned about it, Webb opined, "There's a great Marine Corps saying, 'If you were there, I don't need to explain it to you, and if you weren't there, I can't explain it to you.' That's the divide."

9. Jones, "Time to Disband?"

Bibliography

BOOKS

Adler, Patricia, and Peter Adler. *Membership Roles in Field Research*. Newbury Park, CA: Sage, 1987.

Alway, Joan. *Critical Theory and Political Possibilities: Conceptions of Emancipatory Politics in the Work of Horkheimer, Adorno, Marcuse, and Habermas*. Westport, CT: Greenwood Press, 1995.

Amen, Ra Un Nefer. *Metu Neter*. Bronx, NY: Khamit Corporation, 1990.

Apter, David. *Introduction to Political Analysis*. Cambridge, MA: Winthrop Publishers, 1977.

Arendt, Hannah. *On Violence*. New York: Harcourt Brace Jovanovich, 1970.

———. *The Human Condition*. Chicago: University of Chicago Press, 1958.

———. *The Origins of Totalitarianism*. New York: Harcourt Brace Jovanovich, 1951.

Aronowitz, Stanley. *False Promises: The Shaping of American Working Class Consciousness*. New York: McGraw-Hill, 1973.

Asante, Molefi Kete. *Afrocentricity*. Trenton, NJ: Africa World Press, 1988.

Baillie, James. *Problems in Personal Identity*. New York: Paragon House, 1993.

Baumeister, Roy. *Identity: Cultural Change and the Struggle for Self*. New York: Oxford University Press, 1986.

Beck, Roger. *Planetary Gods and Planetary Orders in the Mysteries of Mithras*. Leiden, New York: E. J. Brill, 1987.

Bentley, James. *Ritualism and Politics in Victorian Britain: The Attempt to Legislate for Belief*. Oxford, UK: Oxford University Press, 1978.

Bernstein, Jay M. *Recovering Ethical Life: Jürgen Habermas and the Future of Critical Theory*. New York: Routledge, 1995.

Best, Steven. *The Politics of Historical Vision: Marx, Foucault, Habermas*. New York: Guilford Press, 1995.

Bishop, Morris. *A History of Cornell*. Ithaca, NY: Cornell University Press, 1962.

Blake, Casey Nelson. *Beloved Community: The Cultural Criticism of Randolph Bourne, Van Wyck Brooks, Waldo Frank, and Lewis Mumford*. Chapel Hill: University of North Carolina Press, 1990.

Bly, Robert. *Iron John: A Book about Men.* Reading, MA: Addison-Wesley Publishing Company, 1990.

Boime, Albert. *The Art of Exclusion: Representing Blacks in the Nineteenth Century.* Washington, DC: Smithsonian Institution Press, 1990.

Bowles, Frank, and Frank DeCosta. *Between Two Worlds: A Profile of Negro Higher Education.* New York: McGraw-Hill, 1971.

Braeten, Jane. *Habermas's Critical Theory of Society.* Albany: State University of New York Press, 1991.

Brecher, Jeremy, and Tim Costello. *Global Village or Global Pillage: Economic Restructuring from the Bottom Up.* Boston: South End Press, 1994.

Brennan, Andrew. *Conditions of Identity: A Study in Identity and Survival.* Oxford, UK: Clarendon Press, 1988.

Brunson, James. *Frat and Soror: The African Origins of Greek Lettered Organizations.* Cleage Group, 1991.

Bulhan, Hussein Abdilahi. *Frantz Fanon and the Psychology of Oppression.* Boston: Boston University Press, 1985.

Buscaglia, Leo. *Personhood: The Art of Being Fully Human.* New York: Fawcett, 1982.

Butler, Elizabeth M. *Ritual Magic.* New York: Cambridge University Press, 1979.

Calasso, Robert. *The Ruin of Kasch.* Cambridge, MA: Belknap Press of Harvard University, 1994.

Calhoun, Craig. *Critical Social Theory.* Cambridge, MA: Blackwell, 1995.

———. *Habermas and the Public Sphere.* Cambridge, MA: MIT Press, 1992.

Carnes, Mark. *Secret Ritual and Manhood in Victorian America.* New Haven, CT: Yale University Press, 1989.

Caron, Charlotte. *To Make and Make Again.* New York: Crossroads, 1993.

Charme, Stuart. *Vulgarity and Authenticity: Dimensions of Otherness in the World of Jean-Paul Sartre.* Amherst: University of Massachusetts Press, 1991.

Chesler, Phyllis. *About Men.* New York: Simon and Schuster, 1978.

Chinoy, Ely. *Automobile Workers and the American Dream.* Boston: Beacon Press, 1955.

Clark, Thomas. *Indiana University: Midwestern Pioneer.* Vol 2. Bloomington: Indiana University Press, 1973.

Cobbs, Price, and William Grier. *Black Rage.* New York: Basic Books, 1968.

Cohen, Anthony. *Self-Consciousness: An Alternative Anthropology of Identity.* New York: Routledge, 1994.

Cook, Ezra. *Red Men Illustrated: The Complete Illustrated Ritual of the Improved Order of Red Men.* Chicago: Ezra A. Cook, 1896.

Cook, Maeve. *Language and Reason: A Study of Habermas's Pragmatics.* Cambridge, MA: MIT Press, 1994.

Cose, Ellis. *A Man's World: How Real Is Male Privilege and How High Is Its Price?* New York: Harper Collins, 1995.

———. *Rage of a Privileged Class.* New York: Harper Collins, 1992.

Crump, William. *The Story of Kappa Alpha Psi.* Philadelphia: Kappa Alpha Psi Fraternity, Inc., 1991.

Cruse, Harold. *The Crisis of the Negro Intellectual.* New York: Quill, 1967.

Dahl, Robert. *After the Revolution: Authority in a Good Society.* New Haven, CT: Yale University Press, 1970.

Denzin, Norman, and Yvonna Lincoln. *Handbook of Qualitative Research.* Thousand Oaks, CA: Sage, 1994.

Dewey, John. *The Public and Its Problems.* New York: Holt and Company, 1927.

Digeser, Peter. *Our Politics, Our Selves: Liberalism, Identity, and Harm.* Princeton, NJ: Princeton University Press, 1995.

Dollard, John. *Caste and Class in a Southern Town.* Garden City, NJ: Doubleday, 1937.

Du Bois, W. E. B. *The Souls of Black Folk.* New York: Library of America, 1903 (1986 printing).

Early, Gerald, ed. *Lure and Loathing: Essays on Race, Identity, and the Ambivalence of Assimilation.* New York: Allen Lane, The Penguin Press, 1993.

Edem, M. *Confused Values in Nigerian Context: Rituals Reveal Mythology.* Lagos: Jeromelaiho & Associates, Ltd., 1993.

Erez, Miriam. *Culture, Self-Identity, and Work.* New York: Oxford University Press, 1993.

Ewen, Stuart. *All Consuming Images: The Politics of Style in Contemporary Culture.* New York: Basic Books, 1998.

Ezorsky, Gertrude. *Racism and Justice: The Case for Affirmative Action.* Ithaca, NY: Cornell University Press, 1991.

Fanon, Frantz. *Black Skin, White Masks.* New York: Grove Press, 1967.

———. *The Wretched of the Earth.* New York: Grove Press, 1963.

Feldman, Allen. *Formations of Violence: The Narrative of the Body and Political Terror in Northern Ireland.* Chicago: University of Chicago Press, 1991.

Foner, Phillip. *W. E. B. Du Bois Speaks: Speeches and Addresses, 1890–1919.* New York: Pathfinder, 1970.

Franklin, John Hope, and Alfred Moss. *From Slavery to Freedom: A History of the Negro American.* 6th ed. New York: Knopf, 1981.

Frazier, E. Franklin. *Negro Youth at Their Crossroads.* Washington, DC: American Council on Education, 1940.

———. *Black Bourgeoisie.* New York: Free Press, 1965.

Fredrickson, George. *The Black Image in the White Mind: Character and Destiny, 1817–1914.* Middletown, CT: University Press of New England, 1971.

Freemasons. *Ceremonials for the Use of the W. M. Grand Lodge of Ancient, Free, and Accepted Masons of the State of Illinois and Its Constituent Lodges.*

Bloomington, IN: Pantograph Printing & Stationary Company, 1931.

Freire, Paulo. *Pedagogy of the Oppressed.* New York: Continuum, 1990.

Gay, G., and W. Barber. *Expressively Black: The Cultural Basis of Identity.* New York: Praeger Publishers, 1987.

Germino, Dante. *Antonio Gramsci: Architect of a New Politics.* Baton Rouge: Louisiana State University Press, 1990.

Giddens, Anthony. *Modernity and Self-Identity.* Stanford, CA: Stanford University Press, 1991.

Gibbs, Jewelle Taylor. *Young, Black, and Male in America: An Endangered Species.* Westport, CT: Auburn House Publishing Company, 1988.

Girard, René. *Violence and the Sacred.* Baltimore, MD: Johns Hopkins University Press, 1989.

Gitlin, Todd. *The Whole World Is Watching: Mass Media and the Making and Unmaking of the New Left.* Berkeley: University of California Press, 1980.

Glover, Jonathan. *I: The Philosophy and Psychology of Personal Identity.* Middlesex, UK: Penguin Books, 1989.

Goldfarb, Jeffery. *The Cynical Society: The Culture of Politics and the Politics of Culture in American Life.* Chicago: University of Chicago Press, 1991.

Gosnell, Harold. *Negro Politicians: The Rise of Negro Politics in Chicago.* Chicago: University of Chicago Press, 1967.

Graham, Lawrence Otis. *Our Kind of People: Inside America's Black Upper Class.* New York: Harper Perennial, 2000.

Gramsci, Antonio. *Selections from the Prison Notebooks.* New York: International Publishers, 1971.

Gratacap, Louis. *Philosophy of Ritual.* New York: J. Pott. 1887.

Gregg, Gary. *Self-Representation: Life Narrative Studies in Identity and Ideology.* New York: Greenwood Press, 1991.

Grodin, Debra, and Thomas Lindlof. *Constructing the Self in a Mediated World.* Thousand Oaks, CA: Sage, 1996.

Gross, Feliks. *The Revolutionary Party: Essays in the Sociology of Politics.* Westport, CT: Greenwood Press, 1974.

Grossberg, Lawrence. *We Gotta Get Outta This Place.* New York: Routledge, 1992.

Habermas, Jürgen. *The Structural Transformation of the Public Sphere.* Cambridge, MA: MIT Press, 1991.

Hacker, Andrew. *Two Nations: Black and White, Separate, Hostile, Unequal.* New York: Charles Scribner's Sons, 1992.

Hall, Stuart. *The Hard Road to Renewal: Thatcherism and the Crisis of the Left.* London: Verso, 1988.

Hamerton-Kelly, Robert. *Violent Origins: Walter Burkert, René Girard, and Jonathan Smith on Ritual Killings and Cultural Formation.* Stanford: Stanford University Press, 1987.

Harris, Middleton. *The Black Book.* New York: Random House, 1974.

Harrison, Bennett, and Barry Bluestone. *The Great U-Turn: Corporate Restructuring and the Polarizing of America.* New York: Basic Books, 1988.

Heidegger, Martin. *Identity and Difference.* New York: Harper & Row, 1974.

Heimbrock, Hans-Gunter, and H. Barbara Boudewijnse, eds. *Current Studies in Rituals: Perspectives for the Psychology of Religion.* Atlanta: Rodopi, 1990.

Hobbes, Thomas. *Leviathan.* New York: Penguin Classics, 1982; orig. pub. 1651.

Hoetnik, Harry. *The Two Variants in Caribbean Race Relations.* London: Oxford University Press, 1967.

Holub, Robert. *Jürgen Habermas: Critic in the Public Sphere.* London: Routledge, 1991.

Horowitz, Helen. *Campus Life: Undergraduate Cultures from the End of the Eighteenth Century to the Present.* New York: Knopf, 1987.

Huntington, Samuel. *Political Order in Changing Societies.* New Haven, CT: Yale University Press, 1968.

Hutchinson, Earl Ofari. *The Assassination of the Black Male Image.* Los Angeles: Middle Passage Press, 1994.

James, George G. M. *Stolen Legacy.* Newport News, VA: United Brothers Communications Systems, 1989.

James, Joy. *Transcending the Talented Tenth: Black Leaders and American Intellectuals.* New York: Routledge, 1997.

Kamler, Howard. *Identification and Character: A Book on Psychological Development.* Albany, NY: SUNY Press, 1994.

Karenga, Maulana. *Introduction to Black Studies.* 3d ed. Los Angeles: University of Sankore Press, 2002.

———. *The Book of Coming Forth by Day: The Ethics of the Declarations of Innocence.* Los Angeles: University of Sankore Press, 1990.

———. *Selections from the Husia: Sacred Wisdom of Ancient Egypt.* Los Angeles: University of Sankore Press, 1984.

Keil, Charles. *Urban Blues.* Chicago: University of Chicago Press, 1966.

Kimbrough, Walter. *Black Greek 101: The Culture, Customs, and Challenges of Black Fraternities and Sororities.* Hackensack, NJ: Fairleigh Dickinson, 2003.

Knowles, Louis, and Kenneth Prewitt. *Institutional Racism in America.* Englewood Cliffs, NJ: Prentice Hall, 1969.

Kopas, Jane. *Sacred Identity: Exploring the Theology of a Person.* Mahwah, NJ: Paulist Press, 1994.

Krueger, Richard. *Focus Groups: A Practical Guide for Applied Research.* Newbury Park, CA: Sage, 1988.

Ladd, Everett. *Negro Political Leadership in the South.* New York: Athenaeum, 1969.

Lapsley, Daniel, and F. Clark Power, eds. *Self, Ego, and Identity.* New York: Springer-Verlag, 1988.

Lasswell, Harold. *Politics: Who Gets What, When, How.* Cleveland, OH: Meridian Books, 1958.

Latif, Sultan, and Naimah Latif. *Slavery: The African-American Psychic Trauma.* Chicago: Latif Communications Group, 1994.

Lee, Alfred. *Fraternities Without Brotherhood.* Boston: Beacon Press, 1955.

Leftkowitz, Mary. *Not Out of Africa: How Afrocentrism Became an Excuse to Teach Myth as History.* New York: Basic Books, 1996.

Lincoln, C. Eric. *The Black Muslims in America.* Boston: Beacon Press, 1961.

Litchman, C. *Official History of the Improved Order of Red Men.* Boston: Fraternity Publishing Company, 1893.

Luckok, H. M. *The Ritual Crisis: How It May Be Turned to the Best Account.* New York: Longmans & Green, 1899.

Lundquist, John. *The Temple: Meeting Place of Heaven and Earth.* London: Thames & Hudson, 1993.

Madell, Geoffrey. *The Identity of the Self.* Edinburgh, Scotland: Edinburgh University Press, 1981.

Madhubuti, Haki. *Black Men: Obsolete, Single, Dangerous?* Chicago: Third World Press, 1990.

Madhubuti, Haki, and Maulana Karenga. *Million Man March/Day of Absence.* Chicago and Los Angeles: Third World and University of Sankore Press, 1996.

Maffesoli, Michel. *The Time of Tribes: The Decline of Individualism in Mass Society.* London: Sage, 1996.

Majors, Richard, and Janet Billson. *Cool Pose: The Dilemma of Black Manhood in America.* New York: Simon and Schuster, 1992.

Mann, David. *A Simple Theory of the Self.* New York: Norton, 1994.

Mannheim, Karl. *Ideology and Utopia: An Introduction to the Sociology of Knowledge.* New York: Harcourt Brace, 1929.

McAdam, Doug. *Political Process and the Development of Black Insurgency, 1930–1970.* Chicago: University of Chicago Press, 1982.

McCall, Nathan. *Makes Me Wanna Holler: A Young Black Man in America.* New York: Random House, 1994.

McCartney, John. *Black Power Ideologies: An Essay in African-American Political Thought.* Philadelphia: Temple University Press, 1992.

McIntosh, D. *Self, Person, World: The Interplay of Conscious and Unconscious in Human Life.* Evanston, IL: Northwestern University Press, 1995.

McMinn, Bobby. *A Content Analysis of the Esoteric Ritual Manuals of National College Social Fraternities.* PhD diss., 1979; Ann Arbor, MI: University Microfilms International, 1979.

Meade, Michael. *Men and the Water of Life: Initiation and the Tempering of Men.* San Francisco: Harper, 1994.

Meehan, Johanna. *Feminists Read Habermas: Gendering the Subject of Discourse.* New York: Routledge, 1995.

Mele, Alfred. *Irrationality: An Essay on Akrasia, Self-Deception, and Self-Control.* New York: Oxford University Press, 1987.

Merton, R., K. Fiske, and P. Kendall. *The Focused Interview.* Glencoe, IL: The Free Press, 1956.

Miller, Toby. *The Well-Tempered Self: Citizenship, Culture, and the Postmodern Subject.* Baltimore: Johns Hopkins University, 1993.

Mishler, Elliot. *Research Interviewing: Context and Narrative.* Cambridge, MA: Harvard University Press, 1986.

Morgan, David. *Focus Groups as Qualitative Research.* Newbury Park, CA: Sage, 1988.

Moore, Jesse. *A Search for Equality: The National Urban League, 1910–1961.* University Park: Pennsylvania University Press, 1981.

Muhammad, Elijah. *Message to the Black Man in America.* Chicago: Muhammad Mosque of Islam, 1965.

Munitz, Milton, ed. *Identity and Difference.* New York: New York University Press, 1971.

Murray, Charles. *The Bell Curve: Intelligence and Class Structure in American Life.* New York: Free Press, 1994.

Newman, Graeme. *Understanding Violence.* New York: Lippincott, 1972.

Nietzsche, Friedrich. *The Birth of Tragedy and the Case of Wagner.* New York: Vintage Books, 1967.

Noonan, Harold. *Personal Identity.* New York: Routledge, 1989.

Nuwer, Hank. *Broken Pledges: The Deadly Rite of Hazing.* Marietta, GA: Longstreet Press, 1990.

Parenti, Michael. *The Sword and the Dollar.* New York: St. Martin's Press, 1989.

Perkins, Linda. *Black Feminism and "Race Uplift."* Cambridge, MA: Institute for Independent Study, Radcliffe College, 1981.

Pollkinghorne, Donald. *Narrative Knowing and the Human Sciences.* Albany: State University of New York Press, 1988.

Prothrow-Stith, Deborah. *Deadly Consequences: How Violence Is Destroying Our Teenage Population and a Plan to Begin Solving the Problem.* New York: Harper Collins, 1993.

Ray, Larry. *Rethinking Critical Theory: Emancipation in the Age of Global Social Movements.* Newbury Park, CA: Sage, 1993.

Ricoeur, Paul. *Oneself as Another.* Chicago: University of Chicago, 1992.

Rifkin, Jeremy. *The End of Work: The Decline of the Global Labor Force and the Dawn of the Post-Market Era.* New York: G. P. Putnam's Sons, 1995.

Ross, Lawrence. *The Divine Nine: The History of African-American Fraternities and Sororities.* New York: Dafina, 2000.

Rothschild, Emma. *Paradise Lost: The Decline of the Auto Industrial Age.* New York: Random House, 1973.

Scheibe, Karl. *Self Studies: The Psychology of the Self and Identity.* Westport, CT: Praeger, 1995.

Schenk, Roy, and John Everingham, eds. *Men Healing Shame: An Anthology.* New York: Springer Publishing Co., 1995.

Shepardson, Francis. *Baird's Manual: American College Fraternities.* Menasha, WI: Collegiate Press, 1930.

Shoemaker, Sydney. *Personal Identity.* Oxford, UK: Basil Blackwell, 1984.

Sklar, Holly. *Chaos or Community: Seeking Solutions, Not Scapegoats for Bad Economics.* Boston: South End Press, 1995.

Stevens, Albert. *Cyclopaedia of Fraternities.* New York: E. B. Treat, 1907.

Stewart, Shelley. *The Road South: A Memoir.* New York: Warner Books, 2002.

Susser, Bernard. *Political Ideology in the Modern World.* Needham Heights, MA: Allyn and Bacon, 1995.

Taylor, Charles. *Sources of the Self: The Making of the Modern Identity.* Cambridge, MA: Harvard University Press, 1989.

Terkel, Studs. *Race: How Blacks and Whites Think and Feel about the American Obsession.* New York: The New Press, 1992.

Tiger, Lionel. *Men in Groups.* New York: Random House, 1969.

Trupp, Andreas. *Why We Are Not What We Think We Are.* New York: Lang, 1987.

Van Gennep, Arnold. *Rites of Passage.* Paris: Nourry, 1909.

Wallace, Michelle. *Black Macho and the Myth of the Superwoman.* New York: Dial Press, 1979.

Walsh, W. *The Ritualistic Reaction in the Present Century.* Liverpool: Protestant Standard, 1899.

———. *Secret Societies of the Ritualists.* Leamington, UK: J. Beck, 1884.

Walton Jr., Hanes. *Invisible Politics: Black Political Behavior.* Albany: State University of New York Press, 1985.

Webb, James. *I Heard My Country Calling.* New York: Simon and Schuster, 2014.

Weigert, Andrew. *Society and Identity: Toward a Sociological Psychology.* Cambridge, UK: Cambridge University Press, 1986.

Weiss, Nancy. *The National Urban League, 1910–1940.* New York: Oxford University Press, 1974.

Wesley, Charles. *The History of Alpha Phi Alpha: A Development in College Life.* Chicago: The Foundation Publishers, 1961.

West, Cornel. *Race Matters.* Boston: Beacon Press, 1993.

———. *American Evasion of Philosophy: A Genealogy of Pragmatism.* Madison: University of Wisconsin Press, 1989.

White, Vernessa. *Afro-American and East German Fiction: A Comparative Study of Alienation, Identity, and the Development of Self.* New York: Lang, 1983.

Wickham-Crowley, Timothy. *Guerrillas and Revolution in Latin America: A Comparative Study of Insurgents and Regimes Since 1956.* Princeton, NJ: Princeton University Press, 1991.

Williams, Raymond. *Marxism and Literature.* Oxford, UK: Oxford University Press, 1977.

Willhelm, Sidney. *Who Needs the Negro?* Cambridge, MA: Schenkman Publishing Company, 1970.
Wilson, James. *Negro Politics.* New York: The Free Press, 1960.

BOOK CHAPTERS, REPORTS, AND SCHOLARLY JOURNAL, MAGAZINE, AND NEWSPAPER ARTICLES

Adler, Patricia, and Peter Adler. "Observational Techniques." In *Handbook of Qualitative Research*, edited by Norman Denzin and Yvonna Lincoln. Thousand Oaks, CA: Sage, 1994.
Allen, Wayne. "The Breakdown of Authority and the End of Community." *Modern Age* 36, no. 2 (Winter, 1994): 139–149.
Applebome, Peter. "Lawsuit Shatters Code of Silence over Hazing at Black Fraternities." *New York Times*, December 21, 1994, B8, B15.
Baker-White, R. "The Politics of Ritual in Wole Soyinka's *The Bacchae of Euripides*." *Comparative Drama* 27, no. 3 (Fall, 1993): 377–98.
Barnes, Bruce. "Our Common Bonds." Paper presented at the Southeastern Intra Fraternity Conference, Atlanta, GA, February 1994.
Barnet, Richard. "Lords of the Global Economy." *The Nation* (December 19, 1994): 754–7.
Bates, Karen. "Elite Fraternity Widens Agenda for Black Men." *Los Angeles Times*, July 18, 1990, E2.
Bhabha, Homi. "Anxious Nations, Nervous States." In *Supposing the Subject*, edited by Joan Copjec: 201–217. London: Verso, 1994.
Carey, James. "Abolishing the Old Spirit World." *Critical Studies in Mass Communications* (March 1995): 82–8.
Carnes, Mark. "Iron John in the Gilded Age." *American Heritage* (September 1993): 37–9.
Carpini, Michael, and Bruce Williams. "The Method Is the Message: Focus Groups as a Means of Examining the Uses of Television in Political Discourse." Paper presented to the International Society of Political Psychology, Washington, DC, July 1990: 11–4.
Cazenave, Noel. "Black Men in America: The Quest for Manhood." In *Black Families*, edited by Harriet Pipes McAdoo: 176–85. Beverly Hills, CA: Sage, 1981.
Collison, Michelle N. K. "Eight Major Black Fraternities and Sororities Agree to End the Practice Of Pledging." *Chronicle of Higher Education* (February 1990): A31.
Copeland, Larry, and Yamiche Alcindor. "Hazing Culture Mars Marching Band's Glamour." *USA Today,* December 16, 2011.
Cox, William. "Joining a Fraternity Should Not Result in Death." *Black Issues in Higher Education* (March 1994): 88.
Dassbach, Carl. "The Origins of Fordism: The Introduction of Mass Production and the Five-Dollar Day." *Critical Sociology* 18 (1991): 77–90.

Davis, Melvin. "Editor's Note." *The Kappa Alpha Psi Journal* (December 1994): 216.

DeLisser, Eleena. "Violent Hazing Threatens Black Fraternities." *Wall Street Journal*, November 18, 1994, B1, B2.

Dionne, E. J. "Building a Beloved Community." *Lexington Herald Leader*, October 18, 1995, A13.

Dostal, Robert. "The Public and the People: Heidegger's Illiberal Politics." *The Review of Metaphysics* (March 1994): 517–56.

Durkheim, Emile. "Social Facts." In *Readings in the Philosophy of Social Science*, edited by M. Brodbeck. New York: Macmillan, 1968.

Frankfurt, Harry. "Identification and Wholeheartedness." In *Perspectives on Moral Responsibility*, edited by John Martin Fischer and Mark Ravizza. Ithaca, NY: Cornell University Press, 1993.

———. "Freedom of the Will and the Concept of a Person." *Journal of Philosophy* (January 14, 1971): 5–20.

Freeh, Louis. "Report of the Special Investigative Counsel Regarding the Actions of the Pennsylvania State University Related to the Child Abuse Committed by Gerald Sandusky." Freeh, Sporkin, & Sullivan, LLP. July 12, 2012. The full report is available online from Penn State at http://progress.psu.edu/the-freeh-report.

Gelles, Richard, and Murray Straus. "Determinants of Violence in the Family: Toward a Theoretical Investigation." In *Contemporary Theories about the Family*, edited by Wesley Burr et al. New York: The Free Press, 1979.

Hall, Stuart. "The Whites of Their Eyes: Racist Ideologies and the Media." In *The Media Reader*, edited by M. Alvarado and J. Thompson. London: BFI Publishing, 1990.

———. "The Toad in the Garden: Thatcherism among the Theorists." In *Marxism and the Interpretation of Culture,* edited by C. Nelson and L. Grossberg. Urbana: University of Illinois Press, 1988.

Harris, Robert. "Grand Polemarch's Message." *Kappa Alpha Psi Journal* (December 1994): 217.

Henry, William. "Pride and Prejudice." *Time,* (June 27, 1994): 20–7.

Herbert, Bob. "The Issue Is Jobs." *New York Times,* May 6, 1995, 19.

Hilliard, Asa. "Pedagogy in Ancient Kemet." In *Kemet and the African Worldview*, edited by Maulana Karenga and Jacob Carruthers. Los Angeles: University of Sankore Press, 1985.

Hoshmand, Lisa. "Alternate Research Paradigms: A Review and Teaching Proposal." *Counseling Psychologist* 17, no. 4 (1989): 3–79.

Howell, George, and Mariano Castillo. "Recommendations for Suspension Preceded FAMU Band Death." CNN, July 6, 2012.

Jacoby, Russell. "The Myth of Multiculturalism." *New Left Review* (Nov–Dec 1994): 121–6.

Jensen, Arthur. "How Much Can We Boost I.Q. and Scholastic Achievement?" *Harvard Educational Review* 39 (Winter 1969).

Jones, Ricky L. "Is It Time to Disband Black Fraternities and Sororities?" *Black Issues in Higher Education* (October 21, 2004).

———. "From *School Days* to *Stomp the Yard*: Why Black Greeks Must Go." *Diverse* (February 7, 2007).

Kimbrough, Walter. "Founding of Black Fraternities and Sororities." Unpublished manuscript, Georgia State University, 1993.

King, W. D. "Dionysus in Santa Barbara: Wallace Shawn's Euripidean Fever." *Theater* (1992): 83–7.

Lord, M. G. "The Greek Rites of Exclusion." *The Nation,* (July 4–11, 1987): 9–16.

Lords, Erik. "Outrage Continues over Fraternities' Racially Offensive Costumes." *Black Issues in Higher Education* (December 6, 2001): 10–11.

Luyster, Robert. "Dionysus: The Masks of Madness." *Parabola* 20, no. 4 (Winter 1995): 43–8.

Maisel, J. M. "Social Fraternities and Sororities Are Not Conducive to the Educational Process." *National Association of Student Personnel Administrators Journal* 28 (1990): 8–12.

Mazzaro, Jerome. "Mnema and Forgetting in Euripides' *Bacchae.*" *Comparative Drama* (Fall 1993): 286–305.

Morin, R. "Whites Found to Have a Distorted Impression of Minorities' Success." *Washington Post*, October 8, 1995, A1, A10.

Murray, Charles. "The Partial Restoration of Traditional Society." *The Public Interest* (Fall, 1995): 122–34.

———. "Affirmative Action Is Racist." In *Racism: Opposing Viewpoints*, edited by Bruno Leone. San Diego: Greenhaven Press, 1986.

Neal, Larry. "Any Day Now: Black Art and Black Liberation." *Ebony* (August 1969): 54.

Nicholson, Oliver. "The End of Mithraism." *Antiquity* 69 (June 1995): 358–62.

Olsen, J. P. "Blood Brothers." *Swing* (February 1995): 49–53.

Peters, John. "Distrust of Representation: Habermas on the Public Sphere." *Media, Culture, and Society*, 15, no. 4 (October 1993): 541–71.

Porteous, Skipp. "The Politics of Spiritual Warfare." *Free Inquiry* (Summer 1992): 16–17.

Roberts, Steven. "Workers Take It on the Chin." *U.S. News and World Report* (January 22, 1996): 44–54.

Schofield, A. "The Search for Iconographic Variation in Roman Mithraism." *Religion* 25, no. 1 (January 1995): 51–66.

Schwartz, H. "Affirmative Action Is Not Racist." In *Racism: Opposing Viewpoints*, edited by Bruno Leone. San Diego: Greenhaven Press, 1986.

Sena, M. "Dionysus as Antidote: The Veils of Maya." *Research in Phenomenology* (Fall 1994): 189–205.

Sharrett, Christopher. "Movies vs. the Media." *USA Today Magazine* 123, no. 2598 (March 1995), p. 37.

Shea, Christopher. "Two More Alumni in Fraternity Charged in Hazing Death." *New York Times*, February 24, 1994, A13, A18.

———. "Brutal Hazing Death Shocks Missouri Campus." *Chronicle of Higher Education* (March 2, 1994): A37–9.

———. "Wall of Silence." *Chronicle of Higher Education* (June 22, 1994): A25.

Simon, Mallory. "Witnesses: FAMU Drum Major Beaten with Drum Mallets in Hazing Gauntlet." CNN, May 25, 2012.

Slakey, Francis. "When the Lights of Reason Go Out." *New Scientist* (September 11, 1993): 49–   50.

Sloan, Allen. "The Hit Men," *Newsweek* (February 26, 1996): 44–8.

Smith, Steven. "Personalities in the Crowd: The Ideal of the Masses in American Popular Culture." *Prospects Annual* 18, no. 19 (1994): 225–87.

Staples, Robert. "Masculinity and Race: The Dual Dilemma of Black Men." In *Black Masculinity*, edited by Robert Staples. San Francisco: The Black Scholars Press, 1972.

Stump, Elenore. "Sanctification, Hardening of the Heart, and Frankfurt's Concept of Free Will." In *Perspectives on Moral Responsibility*, edited by John Martin Fischer and Mark Ravizza. Ithaca, NY: Cornell University Press, 1993.

Tulin, Alexander. "A Note on Euripides' *Bacchae*." *Mnemosyne* 47, no. 2 (April 1994):221–224.

West, Cornel. "Nihilism in Black America: A Danger that Corrodes from Within." *Dissent* (Spring 1991): 221ff.

Whiting, J. M. W., R. Kluckhohn, and A. Anthony. "The Function of Male Initiation Ceremonies at Puberty." In *Readings in Social Psychology*, edited by E. Macooby, T. M. Newcomb, and E. L. Hartley. New York: Holt, 1958.

Wideman, John Edgar. "Dead Black Men and Other Fallout from the American Dream." *Esquire* (September 1992): 149–56.

Williams, John. "Perceptions of the No-Pledge Policy for New Member Intake by Undergraduate Members of Predominantly Black Fraternities and Sororities." PhD diss., Kansas State University, 1992.

Index